From
CURSES
to
BLESSINGS

Books by Ken and Jeanne Harrington

Shift!

Designer Genes

Available from Destiny Image Publishers

From
CURSES
to
BLESSINGS
REMOVING GENERATIONAL CURSES

KEN AND JEANNE HARRINGTON

Used by permission:

Cartoons created by Brenda G. Smith: Wrapped up in sin and Out of prison.

Shannon Harrington created the 3 Generation cartoon.

DESTINY IMAGE® PUBLISHERS, INC.

P.O. Box 310, Shippensburg, PA 17257-0310

"Speaking to the Purposes of God for This Generation and for the Generations to Come."

This book and all other Destiny Image, Revival Press, MercyPlace, Fresh Bread, Destiny Image Fiction, and Treasure House books are available at Christian bookstores and distributors worldwide.

For a U.S. bookstore nearest you, call **1-800-722-6774.**

For more information on foreign distributors, call **717-532-3040.**

Reach us on the Internet: **www.destinyimage.com.**

ISBN 13 TP: 978-0-7684-3634-1

ISBN 13 HC: 978-0-7684-3635-8

ISBN 13 LP: 978-0-7684-3636-5

ISBN 13 E-book: 978-0-7684-9042-8

For Worldwide Distribution, Printed in the U.S.A.

2 3 4 5 6 7 8 9 10 11 / 14 13 12 11

DEDICATION

Mark Steven Michener (1957–2009): Gone Fishing

Lock on the Door (Hebrews 4:7)

His Word has come down through the ages; steadfast in love it is sure.
Men by degrees and stages have come to Him in sin for the cure.
Commissions He gave through the pages
And the prophets would cry from the shores.
To this day the same battle rages, eternal life is the stakes in the war,
Stakes in the war
The Lord always warned of the danger, for you He may not come anymore.
Last chance to receive your savior, how many times He's called before.
He comes in His love not His anger and calls through the cross to the world.
No one need be a stranger; you could come and be a son to the Lord
Daughter of the Lord

Chorus:
But they see nothing and their hearts never change
(They) refuse to open up the door
They hear nothing as they're locked up in chains
In fact they harden their hearts a little more and then they throw
Another lock on the door, lock on the door.

Don't turn away from the savior who called in love to life evermore
The one born in a manger, yes He knows what it's like in the world
He knows you, He's no stranger, and forgiveness from Him is the cure
You can let the battle rage here for the world won't be your home anymore.

Chorus 2:
So if you see something and your heart wants a change
Just choose to open up the door
If you hear something and you're tired of the chains
Don't harden your heart anymore, maybe unlock the lock on the door
Lock on the door.

Lyrics and Music by Mark Michener

Mark ministered the "Curses to Blessings" seminar every chance he got. He loved to bring people into freedom. He was an independent individual [too much so as he told me (Ken) the last time we talked], who lived life to the fullest. Though we were ten years his senior, he always called us "Sister" and "Kenny." Mark believed in the Scripture, "*...greet one another with a holy kiss*" (1 Cor. 16:20 NASB), and would often give us a full-blown kiss when he greeted us. He wrote out the story that appears at the end of Chapter 3 just months before he died.

Mark experienced one of our favorite tales from the "Curses to Blessings" seminar when he was given a man to work with who panicked before the personal ministry time. He left his wife and bolted for the parking lot to avoid having to expose himself. Mark was a bulldog and not about to let his guy get away. He followed the guy to his truck and tried to assure him that it was cool, but there was no way this man was coming back into the church.

So Mark climbed into the truck and proceeded to go through the workbook with him. He gained the man's confidence after a few curses were broken off and a few cigarettes were smoked. They continued smoking and ministering until it was time for the blessings and the guy felt comfortable enough to come in and join the rest of us. Mark was not only a great fisherman, he was a great fisher of men. This book is dedicated in his honor.

We love you, Mark—see you later.

ACKNOWLEDGMENTS

Men occasionally stumble over the truth, but most of them pick
themselves up and hurry off as if nothing ever happened.
—Sir Winston Churchill (1874–1965)[1]

Jeanne stumbled onto the truth of generational curses and blessings that God had put into our path. When we applied that truth, we realized that the Holy Spirit had shown us a key to bring deliverance to anyone who would embrace it. Without God's gentle intervention, our family would have stayed in bondage. We acknowledge that Jesus is the Truth, and we thank Him for revealing a small measure of who He is to us.

The truth is that many people's input was required to allow us to bring this project to completion. We would first like to thank our son, James Harrington, for allowing us to be candid about his journey through his sickness and for writing the poem that appears in the preface. His sickness drove us to seek an answer from God; his victories spurred us on to seek the full depth of the truth concerning generational curses and blessings.

Special thanks to Brenda G. Smith for her wisdom and advice, which she gave as she did the initial edit of this manuscript. Brenda, your tireless assistance makes us appreciate you as a valued friend. Thanks also to Suzanne Harrington for our photo.

We would also like to acknowledge and thank the one hundred plus friends and family of Spruce Grove Community Church who allowed us to practice on them and hone the truths presented in this book. Thank you also for becoming part of the team that has ministered freedom to thousands through the "Curses to Blessings" seminar. Your testimonies have been invaluable, and your enthusiasm has repeatedly inspired us to glorify God for the revelation that He gave us. This stuff "really works"!

Thank you to Destiny Image for your support and encouragement for this project. You have made it possible to take *the good news to all creation* (Mark 16:15 NIV).

ENDORSEMENTS

Many of us probably feel that *curses* is a very spooky word. We tend to think of curses as something dark and evil that God would never be part of. However, in recognizing the vast difference between punishment and consequences, Ken and Jeanne provide real insight into the value that we can gain by identifying and dealing with the evidence of curses (pronounced by God!) in our lives. Backed by Scripture and laced with personal testimonies, this book provides biblically based, practical steps that anyone, regardless of where they are in their Christian walk, can take to gain freedom from the consequences of curses operating in their lives. Having been one of Ken and Jeanne's early guinea pigs during the development of their "Curses to Blessings" seminar, I can wholeheartedly endorse both their character, and the value and effectiveness of this teaching.

—Jim den Otter
Vice President and Partner, Computronix
Edmonton, Alberta and Lakewood, Colorado

It is a great honor to recommend this precious book. I met Ken three years ago when he was in Korea teaching Kingdom finances to a group of business people who were YWAM discipleship training school graduates. He has a strong anointing for raising workplace Christians preparing for the last battle. Personally, I have fought cancer four times in my life. Breaking curses from generations' idolatry and sins was a great help in winning the fourth battle. I thank Ken and Jeanne for this insight that they have received from the Lord; it helped me through this fight. Surprisingly, many Christians, whether they perceive it or not, are affected by generational curses. I know that this book will free many readers from curses and fulfill our faithful Jesus Christ's intentions. Heavenly Father wishes all of His children to live in freedom and happiness. This book will prepare Christians, who are all called to fight with Jesus, to be free from any bondage that the enemy attempts to bind them with, so that they are held back.

—Chang Su Yoo
Managing Director
Alternative Investment Partners
Seoul, Hong Kong, and Tokyo

Jesus said, "*But wisdom is justified of all her children*" (Luke 7:35). What that means to me is that children are the proof of wisdom. Nothing speaks more loudly than stable and productive offspring. This means when a steady stream of healthy individuals come from the same place, you can bet there is something right about it. The wisdom and understanding found in the "Curses to Blessings" course has helped produce that kind of fruit wherever it is taught.

—Marc Brisebois
Senior Pastor, Spruce Grove Community Church
Director, Watchman on the Wall
Spruce Grove, Alberta

It has been our pleasure to have known Ken and Jeanne for some years now. Their revelation and understanding of the function of spiritual structures and how to apply them to everyday situations has been instrumental in our lives. We use their material and their training for all of our ministry staff as well as teaching it to the hundreds of pastors we minister to in our ministry. We have seen firsthand, in our lives, how these amazing truths can set people free and put them on the right path. We personally went through the "Curses to Blessings" course with Ken and Jeanne and apply it in our own lives. We wanted to be totally free in Christ so we could set others free. This truth, of removing generational curses and enacting generational blessings, is for every believer—no matter how mature or how young you are in Christ. If you know the truth, the truth will set you free. Thanks to this awesome couple, we know more truth, and it has set us freer. This teaching should be taught in every Bible school and applied in every church.

—Kim and Lynn Weiler
President, Fe Viva World Missions
Guatemala

In your hands is another *great* book by Ken and Jeanne Harrington. Well researched and thoughtful, this book, *From Curses to Blessings,* will give you great insights into issues that regulate your daily life—for good and for evil. It could change your life…if you let it!

—Stacey Campbell
Prophet, Co-founder, and Director
RevivalNOW! Ministries,
Be A HERO, and Praying the Bible International
Founder & Facilitator, Canadian Prophetic Council
Kelowna, British Columbia
www.revivalnow.com
www.beahero.org

When I met Ken and Jeanne Harrington, the godly character working in them that produces amazing miracles overwhelmed me. Allow them to mentor you as they share powerful revelation on how blessings and curses operate in their book *From Curses to Blessings.* Get ready to receive all the supernatural blessings God has prepared just for you!

—Sid Roth
Host, *It's Supernatural!* TV
Brunswick, Georgia

One of the most frequent questions I get asked as a pastor is, where do you find the most fulfillment in ministry? For me, the answer has always been to see people who are jewels in the rough come into a freedom where they can then shine, as they step into the destiny that God has for them. Ken and Jeanne Harrington's "Curses to Blessings" course is a fantastic tool that helps accomplish this. In fact, I have seen the countenance of people change after the very first curse became annulled in their lives. The fruit of this ministry has radically transformed many and has helped strengthen our church as a whole.

—Pastor Lance Steeves
Team Leader
Cold Lake Community Church
Cold Lake, Alberta

Having read *Designer Genes* and *SHIFT!*, the Harringtons' first two books, I know that their writings originate from the heart of God. I have seen an increase in spiritual momentum as Ken and Jeanne put into writing the revelation they have received. If you want a life of freedom in God, please read *From Curses to Blessings*. It will set you free to live the destiny that God has planned for you.

—Paul Collins
Founder and CEO, Collins Industries Ltd.
Chair of Marketing
Canadian Institute of Steel Construction
Edmonton, Alberta

Today we have good news and bad news.

The good news is that immediately after an all-powerful, all-knowing, all-loving God created man and woman in the garden, He blessed them! The bad news is that the moment they sinned and rebelled against God, curses descended on the earth! And now, even centuries later, man lives with this tragic mix of "blessing" and "cursing." Now, out of the same fountain comes "bitter water" and "sweet." These things ought not to be!!

Once again in their new book, Ken and Jeanne Harrington clearly and accurately show us the way out of this wilderness. They identify the steps we can each take to be free, once and for all, from the "curse," and they reveal the certain path we can take into our promised land! Wow! This is good news!! And as for the bad news? For those who are in Christ, I guess there isn't any!

—Dennis Wiedrick
President, Wiedrick and Associates
Apostolic Ministries
Oshawa, Ontario

Ken and Jeanne's insightful and revelatory writings will give you the tools to remove generational curses and negative influences from your life and release the blessings of God to you and your family.

—Lorne and Rita Silverstein
Directors, Every Home for Jesus
Edmonton, Alberta

Oh, I love it! True Kingdom of God plumbing! I don't need more spiritual power; I just need to remove the old thinking in my heart and mind that prevents the life of God from flowing freely through me. This is certainly a must read for anyone who feels like they have been handed less than the ultimate breakthrough. At the end of this book there is no doubt you will be saying, "Curse? What curse?" Thanks, Ken and Jeanne, your purpose for writing is very well noted.

—Michael Danforth
Founder, Mountain Top International
Yakima, Washington

CONTENTS

FOREWORD

We are entering the most treacherous period in human history. In my whole life, I have never seen morality and the economy deteriorate so rapidly before my eyes.

Yet, even in the midst of great darkness, I know God desires to pour out His blessings on believers and their families. So why do so few Christians seem to walk in the blessings outlined in Deuteronomy 28, and why are so many Christians suffering from the same curses as the world? Shouldn't all Christians be living under an open Heaven of blessings?

This isn't just a matter of enjoying God's blessings; it's part of our calling. The apostle Paul tells us in Romans 11:11 that the job of the Christian is to provoke the Jew to jealousy. If Christians have the same family, financial, and health problems as the world, they will not provoke any Jew to desire what they have.

Ken and Jeanne Harrington have unlocked the door that has prevented so many Christians from receiving the blessings God has for them.

Just as it was during the first Passover when the Egyptians were overtaken by curses and the Jews were overtaken by God's blessings, God is about to shower His blessings on the Body of Messiah one more time. But in order to receive what God has in store, you must be free from all the curses that you have inherited through the sins of your fathers.

When you follow the biblical truths found in this simple yet profound teaching by Ken and Jeanne, God promises to remove every generational curse and pour out His blessings beyond what you can contain.

It's time for you to become "normal" according to Deuteronomy 28 and to move from curses to blessings. As you do, *the LORD will open to you His good treasure, the heavens, to give the rain to your land in its season, and to bless all the work of your hand* (Deut. 28:12 NKJV). That includes God's prosperity on your finances, family, health, and peace.

Get ready to provoke the Jewish people and all people to jealousy as Ken and Jeanne mentor you with their powerful revelation!

—Sid Roth
Host of *It's Supernatural!* TV program

PREFACE

We are not the masters of our own fate; *"Jesus* [is] *the author and finisher of our faith"* (Heb. 12:2). He often comes and interrupts our well-ordered lives with a call to something higher than what we can ever hope for. He will use situations, interruptions, relations, and words that speak to our spirits to accomplish His will. God did that for me (Jeanne) when Jim Goll pulled me out of a crowd and downloaded on me.

Jim Goll (August 2002):

Jeanne, Jeanne, Jeanne, come up here. Tonight we're going to let Jeanne out of the bottle. She is going to get an Elvis anointing, and it's not going to be, "I've been crying in the chapel." It's going to be, "I'm all shook up."

There is going to be a deliverance and inner healing anointing come upon you. It shall come upon you one by one, one by one, one by one. There is going to be a life impartation message given to you. God's going to give you this life impartation of overcoming rejection, in Jesus' name. You shall speak the word, and spirits of suicide, and death wish, and self-hatred, and rejection shall depart. You shall speak the word, and the demons will flee from the people by the thousands, in a moment, in Jesus' name [I'm on the floor]. He shall shod your feet with new shoes [he kicked off both of my shoes, and they went flying]. Just click your heels and dream. Get on the yellow brick road, lady. Click your heels and dream, dream, dream, dream, dream. Don't be afraid, don't be afraid.

This book is part of the dream and will cause thousands of demons to flee as you release it into your family. This book was not developed because we saw a problem in the Church that needed fixing; rather, this book was the result of a cry of desperation that arose within our own family. The greatest changes in our lives, the greatest steps of faith usually come because we get desperate and come to the end of our own resources. This place of relinquishment and total dependence on God is the very place where God loves to intervene. How long we take to arrive at that spot dictates the length of our trial.

The test for us began when our son James became seriously ill with schizophrenia. Nobody had any solutions to the problem, and nobody knew how to minister to either our son or to us. In fact, people started to pull away because they had no answers and felt awkward with the situation. But God was ready, both with a word of hope and a redemptive revelation that would allow us to take this disaster and turn it into a victory of His grace.

I (Jeanne) was before the Lord, reading the Bible, when I came across the Scripture stating that madness was a result of a curse (see Deut. 28:28). I was desperate for a solution to James' affliction of schizophrenia, and I knew if there was an entrance for this problem, there was an exit! I flipped back to what I had just read, but now with revelation, and I saw how the curse started. It had come in through a corporate sin (see Deut. 27:15-26). Not the corporate sin of Israel but the corporate sins of our families. A door had been opened for a curse to come upon our family because none of the family members had repented for breaking God's laws.

I (Ken) had also been searching for the answer to counter this blow to our family. God gave me a word that He was taking James on a journey similar to the one that Israel had experienced. Israel had been in bondage in Egypt until Moses came with the power of God and rescued them. They then embarked on a journey that led them through the wilderness into the Promised Land.

James had also been held captive in the world (represented by Egypt) of bad friends and drugs. God was going to take him out of the bondage and use the desert of schizophrenia to separate both out of James' life. When the desert (the illness) was finished, God would take him into his Land of Promises: his destiny. No timetable was laid out concerning the duration of the trip, only a guarantee that it would be completed.

Now armed with both a word of redemption and a seed of revelation, we started our fight for James' deliverance. The revelation showed us where to start interceding, and the word filled us with an assurance of victory, enabling us to aggressively go after this disease.

As we went through the curses that we found in the Bible and started to repent for our sins and ask forgiveness for our ancestors' sins, God started to remove the effect of the curses and release the blessings. We searched the Scriptures knowing that the answers lay hidden, waiting to be released. Our son, as well as ourselves, immediately started to get more freedom. His need to be in the hospital for months at a time, multiple times a year, ended, and he has never been back since. Excited to see the results, we began experimenting with this revelation on friends and people in the church. We watched as relational healings, physical healings, financial restorations, and tremendous releases began to manifest in their lives. Deliverance from addictions, fears, and torments occurred quickly and regularly.

Removing generational curses is just the first stage in coming out of bondage. Following the steps laid out in this book will remove many of the weights and curses passed down in our Christian walk, but it really deals only with layer one. It is not a "cure all" but is only a tool preparing us to deal with life's other issues as God reveals them. The Old Testament priests were disqualified from ministering if they had unhealed wounds (see Lev. 21:21); Jesus has the authority to heal because He was wounded for us and is now healed (see 1 Pet. 2:24). God doesn't want us to waste our sorrows; He wants to redeem them. He wants to use those very places where we have been wounded to gain the power and authority to heal others. But we must be healed first ourselves.

This book can be the beginning of an exciting journey. God will bless you as you allow old wounds to be opened up. God wants to remove the scars so that He can restore the proper functioning of the whole body. We present the many testimonies in this book as an inspiration to you of the power of God to *"destroy the works of the devil"* (1 John 3:8). We marvel at the wonderful work of the Holy Spirit in each and every life. James, who is the inspiration for this book, wrote this poem for you. In his own words, he is describing the process whereby we claim our inheritance in God's covenant.

"Angel Tread; We Proclaim"

An author, a finisher
A plea in heart
With wisdom planned
We will stand
A place of repentance
A will towards contentment
What gifts to acclaim our right?
When power transfers to might
A character heart
An inner plan
Who else can claim the man
To ensure a place
Amongst a new face
Presenting wisdom to the right
We stumble in darkness
We stand and fight
A man's journey for a goal
What can we finish
What game can we play?
What will make a pure heart stay?
We claim we know
We claim to stand
When we destroy a common land

Hearts are wrought
We don't know why
A force that's right
Changed to might
The privilege is up to man.

—James A. Harrington, 2009

Love,

Ken and Jeanne Harrington

INTRODUCTION

Jeanne and I (Ken) were ministering in our home to a couple from another church, who were in their mid-40s. They were experiencing some relational problems that tied back into the way they had connected with their respective mom and dad. The husband in particular was having trouble accepting some of the concepts we were trying to deal with. He had not initiated this ministry—his wife had; and though he was trying, his heart was not in it. After several vain attempts to break through into some of his strongholds, he excused himself to go for a bathroom break. His wife decided she also needed a break, so we showed her our home's main floor washroom and led him to the upstairs one. Shortly the wife returned, but the husband, who obviously had more to deal with, took much longer. We encouraged her as she waited for her husband to finish upstairs. Eventually we heard the toilet upstairs flush, but no husband appeared. The toilet flushed again, followed by a few choice expletives and some hurried steps.

"I plugged the toilet, and it's running all over the place!" he yelled. I rushed upstairs, pulled the top off the toilet, and flopped down the flapper to stop the flow of water. A huge quantity of water, along with various floating articles, had escaped. It flooded the entire bathroom, ran down through the heating pipe access hole in the floor, and inundated the kitchen cupboards below. We calmly assured them that it could all be cleaned up, as we pulled the polluted dishes out of the cupboards. When we started to mop up the bathroom and kitchen, the couple, with many apologies, beat a hasty retreat. Though we offered, some embarrassment prevented them from returning and receiving any further ministry.

The Bible often uses water to represent the Holy Spirit. Jesus said that *"out of* [your] *belly shall flow rivers of living water...this spake He of the Spirit, which they...should receive"* (John 7:38-39). John the Baptist said that he baptizes with water, but that Jesus would *"baptize...with the Holy Ghost, and with fire"* (Matt. 3:11). Jesus added that the disciples would *"receive power, after that the Holy Ghost is come upon you"* (Acts 1:8). These Scriptures present the baptism of the Holy Ghost as a baptism of power. We wrongly assume that in every situation, more power will be beneficial. God was showing us that is not always the case.

The mess in the bathroom was not created from the plugged toilet, though that was a problem. The mess came from the addition of the extra flush of water. It is the same in our lives: the more power or authority we have, the greater the mess that the issues, or blockages, in our character creates. Today's media blasts the sins and indiscretions of every celebrity across newspaper pages, television screens, and computer monitors. It is one thing for me to lose my cool and explode at my wife in the privacy of my home. I can repent, apologize in private, and quietly heal the situation. It is another to have all those weaknesses automatically exposed to the world. Jeanne has often said, when I am flying off the handle, "If only your fan club could see you now!" The declarations of the President of the United States can influence the stock market; mine seldom go past my personal or family circles. Such is the nature of power.

Through the bathroom mess, which created the husband's initial embarrassment and subsequent panic, irritated us, we realized that God had just presented us with a prophetic picture. This was a perfect illustration of the state that most of us are in: we are plugged up. Plugged up with wrong thinking, judgments, unforgiveness, fears, traditions, and bad experiences. Just as that hapless husband thought more water would fix the problem, we think that if we have more power we can remove any obstacle. Lack of power is not the problem; our plugged up system is the problem. We need a solution to our problem so the Holy Spirit's power doesn't create a mess in our lives and in the lives of those we touch.

"Problems" or "Sins"?

The solution we want to present is to call our problems *sin*. If I have a problem, I will have that problem all my life. If I have a sin, I can ask forgiveness, repent, and be free of it today. We prefer the term *problem* because that term does not carry any stigma with it. Unfortunately, it also provides no solution. Sin, on the other hand, has the blood of Jesus as its solution. You cannot apply the blood to a problem, only to a sin.

The people of Israel applied the blood to their doors on the night that God executed judgment *"against all the gods of Egypt"* (Exod. 12:12). God said, *"When I see the blood, I will pass over you, and the plague shall not…destroy you, when I smite the land of Egypt"* (Exod. 12:13). This passing over was a type or foreshadowing of what Jesus does in reality when He, *"Christ our passover is sacrificed for us"* (1 Cor. 5:7). His blood allows our judgment to be applied to Him and frees us, as families, to enter into the blessings that belong to Him.

Though we had not made the mess in the bathroom, it was our house, and we had to clean it up. It is the same in families: the messes we must clean up are not always originated by us. It is interesting that the Hebrew root for house and family is the same: *bayith*,[1] from the root *banah*,[2] meaning to build. When King David was attempting to build a house for God, the prophet said to David that *"The Lord tells you that He will make you a house…*[He] *will set up your seed after you…and* [He] *will establish his kingdom"* (2 Sam. 7:11-12 NKJV). David's family was to be his house.

God always works with families. That is how He divided the earth: *"These are the families of the sons of Noah after their generations, in their nations: and by these were the nations divided in the earth after the flood"* (Gen. 10:32). God said in Abraham and in his seed *"shall all the families of the earth be blessed"* (Gen. 28:14). God delivered the whole nation of Israel at the time of the Passover by their families (see Exod. 12:7,21) and divided the promised land the same way (see Num. 33:54).

As the blessings of favor and inheritance come down family lines, so curses of bondage, robbery, and addictions descend the same way. God wants to move us where, as a family, we can break free of our bondages and enter into the *"glorious liberty of the children of God"* (Rom. 8:21). This book, *From Curses to Blessings,* will deal with both the principles and the practical means to accomplish this transformation. We will explore the seeming contradiction between application of law and grace and will share some of the countless testimonies of people who have applied the truths we are about to share.

Freedom is a journey, not a destination; it is a way of thinking that aligns with the Word of God. That is why we are told to *"walk in newness of life"* (Rom. 6:4), to *"walk not after the flesh, but after the Spirit"* (Rom. 8:1), and to *"walk by faith, not by sight"* (2 Cor. 5:7). Moving out of generational curses is only one step on our journey of freedom, but without it we will be frustrated by why we don't seem to get victory in our lives.

John the Baptist prepared the way for Jesus as he proclaimed righteousness to Israel. John's preaching and baptisms brought about a gift of repentance that opened the way for the coming of the Lord. From this book we pray a gift of repentance will arise within your spirit and that you will prepare the way of the Lord in your life and that of your family.

We pray that you will enter into a clear flow of the Spirit and apprehend the destiny that belongs to your family. We pray that as you break off the last vestiges of the law that the grace of God will lift your spirit until you know that you are *"blessed…with all spiritual blessings in heavenly places in Christ"* (Eph. 1:3).

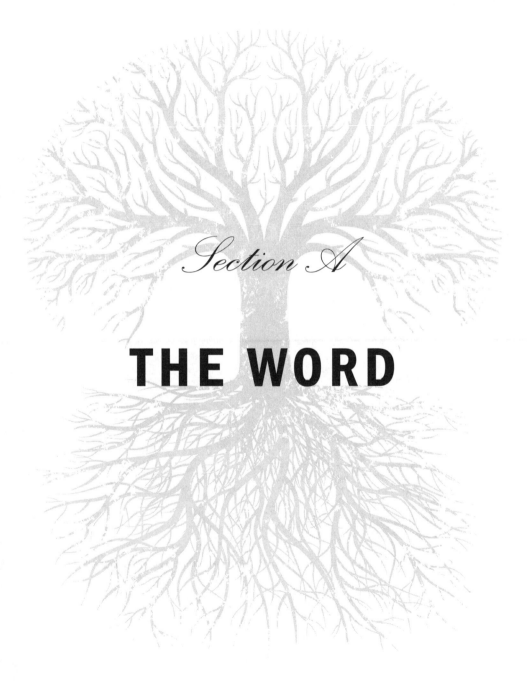

Section A

THE WORD

Chapter 1

ARE WE CURSED?

The night is dark and dreary, the cave dank and smoky, as three witches with warts and hooked noses flit around a steamy pot.

> Round about the cauldron go,
> In the poison'd entrails throw.
> Toad, that under cold stone
> Days and nights has thirty-one
>
> Swelter'd venom sleeping got,
> Boil thou first i' the charmed pot.
>
> Double, double, toil and trouble,
> Fire burn, and cauldron bubble.
>
> Fillet of a fenny snake,
> In the cauldron boil and bake.
> Eye of newt and toe of frog,
> Wool of bat and tongue of dog,
>
> Adder's fork and blind-worm's sting,
> Lizard's leg and howlet's wing,
> For a charm of powerful trouble,
> Like a hell-broth boil and bubble.

Double, double, toil and trouble,
Fire burn and cauldron bubble.[1]

This scene from Macbeth, with the three old hags cackling around a boiling caldron, is what we often conjure up when we think of curses. These malevolent utterances of evil seemingly do, in certain circumstances, affect some people. The Bible says that God *"made us to sit together in heavenly places in Christ"* (Eph. 2:6), *"far above all principality, and power, and might, and dominion…in this world"* (Eph. 1:21). As long as we are in Christ, we are free from the effects of these kinds of curses.

Yet if we check the following list of consequences (see Deut. 28:15-68) associated with curses, we see that many of these apply to us.

- Problems conceiving

- Depression

- Tumors

- Work problems

- Persecution

- Fever

- Tuberculosis

- Inflammations

- Fear

- Lack of answered prayer

- Insanity

- Confusion

- Blindness

- Sores that won't heal

- Marital problems

- Infidelity

- Financial problems

- Accidents

- Violence

- Robbery

- Oppressive government

- Discrimination

- Poverty

- Destruction

- Business failure

- Deprivation

Add to that list all the diseases that flow down family lines from deleterious genes, including diabetes, heart disease, cancers, cystic fibrosis, hemophilia, Down syndrome, sickle cell anemia, muscular dystrophy, and many, many more. Sickness and death are a result of the fall of man and the consequent curse that was imposed upon creation. Yet *"Christ hath redeemed us from the curse of the law, being made a curse for us"* (Gal. 3:13). He *"took our infirmities, and bare our sicknesses"* (Matt. 8:17). Why, if grace has supplanted the curse, do we still suffer its effects?

The Law! All the laws! The law of sin and death (see Rom. 8:2), the laws of sowing and reaping (see Gal. 6:7-8), the law of increase (see Hos. 8:7), and the law of Moses (see 2 Cor. 3:6) all conspire against us to bring us into bondage and death. Even the second law of thermodynamics[2] tells us our universe is running down. Death of one kind or another is everywhere; only the *"Spirit gives life"* (2 Cor. 3:6 NKJV).

The Bible says that the *"law is holy, and the commandment holy, and just, and good...But sin...[was] working death in me by that which is good"* (Rom. 7:12-13). The *"law was our schoolmaster to bring us unto Christ, that we might be justified by faith. But after that faith is come, we are no longer under a schoolmaster"* (Gal. 3:24-25). However, we keep ourselves under *"the law [which] is not of faith: but...Christ hath redeemed us from the curse of the law...that the blessing of*

Abraham might come...through Jesus Christ; that we might receive the promise of the Spirit through faith" (Gal. 3:12-14).

The law is like the first gear in a five-speed transmission. It is necessary to get the car moving, but once that gear has reached its maximum RPM it becomes the biggest hindrance to the car reaching its highest speed. In fact, if the car gets stuck in first gear, it will cause the whole engine to burn up. The effort to live by the law is actually a work of the flesh. Paul said, *"When we were in the flesh, the motions of sins, which were by the law, did work in our members to bring forth fruit unto death"* (Rom. 7:5). Paul is even more forceful by declaring that *"Christ is become of no effect unto you, whosoever of you are justified by the law; ye are fallen from grace"* (Gal. 5:4).

Operating in the flesh (not in the Spirit) is the conduit that allows curses to flow into our lives. Being part of the family of man allowed death to reign *"from Adam to Moses, even over those that had not sinned according to the likeness of the transgression of Adam. For...by the one man's offense many died"* (Rom. 5:14-15 NKJV). Thus, even though we don't sin in the particular way that Adam did, we come under the consequence of that sin. In Jesus, that judgment is reversed, and His righteous acts are now transferred to us (see Rom. 5:17). However, where we don't walk in faith to access the grace of the Spirit, we fall out of that grace back into the realm of the curse.

The Word says, *"the curse causeless shall not come"* (Prov. 26:2). Without an open door, the thief cannot come *"to steal...to kill, and to destroy"* (John 10:10). Yet we seem to suffer from many afflictions that we do nothing to initiate. Just as Adam and Jesus' actions affected all of mankind, so on a micro-scale our individual ancestors' actions can connect us to the consequences of their sins or their righteousness.

There is a common theme used in the Old Testament for the various words translated as curses. The first mention of a curse is in Genesis 3:14-17 where God curses both the snake and the ground. The Hebrew verb *ârar* is used and the meaning is to execrate.[3] Execrate is derived from the Latin *execrates:*[4] *ex*-meaning out, and *sacrare*—meaning consecrated, from the root *sacer*—meaning sacred.

Thus the root of the verb "to be cursed" means to be removed from a consecrated or sacred position. A similar idea is portrayed in other Hebrew words translated as curse: *meêrâh,*[5] *qelâlâh,*[6] and *qâlal.*[7] Here the meaning is to lightly esteem or bring into contempt. A curse always lowers who we are.

The result of the original curse:

1. The snake lost his position:

   - He was demoted to the lowest among the animals.

   - He had to go on his belly and eat dust.

   - He became the enemy of man.

2. The ground lost its fruitfulness:

   - It now would produce thorns and thistles.

3. The woman lost her place:

   - She came under her husband.

   - Childbearing would be worrisome and difficult.

   - She would now die.

4. The man lost his position:

   - He was driven out of the Garden.

   - Now he had to toil to eat.

   - He would now die.

God did not curse Adam or Eve; He cursed the snake and the ground, but Adam and Eve had to live under the consequence of the curses. We tend to think that God is like us; if we curse someone or something, it is because we are angry and want punishment to fall. But God *"so loved the world* [cosmos],[8] *that He gave His only begotten Son…God sent not His Son into the world to condemn the world; but that the world through Him might be saved"* (John 3:16-17). If God loves us and died for us, then the curse He sent was not for our punishment but for our salvation. His curses have redemptive purpose. God's curses are like

"Wrong Way" road signs, signaling that we are on the wrong side of the highway and that if we continue down this track, someone is going to get killed. As we saw earlier, the curse removes us from our exalted position in the heavenlies, our sacred place, and entangles us in satan's realm. Grace or favor was the original state that Adam and Eve enjoyed. Jesus came to restore that state. Through Adam we have literally fallen from grace.

That picture is laid in the tabernacle where the law, the Ten Commandments, is placed in the ark under the mercy seat or the throne of grace (see Exod. 25:21 and Heb. 4:16). If we refuse grace, we are lowered to the realm of the law and our own efforts. God knew that in such a state we would die.

Genesis 3:22 reveals a discussion that took place between members of the Godhead, in which the danger of letting man remain in his fallen state eternally becomes apparent. The solution was to drive him away from the Garden (the blessing) and the tree of life so he would die (the curse), thus allowing him to be resurrected in a different state. That was not an act of revenge, but an act of redemption.

Through His death on the cross, Jesus, *"by whom also we have access by faith into this grace wherein we stand"* opened up the way (Rom. 5:2). The problem is we don't access that grace in every area of our lives, and neither did our ancestors. Sin does not evaporate,[9] and neither do the consequences. If no one in the family has brought the sin to the cross and repented, it will continue to pass down the family line. It is God who visits *"the iniquity of the fathers upon the children unto the third and fourth generation"* (Exod. 20:5).

The Hebrew word for iniquity is *âvôn:*[10] perverse, evil, fault. The root is *âvâh:*[11] to crook, do amiss, pervert, do wrong. God is desirous to remove the iniquity or the perverted bent in a family line so that the family can walk in its destiny. Destiny is more corporate than personal. Only once after Isaac is born is the God of Abraham ever mentioned without including Isaac and Jacob. Even then, the passage is speaking corporately about the people of the God of Abraham, his offspring (see Ps. 47:9). The blessings of Abraham were also for Isaac and Jacob and their children.

God is the God of the generations. In the Ten Commandments, God linked long life to generational honoring (see Exod. 20:12). His purpose for sending

Elijah, who is to prepare the way of the Lord, is to *"turn the heart of the fathers to the children, and the heart of the children to their fathers, lest I come and smite the earth with a curse"* (Mal. 4:6). That curse comes when the first generation rejects the next, and the next refuses to honor the first. The seed of the curse is planted in this kind of animosity. Like all seeds, they will grow and produce fruit. God allows that fruit to ripen so that it becomes obvious that something is wrong and to allow it to be extricated without destroying the good fruit (see Matt. 13:29).

Satan would like to keep the fruit hidden until it brings death. For when an evil desire has conceived, it gives birth to sin; and sin, when it is full-grown, gives

birth to death (see James 1:15). God said, *"I sought for a man among them, that should make up the hedge, and stand in the gap before me for the land, that I should not destroy it: but I found none"* (Ezek. 22:30). It is God's mercy to past generations that He allows the present generation to stand in the gap for the family and repent of past sins. It is His goodness to the present generation that God *"keeps covenant and mercy for a thousand generations with those who love Him and keep His commandments"* (Deut. 7:9 NKJV).

Family was God's idea from the beginning. God said, concerning the past heroes of the faith, that *"these all, having obtained a good report through faith, received not the promise: God having provided some better thing for us, that they without us should not be made perfect"* (Heb. 11:39-40). In fact, it is this presence of our families: this *"great cloud of witnesses"* (Heb. 12:1a), that empowers us to *"lay aside every weight, and the sin which so easily ensnares us, and let us run with endurance the race that is set before us"* (Heb. 12:1b NKJV). We are running a race, but it is a relay race with our family. We may be called to make up a leg that was run poorly or benefit from a leg that was run with excellence. The team, not the individual, will claim the prize.

Jesus alluded to this cross-generational unity when He said, *"I do not pray for these alone, but also for those who will believe in Me through their word: that they all may be one"* (John 17:20-21 NKJV). Dealing with generational curses helps fulfill that prayer of Jesus and mirrors the relationships in our families, which exists amongst the Father, Son, and Holy Spirit.

Chapter 2

OPEN DOORS

I am persuaded, that neither death, nor life, nor angels, nor principalities, nor powers, nor things present, nor things to come, nor height, nor depth, nor any other creature, shall be able to separate us from the love of God, which is in Christ Jesus our Lord
(Romans 8:38-39).

Even though no power in Heaven and earth can keep us out of the love and will of God, our attitudes and our words can. They will dictate what God can do for and through us.

When Israel was traveling through the wilderness,

...the people became impatient because of the journey. The people spoke against God and Moses, "Why have You brought us up out of Egypt to die in the wilderness? For there is no food and no water, and we loathe this miserable food." The Lord sent fiery serpents among the people and they bit the people, so that many people of Israel died (Numbers 21:4-6 NASB).

They were in a desert that had no food or water and was full of snakes (see Deut. 8:15). But until now, God had supplied food and water and had provided protection against the snakes. Their murmuring had broken down their hedge of protection, and the snakes, which were always there, now had access (see Eccles. 10:8). Israel didn't trust God even though He had delivered them and cared for them in the desert for 40 years. Their lack of trust blinded them to God's goodness and thus to His protection.

We often see what we want to see, and hear the fears in our hearts louder than we hear God. Often those fears become the voice of God to us. When I (Jeanne) was younger, because of a bad experience in another relationship, I didn't trust my husband with women even though he had been faithful for over twenty years. My fears caused me to "hear God" telling me to drive down to a particular hotel where I would find Ken cheating on me.

I went, and sure enough, there was his truck parked out in front of the hotel. I was so furious that I spun around and plotted a strategy to trap him in whatever pathetic lie he might try to weave. I had prophetically heard to go and had seen the evidence to prove my suspicions.

When Ken came home, I sweetly asked him how his day went and whether he had to come into town for anything. He calmly replied that the day had been like any other day, and no, he had been at work the whole time. I blew up and confronted him with my word from God and how I knew he was lying because I had seen his truck outside the bar at the hotel.

He took me outside and showed me the truck he had driven home. It was not his usual truck. He explained that one of his men had taken his truck into town to get the brakes done and that the brake shop was next to the hotel where I had spotted the truck. I had believed a lie, and my fears opened the door to listening to the enemy. *"There is no fear in love; but perfect love casts out fear, because fear involves torment"* (1 John 4:18 NKJV). If we have no peace and are walking in fear, we have opened an access for the enemy to come in.

The good news is that if there is an access point that allows the enemy in, then there is an exit point. We must be brutally honest concerning our families and ourselves if we expect to rout satan from his stronghold within us. We are going to look at several of these doors and learn how to close them from further access.

The Door of Occult Activity

The term *occult* comes from the Latin *occultus*, which means concealed[1] or hidden from the eyes of understanding. The modern application of the term alludes to various forms of the black arts of magic and astrology.

According to Scripture there are three basic branches of occult activity:

1. The witchcraft or power branch includes

   hypnosis,[2] mind control, parakinesis,[3] voodoo, telekinesis, "touch" healing, table tipping, astral projection, levitation, witchcraft, martial arts (those that meditate on gods).

2. The divination or knowledge branch includes

   astrology, automatic writing, channeling, crystal balls, ESP, clairvoyance, color therapy, pendulum divining, handwriting analysis, kabbalah, horoscopes, iridology, mediums, mind reading, omens, séances, numerology, palm reading, phrenology, telepathy, tarot cards, tea leaf reading, false religions, occult books, water witching.

3. Sorcery using physical objects can include

   amulets, ankhs, charms, crystals, hallucinogenic drugs, hex signs, lucky symbols, Ouija boards, pagan fetishes, religious artifacts, zodiac charms, talismans.

Though many of these objects or actions are in themselves seemingly innocent, they are, nonetheless, the doors or access points for demonic activity. It was for these very practices that the original inhabitants of Canaan were ejected. God commanded Israel that when they came into the land that they were not to

> *...learn to follow the abominable practices of these nations. There shall not be found among you anyone who makes his son or daughter pass through the fire, or who uses divination, or is a soothsayer, or an augur, or a sorcerer, or a charmer, or a medium, or a wizard, or a necromancer. For all who do these things are an abomination to the Lord and it is because of these abominable practices that the Lord your God is driving them out* (Deuteronomy 18:9-12 AMP).

The object of all occult activities is to uncover hidden knowledge and use that knowledge to control people and situations for some form of profit or advantage. God has ordained that we draw our knowledge from the Holy Spirit and use it to advance the Kingdom. These practices allowed demonic activity to overtake the Canaanites, and it corrupted them sexually (see Lev. 18). God said,

> *...for in all these the nations are defiled...and the land is defiled: therefore I visit the iniquity...upon it, and the land itself vomiteth out her inhabitants. ...therefore keep My statutes and judgments... that the land spue you not out...when ye defile it, as it spued out the nations that were before you* (Leviticus 18:24-28).

It is interesting that it took four generations of iniquity before the land, and God, brought judgment. God told Abram that his people would be slaves in Egypt: *"But in the fourth generation they shall return here, for the iniquity of the Amorites is not yet complete"* (Gen. 15:16 NKJV). This four-generation cycle is crucial when dealing with sin, curses, and judgments, as we will see later.

Had the Amorites repented, God could have dealt differently with them. If we have been involved in occult activity, we also need to repent of our sin. That will remove the iniquity from us but not the demons associated with it. Neither will it close the door that we have opened. We must aggressively cast out whatever demonic beings we let in and renounce our involvement to shut off further access. Paul said that when the Gentiles sacrifice to idols, they are actually sacrificing to demons. He said the idol is nothing and the sacrifice is nothing, but the act constitutes demon worship:

> *Do I mean then that a sacrifice offered to an idol is anything, or that an idol is anything? No, but the sacrifices of pagans are offered to demons, not to God, and I do not want you to be participants with demons* (1 Corinthians 10:19-20 NIV).

The occult games we play may seem innocent, but the spirit realm takes it seriously, for that is their door into this realm.

I (Jeanne) had a relative come to me for prayer. She was not a Christian but had heard that I prayed for ladies who could not conceive. She and her husband wanted a baby but were not having any success. She asked me if I would pray for her to conceive. Ken had shared Christ with them over the last few months, but they had not yet made a commitment. I knew that the inability to conceive was a part of the curse (see Deut. 28:18), so I asked her if she wanted to give her life to the Lord. She was reluctant and repeated that she just wanted to have a baby.

As we were sharing, the Lord brought her involvement with teacup reading to my mind. I pulled out the Bible and spoke to her.

"Do you remember when you used to do teacup reading to determine your future?" I asked. She nodded.

"The Bible says that is an abomination to the Lord."

I showed her this passage in the Bible:

> ...*There shall not be found among you anyone who makes his son or his daughter pass through the fire, or one who practices witchcraft, or a soothsayer, or a sorcerer, or one who conjures spells, or a medium, or a spiritist, or one who calls up the dead. For all who do these things are an abomination to the Lord* (Deuteronomy 18:10-12).

"Teacup reading is interpreting omens, and God hates it."

"I never knew!" she exclaimed.

I led her in a prayer of repentance, and she received forgiveness.

Immediately, she asked, "What can I do to get saved?"

The demonic structure that was blocking her from receiving Jesus as her Savior was broken, and the light of God was able to penetrate. I led her in a prayer of repentance and commitment to God, and she received Jesus as her Savior. Now I had a liberty to pray for the baby she wanted. Less than a year later they had a son.

God allowed the operation of the curse in her life to bring her to a place of repentance that destroyed a stronghold that her family had participated in for generations. God always wants to bless; when we see the opposite functioning in our lives, we need to ask God, "Why?" so that we can remove whatever demonic structure is blocking the flow of blessings from Heaven. Remember that *"all things work together for good to them that love God, to them who are the called according to His purpose"* (Rom. 8:28).

The Door of the Broken Will

The will is the soul's natural defense against any spiritual invasion. It is the inspector to which everything that passes into the heart must submit. God never bypasses the will, but satan always tries.

The will is much like the skin. If there is no break in the skin, then the germs present in the air cannot penetrate and cause an infection. Cut yourself, fail to clean the cut, and your body will be invaded by germs or bacteria. If the will is intact, spirits in the air cannot enter. Break the will, and anything that is floating around may enter. The will may be breached through a major trauma, such as sexual abuse or the death of a spouse, where the survivor may simply want to die. It can also be breached by an event that creates tremendous fear. The will is sometimes set aside (as in a hypnotic encounter) or seduced (as in a mob situation). Examples of situations where a will may be broken could include rape, sexual or emotional abuse, a vicious animal attack, or being subjected to constant violent arguments. Many of the roots for demonic oppression are linked to these events occurring in early childhood or even during prenatal traumas.

Forgiveness of the abusers is the first step in pulling out the roots of the abuse. Forgiveness is an act, not a feeling; it in no way absolves the perpetrator of their sins but cuts the cords that bind the abuser to the victim. If our well-being is dependent on another's reactions, then in many ways he or she still controls and manipulates us. The healthy response is to refuse to allow anyone to rent space in my brain. This will likely require the healing of some memories, but that is beyond the scope of this book.[4]

When we forgive, we are like a company that is writing off a bad debt. Rather than leaving it on the books and frustratingly trying to collect, we simply rack it up as uncollectible. That does not mean we send a note and say, "It's OK; we don't care anymore." It simply means we won't waste any more resources or time on the debt, and it won't show up on our balance sheets anymore.

The Door of Overt Sin

"Submit yourselves therefore to God. Resist the devil, and he will flee from you" (James 4:7). Submission is the state where you have placed yourself under authority or yielded to that authority. If you are not submitted to God, then you have no power to remove satan from your life or situation. Paul asked the believers, *"Do you not know that when you present yourselves to someone as slaves for obedience, you are slaves of the one whom you obey, either of sin resulting in death, or of obedience resulting in righteousness?"* (Rom. 6:16 NASB). This verse stresses that you actually become the enemy's servant if you indulge in sin. Habits we can't break are an indication of demonic activity in our lives. Examples of overt sins that might lead to demonic oppression might include constant viewing of pornography, repetitive lying, slander, or rebellion. Any of these might provide an open door to demonic intrusion.

Sin is the fruit, not the root, of our problems. Sin will cause other problems, but ultimately we must find what was planted in our hearts that produced our sin actions. The first step in the healing of overt sin is to confess that it is sin—not a lifestyle, not a problem, not a lack of discipline, and not a lapse. It is sin. If I have a problem, I will have a problem all my life. If I have a sin, I can repent and get rid of it today.

Confess, repent, and denounce any demonic activity that may have driven that sin into an addiction. Then close any doors that allowed the enemy to suggest that you can do it again. This is not to be an exercise of will power but of faith—faith in what Jesus did on the cross when He *"condemned sin in the flesh:* [made a way] *that the righteousness of the law might be fulfilled in us, who walk not after the flesh, but after the Spirit"* (Rom. 8:3-4). Trying to fulfill the law is an effort of the flesh; faith in the work of the cross is a fruit of the Spirit.

The Door of Offence

Offence comes from the Greek *skandalon*[5] meaning "bait stick." It suggests the picture of a trap for a bird or small animal held up by a stick baited with some food. If the animal takes the bait, it is immediately trapped. It is a snare that is triggered by the animal's own action. Interestingly *skandalon* is also the root for the English word *scandal*. It is a wrong action initiated by a wrong motive that traps someone in scandal or disgrace. James writes, "*But every man is tempted, when he is drawn away of his own lust, and enticed. Then when lust has conceived, it bringeth forth sin: and sin, when it is finished bringeth forth death*" (James 1:14-15). Had we seen the outcome, we never would have taken the bait.

If we take offence (the bait) at some situation, we are trapped. Jesus made a hard statement about eating His flesh and drinking His blood (see John 6:50-66). Many were offended and stopped following Him. The Latin *offendere*[6] means "to strike against." That was what Jesus was doing, striking against or smashing their traditional mindsets. In the Jewish mind, eating human flesh and drinking blood was an abomination. They could not reconcile Jesus' words with their traditions. Their traditions then "*made the commandment of God of none effect*" (Matt. 15:6 NKJV).

The parable of the sower emphasized that those who were offended had no root in them and would produce no fruit (see Matt. 13:21). Our temptation is to always blame others, but Jesus clearly puts the emphasis on our own responses. Often offences are an indication of a religious spirit being present (believing that how we think and judge is how God thinks and judges); in fact, the opposite is true (see Isa. 55:8-9). Offence is a product of pride. Our friend Jim received the revelation that "you can be wounded in humility, but you can only be offended in pride."[7] If you stub your toe on a chair, it will hurt; if you kick the chair afterward, you are still hurt, but so is your pride. Even worse than our taking offence for what is done to us is taking secondhand offence for what is done to others. The problem with secondhand offence is that it is next to impossible to be free from it. If we are mistreated and get offended, we can always go to the offender and be reconciled. If we take secondhand offence, we have no way of knowing when the situation has been settled and no one is going to apologize to us to bring resolution. All the participants in the conflict may be at peace, but we are still stuck, seething in the snare because we took secondhand offence.

I (Ken) had to discipline someone for an indiscretion, but the correction was not well received and caused many hard feelings. Later we were able to talk it out, and, even though we didn't agree about what happened, we were able to reconcile. Problems started to spring up when other people got involved. While the man was processing his own offence, he had shared the situation with some other people.

I became the enemy for hurting their friend. Nobody came to me with their anger; they only listened to the complaints of a wounded friend. All rumors are lies, and rumors are what you get when you listen to only one side of an argument. I have been stung so many times, accepting one version of an event as the real news (the truth), when in fact it was only an editorial. Only later, when I heard the whole story, was I able to rightly discern the truth. *"The first one to plead his cause seems right, until his neighbor comes and examines him"* (Prov. 18:17 NKJV).

We get stuck in secondhand offence because we will not obey the word that says, *"If your brother wrongs you, go and show him his fault, between you and him privately"* (Matt. 18:15 AMP). We usually don't go to him at all, and we are not very private when we are exposing a perceived sin to anyone who will listen. Love covers; hatred exposes.

> *Nothing is [so closely] covered up that it will not be revealed, or hidden that it will not be known. Whatever you have spoken in the darkness shall be heard and listened to in the light, and what you have whispered in [people's] ears and behind closed doors will be proclaimed upon the housetops* (Luke 12:2-3 AMP).

If we would employ the safeguards that the Scriptures put in place to deal with conflicts, the Church would be able to walk in love and unity. Beware the bait of satan.

The Door of Generational Curses

This is the main topic of the first section of this book. The next several chapters will deal with various aspects of this door into our families.

Chapter 3

OUR BIRTHRIGHT

In the near future, the Baby Boomers will be the recipients of the largest intergenerational transfer of wealth in the history of the U.S.A., if not the world. The next 50 years will see at least $41 trillion pass to the next generation, estimates Paul Schervish, director of the Center on Wealth and Philanthropy at Boston College.[1] The former generation learned to save, fight, and work for what they earned. They endured the Great Depression, World War II, and the battle against communism to create an inheritance to pass on.

Inheritance—the word speaks of hope and promise, the blessing of one generation to the next. Jeanne and I have both received an inheritance in the last few years. They were not huge because we both have large families (Jeanne's—seven siblings; Ken's—five), but they were welcome and appreciated. My (Ken's) mother (healthy at 90) decided to divide the assets from the sale of her house with her children.

The Bible says, *"A good man leaves an inheritance to his children's children"* (Prov. 13:22 NKJV). We have already transferred some of our inheritance to our children, fulfilling that Scripture. But money is not the only thing that gets passed down. We pass down our genetics: tall or short; stout or thin; straight hair or curly; black, white, red, brown, or yellow skin; our intelligence or lack thereof; our emotional disposition or temperament; and even our character.

On the negative side, we can bequeath our children genetic diseases, financial obligations, social disadvantages, and cultural and spiritual baggage. We may have endued them with negative attitudes, spiritual deprivation, and toxic memories. They may hate us because of some real or perceived hurt, which will taint their marriages, their relationships with their children, and their attitudes toward authority, especially God. Even the money may turn out to be a curse if they have not been trained to handle it.

God views our attitudes to our inheritance as having great importance. Isaac's sons, Esau and Jacob, had attitudes concerning their birthrights that were poles apart. Esau sold his birthright (the double portion inheritance) to Jacob for *"bread and stew of lentils...thus Esau despised his birthright"* (Gen. 25:34 NKJV). Jacob, however, was willing to lie, cheat, and steal to get both the blessing and the birthright.

On the surface, it would appear that Esau was just passive concerning these things, and that Jacob was greedy for them. That would, by default, make Esau more righteous, but God said, *"I loved Jacob, and I hated Esau...and laid his... heritage waste"* (Mal. 1:2-3). Not only did Esau not get his rightful inheritance, but he also lost what he did get. Why? God saw him as a profane or base[2] person with no spiritual insight or bent: *"He was rejected: for he found no place of repentance, though he sought it carefully with tears"* (Heb. 12:17). Esau couldn't repent or change his mind[3] concerning his inheritance, even when he tried. He did not value what God valued, which was the cross-generational link, which we will explain in a moment.

Jacob, though he had many character flaws, coveted being in the flow that connected him to the blessing and the family destiny. That strong desire is what God prizes. Paul said we were to *"pursue love, and desire* [literally, *covet*][4] *spiritual gifts"* (1 Cor. 14:1 NKJV). God was saying concerning Jacob, "I like this guy. We will have to tweak his character, but I like this guy." Jesus reacted the same to the disciples after they displayed selfish ambition, territorialism, and a murdering spirit (see Luke 9:46-56).

I would have sent the disciples back for more basic training had I seen those traits, but Jesus wasn't worried about their deficiencies. In fact, He *"appointed seventy others"* (Luke 10:1) just like them and sent them out. God likes it when we like what He likes and hate what He hates. *"The fear of the Lord is to hate evil"*

(Prov. 8:13), and *"the fear of the Lord is the beginning of wisdom"* (Ps. 111:10). Therefore the beginning of wisdom is to hate evil or what God hates. That hatred of evil is just the first step in our transformation into thinking like God.

We only hate in others what is already in us. The Word makes it clear that we *"who judge are habitually practicing the very same things"* (Rom. 2:1 AMP). If we hate it in others, we have it in us. It takes a thief to know one. We will, if we are zealous of what God wants, be able to cleanse it in ourselves when God reveals it to us. Jacob and Jesus' disciples were able to step into their destinies not because they were righteous in their actions, but just the opposite. They stepped in because they were hot after *"the hope of His calling, and...the riches of the glory of His inheritance in the saints"* (Eph. 1:18).

God is desirous to link the generations so that true wealth, not just money, might flow to the third generation. Even though the promises were given to Abraham, they were reaffirmed to Isaac (see Gen. 26:24) and to Jacob (see Gen. 32:9-29). God is always referred to as the God of Abraham, Isaac, and Jacob. The longer the generational connection, the greater the blessings or the curses flow. The first generation has incremental increase; the second multiplies; and the third is designed to go exponential. Abraham had Isaac; Isaac had Esau and Jacob; Jacob had the 12 patriarchs. God wants to establish this pattern: get the blessing to the third generation and beyond. Satan is attempting to block this cross-generational blessing.

Paul said that God's *"invisible attributes...have been clearly seen, being understood through what has been made"* (Rom. 1:20 NASB). He is in essence saying that the natural mirrors the spiritual. This allows us to discern the reality of spiritual truths and principles by observing what is transpiring around us in our physical world. A perfect example of cross-generational blessing is seen in the transfer of wealth. That transfer can be either a curse or a blessing.

"Almost everybody knows a family or has seen a case where the money hurt somebody in the family, or the kids or grandchildren blew it all," says Rodney Zeeb, an attorney and co-author (with Perry L. Cochell) of *Beating the Midas Curse,* a reference to the destructive relationships with money that splinter some families.[5]

So widespread is the problem that six out of ten affluent families will lose the family fortune by the end of the second generation, Zeeb suggests. And nine out of ten will have depleted the family wealth by the end of the third generation. It's a modern-day drama summed up in an ancient Chinese adage: "Wealth never survives three generations." Nineteenth-century Americans updated it to read, "From shirtsleeves to shirtsleeves in three generations."[6]

This battle to get the blessings transferred is played out, first, in that which is natural, and afterward, in that which is spiritual (see 1 Cor. 15:46). Very few families have achieved what Abraham, Isaac, and Jacob did: transfer the callings and blessings past the third or fourth generation. Satan's plan is to cut off the spiritual heritage so it does not get to the third generation and extrapolate into massive authority and power in the fourth, as it did in Joseph's life.

We can see how satan applied this strategy against the kings of Israel. After God removed King Saul, whom He *"gave in...anger, and took...away in...wrath"* (Hos. 13:11), Judea had one continuous line of kings that came down David's lineage. Israel was a different story. They were unable to extend a kingly house past the third generation, with one exception: King Jehu. Jehu destroyed Baal out of Israel, thus the Lord said,

> *...Because you have done well in doing what is right in my eyes and have done to the house of Ahab all that was in My heart, your sons shall sit on the throne of Israel to the fourth generation* (2 Kings 10:30 NKJV).

Jehu started out well but *"took no heed to walk in the law of the Lord...with all his heart"* (2 Kings 10:31). His sons continued in their father's footsteps and *"did that which was evil in the sight of the Lord"* (2 Kings 13:2). God kept His Word and allowed Jehu's line to last to the fourth generation though the last, Zachariah, reigned only six months before he was slain (see 2 Kings 15:8-12). Unfortunately, no one ever dealt with the original sin of Jeroboam, therefore, *"the Israelites persisted in all the sins of Jeroboam and did not turn away from them until the Lord removed them from His presence"* (2 Kings 17:22-23 NIV).

Unlike Israel, Judea never endured more than two consecutive reigns of evil kings, until the very end. This allowed continuous generational repentance and cleansing to occur and kept the blessings that fell on David intact. God always deals with a people through their leaders (see 2 Sam. 24:1). As the kings went, so went the nation; when the kings repented, so did the people; when the kings became apostate, the people followed. The kings' actions, because of their authority and position, representing the kingdom, opened the door for satan to come in and entice the people to sin. The king affected all the institutions that fell within his jurisdiction as a father affects the generations that follow him.

God's initial institution on the earth was the family, and it is within that framework that He intends to bless the nations.

> *The Scripture, foreseeing that God would justify the Gentiles by faith, preached the gospel to Abraham beforehand, saying, "In you all the nations shall be blessed." So then those who are of faith are blessed with believing Abraham* (Galatians 3:8-9 NKJV).

This is so *"the promise might be sure to all the seed...who are of the faith of Abraham, who is father of us all"* (Rom. 4:16 NKJV). By believing in and relying on Jesus, who is the seed of Abraham, we enter into all that belongs to him.

> *For the promise that he would be the heir of the world was not to Abraham or to his seed through the law, but through the righteousness of faith* (Romans 4:13 NKJV).

The antithesis of honoring our ancestors and entering into their destiny and their blessings is to dishonor them and enter into their judgments. Jesus challenged the Pharisees on their cross-generational accusations. They were a multi-generational religious order that prided themselves on keeping the law. Jesus warned them because they chose to distance themselves from the iniquities and the consequences of the past.

> *Woe to you, scribes and Pharisees, hypocrites! Because you build the tombs of the prophets and adorn the monuments of the righteous, and say, "If we had lived in the days of our fathers, we would not*

have been partakers with them in the blood of the prophets." Therefore you are witnesses against yourselves that you are sons of those who murdered the prophets. Fill up, then, the measure of your fathers' guilt (Matthew 23:29-32 NKJV).

The accusation that the Pharisees made against their fathers was the catalyst for their own judgment. They were tied cross-generationally to the actions of their fathers, and God wanted someone to take the responsibility and clean the slate for the family. Their effort to expunge themselves from the family's and organization's guilt guaranteed that those same sins would continue down the line and engulf them.

Serpents, brood of vipers! How can you escape the condemnation of hell? Therefore, indeed, I send you prophets, wise men, and scribes: some of them you will kill and crucify, and some of them you will scourge in your synagogues and persecute from city to city, that on you may come all the righteous blood shed on the earth, from the blood of righteous Abel to the blood of Zechariah, son of Berechiah, whom you murdered between the temple and the altar. Assuredly, I say to you, all these things will come upon this generation (Matthew 23:33-36 NKJV).

The Bible is clear that *"in whatever you judge another you condemn yourself; for you who judge practice the same things"* (Rom. 2:1 NKJV). Their accusations married them to the judgment coming against their forefathers' sins; their intercession would have joined them to the blessing. Their independence and pride blinded them from accepting any generational guilt. As a result, they became *"experts at setting aside the commandment of God in order to keep* [their] *tradition"* (Mark 7:9 NASB). The rigid keepers of the law actually became its enemies: *"Woe to you, scribes and Pharisees, hypocrites! For you pay tithe of mint and anise and cummin, and have neglected the weightier matters of the law: justice and mercy and faith"* (Matt. 23:23 NKJV). They lost the spirit of the law and thus their birthright.

The Title Deed

The birthright is similar to a title deed. On a title deed is written the property's  boundaries (the extent of your authority), a time line for development (your lifetime), and building plan or end use (your purpose). Ideally, your title deed would be free and clear of encumbrances, and you could immediately start to fulfill God's purpose in your life with no restrictions or hindrances.

In an ordinary title deed for an actual piece of property, this isn't the case. You may discover that the previous owner failed to pay some bills and a lien was on the title deed. The bank may also hold a mortgage against it. The back fence may be in the wrong location, and the deck may not conform to the building code. You may even dig around preparing to plant a garden and discover a barrel of toxic waste buried in the backyard. You didn't place any of these restrictions on the title or bury the toxic waste, but as owner you are left with the consequences.

So, in our lives, we will not be allowed to build the house (the destiny) that God has for us until we deal with the encumbrances remaining on the title deed. Since God is the builder of our lives, it is He who is looking for someone to *"stand in the gap"* (Ezek. 22:30) and remove the liens and restrictions that have been placed on the family's house. God is just and must dispense justice (foreclose) if no one will repent and ask forgiveness, break the curses, and allow Him to show mercy.

This is what happened to Israel because they

> *...persisted in all the sins of Jeroboam and did not turn away from them until the Lord removed them from His presence, as He had warned through all His servants the prophets. So the people of Israel were taken from their homeland into exile in Assyria, and they are still there* (2 Kings 17:22-23 NIV).

God had to "foreclose" on the house of Israel because no one would repent and remove the sins of their fathers. God *"rejected...afflicted...and delivered them into the hand of spoilers, until He had cast them out of His sight"* (2 Kings 17:20).

Many of us find ourselves in this situation. We struggle to live a victorious Christian life, but at every turn we hit a roadblock. Our attitudes are wrong; we can't receive grace, can't forgive; our temper is uncontrollable, as is our tongue. Certain temptations are always overwhelming, satan continually harasses, and we can't seem to get into God's presence or tap into His power. In short, the victorious life has eluded us, and we are captive to the iniquities of our fathers.

This is the scenario that results from generational curses, but there is a solution: repent and ask forgiveness. Daniel did this for Judah and delivered them from their captivity in Babylon. He read the prophecy of Jeremiah and realized why the judgment had come to Judah and its duration (see Dan. 9:2).

He prayed,

> *Then I set my face toward the Lord God to make request by prayer and supplications, with fasting, sackcloth, and ashes...I prayed to the Lord my God, and made confession..."O Lord, great and awesome God... we have sinned and committed iniquity, we have done wickedly and rebelled, even by departing from Your precepts and Your judgments. Neither have we heeded Your servants the prophets, who spoke in Your name to our kings and our princes, to our fathers and all the people of the land....O Lord, to us belongs shame of face, to our kings, our princes, and our fathers, because we have sinned against You... and for the iniquities of our fathers, Jerusalem and Your people are a reproach to all those around us....O my God, incline Your ear and hear; open Your eyes and see our desolations, and the city which is called by Your name; for we do not present our supplications before You because of our righteous deeds, but because of Your great mercies. O Lord, hear! O Lord, forgive! O Lord, listen and act! Do not delay for Your own sake, my God, for Your city and Your people are called by Your name"* (Daniel 9:3-19 NKJV).

Notice how he prayed: *we have sinned…we have done wickedly…neither have we heeded.* He spoke as if he had done those things, and he had, in his ancestors. We are connected to them because we are one family and have a common destiny. The writer of Hebrews confirmed this view when he wrote,

> *Levi [the father of the priestly tribe] himself, who received tithes (the tenth), paid tithes through Abraham, for he was still in the loins of his forefather [Abraham] when Melchizedek met him [Abraham]* (Hebrews 7:9-10 AMP).

This principle was revealed recently to one of our workers during a "Curses to Blessings" seminar.

Mark Michener Testimony

I was ministering the "Curses To Blessings" seminar at our local church and was assigned to a young man about 20 years old. Though I had seen him attending our church, I did not know him. I asked him where he came from and about his past. He had been raised in foster homes all his life and had no idea who his mother or father were or his family history. I recall stating that it doesn't really matter whether we do or don't know the past; this works if we break off any generational curses from continuing to operate in our lives.

He knew of a couple of issues he was struggling with as a young Christian, and we planned to focus some time on these when we got to them in the worksheets. It wasn't too far into the ministry time, when I looked up at him as we were seated in chairs facing each other. I saw in the Spirit a literal row of men standing behind this young man. At first, I just said in my spirit, "Lord, what's this?" They were all looking forward, leaning around each other, taking great interest in what was going on. I said again, "Lord, what's going on here? Who are these guys?"

Immediately, I sensed in the Spirit that these were this young man's fore-fathers. I could see at least six or seven of them. They had this look on their faces of deep, genuine concern, and I asked the Lord what this was.

These fathers of this young man had obviously passed on from this earth. Now they had a whole new appreciation about the issues in their lives which they never overcame and which ultimately greatly affected their destinies. Because of their failures, they had passed them down, not only to each other, but also to this young man. Now they saw and knew in all reality that here was a chance to set the record straight and regain the destinies lost.

God sees us doing what our forefathers did—the good and the bad—and has left the consequences of the iniquity for us to deal with. This is the challenge we face for our families, our churches, our businesses, and our nations: undo the bad; reap the good. We must stand in the gap for our families if we are ever going to achieve our corporate and individual destinies. Identificational repentance is how we honor our forefathers and express the love of Jesus to our families without accusing them.

Chapter 4

FRUITS OR ROOTS

The apples were hanging, enticingly red and ripe, on the tree. Our two-year-old asked, "Can I pick an apple from the apple tree?" Even a two-year-old knows that apples grow on an apple tree and oranges grow on an orange tree. Jesus said, "*every tree is known by his own fruit*" (Luke 6:44). He applied this to people, saying, "*Beware of false prophets, which come to you in sheep's clothing, but inwardly they are ravening wolves. Ye shall know them by their fruits*" (Matt. 7:15-16).

Our fruits are the things hanging from the trees of our lives. They are obvious, even to a two-year-old. If we manifest anger all the time, we have an angry tree in us; if we display lust, we are growing a lust tree. If people can see our fruit, we can't say, "I don't have a problem; I only did it once; I didn't mean what came out." Fruit only grows on mature trees. If we have that fruit, we have a mature root of that sin in our character.

God has been talking to me (Ken) about the sarcastic, facetious comments I make to people in jest. I have learned that in jest there is truth: we use a joke to hide the truth we want to say. God told me this is actually the fruit of a negative speech pattern that I have. Most of my attempts to stop speaking in this manner have led to my blurting out something even more offensive than usual. God was showing me that my attempts to deal with my fruit would not change my nature.

Paul agrees when he says,

...[Why do you submit to rules and regulations?—such as] do not handle [this]; do not taste [that]; do not even touch [them]; referring to things all of which perish with being used. To do this is to follow human precepts and doctrines. Such [practices] have indeed the outward appearance [that popularly passes] for wisdom, in promoting self-imposed rigor of devotion and delight in self-humiliation and severity of discipline of the body, but they are of no value in checking the indulgence of the flesh (the lower nature). [Instead, they do not honor God but serve only to indulge the flesh] (Colossians 2:20-23 AMP).

Fruit Reproduction

Our natural tendency is to try and cut off the bad fruit in our lives. If we don't like what we are doing, we try to prune or limit our actions. The logic is that if we have developed a habit of thinking or acting poorly, we can develop another habit of acting properly. The theory is good, but the reality is different.

Suppose we are attempting to shed some unwanted pounds. We decide a little increase in exercise and a little decrease in calories will fix the problem. Soon we are walking, doing an aerobics routine, and singing "Hello, diet; Hello, diet." Our resolve is high, and the first day's results are encouraging. "Nothing to this," we declare. In fact, it seems probable that a clothing size or two may soon be shed.

The next day, the kids start fighting, there are a few extra problems at work, and the car needs to go in for a brake job. Finally, after a long frustrating day, we flop down on the couch to relax, watch a little television, and have a snack to de-stress. Then it hits us, no snacks allowed! Even though we decide to stick to our guns, the fridge refuses to cooperate and keeps calling our name. Eventually, we decide, "One little piece and the cravings will be over. I'll cut myself off gradually; cold turkey is not a good approach anyway."

We're now in a battle with ourselves and the rules of conduct that we established. These food laws that we promised to obey were hatched in a time of peace, a time with no pressure, just determination. They get tested in a time of war, in the time of strong desire. The more we decide not to think about food, the more intensely we do. Soon we are not only battling our desires, we are battling our resolve. What is the problem? We tried to attack the fruit rather than the root of the problem.

Diets are not effective because a diet must be a lifestyle, not an event. Wendy Bumgardner says, "On many diets, you are not eating the way you will eat for the rest of your life. You eat foods you may not like very much…you know this is 'just for the diet' rather than finding healthier foods."[1] The same occurs with any change; we can't change our actions without first changing the source of those actions: the root, which is our thought life.

Our thought life is the root of our being. Proverbs says, as a man *"thinks in his heart, so is he"* (Prov. 23:7 NKJV). It is like a river that flows through us, carrying us along. If we don't like where our thoughts are taking us, we may decide to stop the flow by building a dam. For a while it seems to work; the river does not continue down the same old path. We've changed; problem solved! While we are celebrating our victory, the source of the river—our thoughts, which reflect our heart attitude—is still feeding the flow of the river.

We are shocked when the dam overflows, or is no longer able to restrain the pressure and breaks, or the river simply carves out a new channel, a new expression. If the source of the river, our flesh, is not stopped, the river is not stopped. It is just restrained for a season. In nature, such a foolish plan would never be considered. The consequences of the river flowing across the landscape, with no natural banks to contain it, would be devastating.

Fleshly efforts to curb an action empower the opposite to happen. Paul said, *"the strength of sin is the law"* (1 Cor. 15:56). Our attempts to do things right (the Law) actually strengthens the sin we are trying to cut off or prune. Fruit growers understand this principle. They prune fruit trees, not to get rid of bad branches and bad fruit, but to stimulate increased production of the fruit.

Our attempts to prune our bad fruit, such as curbing our anger, will actually increase our anger. This is because the root, which was not touched in the pruning process, is now supplying fewer branches, thus making the remaining branches capable of producing more bad fruit. The church has challenged new and mature Christians alike to stop smoking, stop drinking, stop running around, all with very little success. Some actions are changed, but none of the "bents" in the people are changed. God changes the bents to empower us to change our actions. We must be human beings before we can be human doings. *"He who is slow to anger is better than the mighty, and he who rules his spirit than he who takes a city"* (Prov. 16:32 NKJV). Who we are is more important to God than what we do.

Jesus knew that the problem was not the external fruit; that was only an indication of the internal root.

> *...Those things which proceed out of the mouth come forth from the heart, and they defile the man. For out of the heart proceed evil thoughts, murders, adulteries, fornications, thefts, false witness, blasphemies. These are the things which defile a man* (Matthew 15:18-20).

The Bible has a solution for the problem: cut off the root!

The sources of our iniquities are often found even deeper than at the levels of  our own experiences. They are often rooted in our family lines. Sayings like, "He is a chip off the old block," or "The apple doesn't fall far from the tree" are based on this truth. I (Ken) remember overreacting to one of my boys. I was angry and thus reacted too harshly with him. After the anger subsided and I cooled down, a revelation smote my heart: "I'm just like my dad." My judgments against my father had opened the door for me to condemn myself, for the Bible says, *"...you who judge are habitually practicing the very same things [that you censure and denounce]"* (Rom. 2:1 AMP). Cross-generational judgments guarantee that God will visit *"the iniquity of the fathers upon the children...unto the third and the fourth generation"* (Exod. 34:7).

One of our friends even suggested that in their family, characteristics seem to be inherited according to birth order. The second child in successive generations inherited chronic sickness while a sarcastic wit was the mark of the third.

Abraham put his wife in a harem (twice); Isaac did the same to his wife. The Bible is full of sins being passed down from generation to generation. Jeroboam, the king of Judah, *"walked in all the sins of his father"* (1 Kings 15:3). Ahab, the king of Israel, *"walk[ed] in the sins of Jeroboam"* (1 Kings 16:31). Families continue in their bent or iniquity until someone addresses the root sin.

Even in Jesus' genealogy, the men often married women who were outcasts in Jewish society: Tamar, who prostituted for her father-in-law; Rahab, who also was a prostitute and a Canaanite, both of which made her an outcast; Ruth, who, as a Moabite, was not allowed into the congregation of Israel (see Deut. 23:3); and Bathsheba, who was an adulterer (see Matt. 1:1-16). Interestingly, these outcasts were the only women the Scriptures recorded in Jesus' line. God was not worried about their reputations, just their character. Jesus continued to supply ammunition for the family's reputation to suffer. He *"made Himself of no reputation, and took upon Him the form of a servant"* (Phil. 2:7).

To the Pharisees, reputation was everything. In one confrontation with Jesus, the Pharisees first claimed Abraham as their father and then challenged Jesus' legitimacy by sneering, *"We were not born of fornication; we have one Father—God"* (John 8:41 NKJV). Jesus countered,

> *If God were your Father, you would love Me, for I proceeded forth and came from God....You are of your father the devil, and the desires of your father you want to do* (John 8:42,44 NKJV).

The fruit hanging from their trees identified the roots in the ground of their heart.

John the Baptist also lashed out at the Pharisees when they came to be baptized:

> *Brood of vipers! Who warned you to flee from the wrath to come? Therefore bear fruits worthy of repentance, and do not think to say to yourselves, "We have Abraham as our father." For I say to you that God is able to raise up children to Abraham from these stones. And even now the ax is laid to the root of the trees. Therefore every tree*

which does not bear good fruit is cut down and thrown into the fire (Matthew 3:7-10 NKJV).

The Pharisees were depending on their lineage as their badge of authority and righteousness. They were masters of keeping the law but not of changing their hearts. Jesus once exploded on them, saying,

> *...you Pharisees clean the outside of the cup and of the platter; but inside of you, you are full of robbery and wickedness...woe to you Pharisees! For you pay tithe of mint and rue and every kind of garden herb, and yet disregard justice and the love of God* (Luke 11:39-42 NASB).

God is vitally interested in our lineage. It is the key to achieving our destiny, for our personal destiny is entwined with our family's destiny. That is why John the Baptist said, *"God is able to raise up children to Abraham from these stones"* (Matt. 3:9 NKJV). God's intent is to have children of faith, and He will go to extraordinary lengths to achieve that end. Satan is just as determined to cut off the family continuum as God is to extend it.

The removal of fathers has the most devastating effect on the blessing of the family. New statistics show that an estimated "80 percent of all African-American children will spend part of their childhood living apart from their fathers." Seventy percent of African-American children are born to unmarried mothers, and 40 percent of all children, regardless of race, live in homes without fathers.[2] The high rate of absent black fathers has a generational component.

A slave mentality is a thought pattern that persists even after the slavery has been eliminated. The generation that escaped from Egypt could not shake that mentality. They never accepted the responsibility that freedom gave them, always remembering "the good old days" with *"the fish which we ate freely in Egypt, the cucumbers, the melons, the leeks, the onions, and the garlic"* (Num. 11:5 NKJV). Because of this false, rosy memory, they were always attempting to return to Egypt (see Num. 14:4). Similarly, many of the slaves in the South stayed on their plantations even after they were freed because they didn't know any other life.

Part of this slave mentality was an inability of the men to bond to their families. This mentality was due mainly to the fact that when the men were sold to other plantations, the women and children stayed with the former masters. By not bonding, the men could survive emotionally when they were ripped away from their families. This nonbonding, generational mindset has persisted to this day and is actually increasing. Since 1940, rates of divorce and nonmarriage have soared among Black adults, and, as a result, the percentage of Black children born to unmarried mothers has risen from 17 to 70 percent.[3]

The effects on the family, especially the Black family, have been devastating. The following statistics give an indication of the carnage satan has wrought by disconnecting fathers of all ethnic backgrounds.

- 61 percent of all child abuse is committed by biological mothers.

- 25 percent of all child abuse is committed by natural fathers.[4]

- 46.9 percent of non-custodial mothers totally default on support.

- 26.9 percent of non-custodial fathers totally default on support.

- 20.0 percent of non-custodial mothers pay support at some level.

- 61.0 percent of non-custodial fathers pay support at some level.

- 7.0 percent of single custodial mothers work more than 44 hours weekly.

- 24.5 percent of single custodial fathers work more than 44 hours weekly.

- 46.2 percent of single custodial mothers receive public assistance.

- 20.8 percent of single custodial fathers receive public assistance.[5]

- 90.2 percent of fathers with joint custody pay all the support due.

- 79.1 percent of fathers with visitation privileges pay all the support due.

- 44.5 percent of fathers with no visitation pay all the support due.

- 37.9 percent of fathers are denied any visitation.

- 66.0 percent of all support not paid by non-custodial fathers is due to inability to pay.[6]

- 50 percent of mothers see no value in the father's continued contact with his children.[7]

- 40 percent of mothers reported that they had interfered with the father's visitation to punish their ex-spouse.[8]

- 63 percent of youth suicides are from fatherless homes.[9]

- 85 percent of all children who exhibit behavioral disorders come from fatherless homes.[10]

- 80 percent of rapists motivated with displaced anger come from fatherless homes.[11]

- 71 percent of all high school dropouts come from fatherless homes.[12]

- 70 percent of juveniles in state-operated institutions come from fatherless homes.[13]

- 85 percent of all youths sitting in prisons grew up in a fatherless home.[14]

Translated, this means that children from a fatherless home are

- 5 times more likely to commit suicide

- 32 times more likely to run away

- 20 times more likely to have behavioral disorders

- 14 times more likely to commit rape

- 9 times more likely to drop out of school

- 10 times more likely to abuse chemical substances

- 9 times more likely to end up in a state operated institution

- 20 times more likely to end up in prison[15]

This generational curse is spreading in all levels of society, all races, and all creeds. Each successive generation multiplies the devastation. If we repent, ask forgiveness, and get healing, the opposite will occur, and we will pull our families out of the morass into which they have fallen. We are running a marathon of a relay race, not an individual sprint. We may receive the baton after a disastrous lap or one that was run with excellence.

I (Ken) had a dream 25 years ago about an elderly gentleman who was near the end of his lap. Harold had run with patience and integrity. He left a spiritual inheritance that had positioned his family to step into the things of God. In the dream, we were praying together in the Spirit. Harold was excited, jumping up and down, declaring the glory of God as he prayed in tongues. I woke up with my heart thumping and my spirit singing; it was so real.

The problem was that Harold was from a traditional church and, though he was filled with the Spirit, he did not speak in tongues or even approve of it. It was not long after this dream that he passed away. I often thought back on that dream, wondering what its significance was, but I had no answers, until the other day. Harold's grandson, Derek, a grandfather himself, and his son Nathan, were praying with us for an upcoming "Curses to Blessings" seminar.

The Spirit took Derek to a passage in the Bible, which says,

> *...lift up your eyes and look at the fields, for they are already white for harvest! And he who reaps receives wages, and gathers fruit for eternal life, that both he who sows and he who reaps may rejoice together. For in this the saying is true: "One sows and another reaps." I sent you to reap that for which you have not labored; others have labored...and you have entered into their labors* (John 4:35-38 NKJV).

I looked at both of them, lost in the Spirit, interceding for people they had never met, and realized this was the meaning of the dream. Harold's offspring, two and three generations out, were waving the baton that great grandfather had carried so valiantly, those many years before. I know he is still jumping up and down with excitement in Heaven declaring the goodness of God.

Hebrews speaks of the faithful saints who both conquered and suffered for God:

...of whom the world was not worthy....And all these, having gained approval through their faith, did not receive what was promised, because God had provided something better for us, so that apart from us they would not be made perfect. Therefore, since we have so great a cloud of witnesses surrounding us, let us also lay aside every encumbrance and the sin, which so easily entangles us, and let us run with endurance the race that is set before us... (Hebrews 11:38–12:1 NASB).

This *"cloud of witnesses"* is our ancestors, both spiritual and natural, who are waiting at the finish line for us to complete the race that they started. God will crown us together because we are one.

Chapter 5

KINGDOM CLASH

Behold Your King

Jesus' entry into this world created a clash of kingdoms that has echoed down through the ages: *"For this purpose the Son of God was manifested, that He might destroy the works of the devil"* (1 John 3:8). The Kingdom of light invaded the kingdom of darkness with the sole intent of obliterating that realm and rescuing all the captives. God...

> *...has qualified us to be partakers of the inheritance of the saints in the light. He has delivered us from the power of darkness and conveyed us into the kingdom of the Son of His love* (Colossians 1:12-13 NKJV).

A Kingdom ruled by God was a foreign thought to Israel even though God intervened and led them out of Egypt *"like a flock by the hand of Moses and Aaron"* (Ps. 77:20). The laws and the statutes, the marching orders, and the battle orders all came through Moses as the oracle of God. Twenty-five times it is recorded that *"by the hand of Moses"* the Lord commanded, spoke, numbered, directed, and promised Israel.[1] Humility allowed Moses to manifest the Presence while not grasping at the glory that he stood in. Never again did a man occupy that position until Jesus stepped into time.

Moses prophesied Jesus' coming, saying, *"The Lord your God will raise up for you a prophet...from the midst of your brethren like me [Moses]; to him you shall listen"* (Deut. 18:15 AMP). That is God's plan, to rule through an anointed man or woman who hears and declares His will. Jesus' rule is the fulfillment of that prophecy, but Israel had long before rejected God dwelling among them.

Observing God's power in delivering them from Egypt and His awesome presence on Mount Sinai had unnerved Israel. They told Moses, *"You speak with us, and we will hear; but let not God speak with us, lest we die"* (Exod. 20:19 NKJV). Later, when they demanded of Samuel, *"Make us a king to judge us like all the nations"* (1 Sam. 8:5 NKJV), God took it personally. He told His prophet Samuel, *"They have not rejected you, but they have rejected Me, that I should not reign over them"* (1 Sam. 8:7 NKJV). Israel wanted God to rule in Heaven, but they were seduced into desiring an earthly king for their earthly kingdom. Direct rule by God was too intimidating to consider.

Jesus said,

> *The scribes and the Pharisees sit in Moses' seat. Therefore whatever they tell you to observe, that observe and do, but do not do according to their works; for they say, and do not do* (Matthew 23:2-3 NKJV).

They were *"holding to a form of godliness, although they...denied its power"* (2 Tim. 3:5 NASB). They were stewards of the Kingdom, waiting for the King, but they refused to yield to the King when He arrived. They said,

> *If we let Him thus alone, all men will believe on Him: and the Romans shall come and take away both our place and nation....Then from that day forth they took counsel together for to put Him to death* (John 11:48,53).

Thus both Israel and Rome set themselves in opposition to the establishment of the Kingdom of Heaven. Daniel had prophesied years before that the

> *...God of heaven will set up a kingdom which will never be destroyed, and that kingdom...will crush and put an end to all these kingdoms, but it will itself endure forever* (Daniel 2:44 NASB).

The stage was set for the divine confrontation that was about to occur.

Spreading the Light

Jesus came, fulfilling the words of Isaiah:

> *...the people which sat in darkness, saw great light; and to them which sat in the region and shadow of death light is sprung up. From that time Jesus began to preach, and to say, Repent: for the kingdom of heaven is at hand* (Matthew 4:16-17).

Jesus was the Light, and everywhere that He went that Light pushed back the darkness. Sickness fled; demons fled; lack fled. Nothing could stand before the Light.

Even though there was an outward manifestation, Jesus' primary goal was to shine that light into men's hearts. He said, *"The kingdom of God does not come with observation...for indeed, the kingdom of God is within you"* (Luke 17:20-21 NKJV). The battle is within us to *"overcome evil with good"* (Rom. 12:21 NKJV); that is our calling. Jesus declared that God *"hath sent Me to heal the broken-hearted, to preach deliverance to the captives, and recovering of sight to the blind, to set at liberty them that are bruised"* (Luke 4:18). That Light pushed back the darkness, making elbow room in the spirit for repentance to flow as that Light illuminated the dark recesses of men's hearts.

The Light is in us to battle, and we

> *...overcome (conquered) him by means of the blood of the Lamb and by the utterance of [our]...testimony, for [we]...[do] not love and cling to life even when faced with death* (Revelation 12:11 AMP).

To paraphrase, "We overcome satan when we are not afraid and declare what the Word says the blood does." The momentum in this battle turns our way as we cast *"down arguments and every high thing that exalts itself against the knowledge of God, bringing every thought into captivity to the obedience of Christ"* (2 Cor. 10:5 NKJV).

Our mental kingdom clashes mirror the bigger battle that is transpiring in Heaven. Two events, concerning the saints, occur continually before the throne where Jesus *"always lives to make intercession for them"* (Heb. 7:25 NKJV), and satan *"accuse*[s] *them before our God day and night"* (Rev. 12:10 NKJV). It is like a scene from a courtroom. Satan is the adversary or opponent bringing suit[2] in this legal battle, and Jesus is the advocate or defense attorney pleading our case.[3] Jesus' intercession is removing the accusations, allowing us to align our thinking with His.

If we think like He thinks, we will also do what He is doing: interceding. God has *"reconciled us to Himself through Jesus Christ, and has given us the ministry of reconciliation"* (2 Cor. 5:18 NKJV). Because we have been given this ministry, we can go into the courtroom in Heaven, stand in proxy, and intercede for another. In that place we can enter a plea, for *"we are ambassadors for Christ, God making His appeal as it were through us; we [as Christ's personal representatives] beg you for His sake to lay hold of the divine favor [now offered you] and be reconciled to God"* (2 Cor. 5:20 AMP). Just as in an earthly court, our words carry weight and are recorded as truth.

Love Intercedes

The company Ken worked for sent us to a Christian function and put us up in a hotel in the city where we had previously resided. We walked past the bar as we returned to our room, following the function's banquet. I (Jeanne) noticed a girl from our former church in that city, sitting in the bar. She looked lonely and pained even though she was laughing and flirting with the man she was sitting with. She had obviously been drinking and was looking for companionship. She never saw us as we passed.

I could not get her out of my mind. I wasn't judging her, but I sensed her pain, which went so deep into my soul. The whole night I hardly got any sleep as I travailed in prayer for her. Instead of this being a time of fun and relaxation, away from the kids with my husband, it became an all-out battle. That night, I stood in the gap for this young woman. I asked God to supply a Christian man for her who would love her and be a good covering.

A year later, we were transferred back to that city and returned to our old church. There was that same woman, but now so different and married to a fine Christian man. God had heard and answered my prayers for her. He needed someone to intercede and invite Him into the situation before a disaster occurred. I could have gone to the girl and confronted her sin; I could have gossiped and told members of the church what I had seen. Instead I interceded on her behalf.

Love covers; it does not expose. That young lady never knew that I prayed that entire night for her. She never even knew that we were there, but God knew and had arranged our encounter. God wants you to stand in for your friends and family so that they can be free from the attacks of the enemy and walk in freedom.

Anyone can come to court and accuse, but only those with authorization can defend. The advocate must be acknowledged by the court to be able to speak on the defendant's behalf. We must identify ourselves with the defendant, not accuse. Jesus was *"made like unto His brethren...to make reconciliation for the sins of the people"* (Heb. 2:17).

When interceding, we also must identify with, or be made like the people we are

praying for, to have a right to stand in proxy. We may not have done the same sin, but we have the same roots that manifest in our own sins. We cannot say, "I don't know how they could do that." We know very well why they did it, if we are willing to examine our heart, because we *"who judge practice the same things"* (Rom. 2:1 NKJV).

We may never have gone through a divorce, but we have all hardened our hearts, which Jesus says was the main cause of divorce (see Matt. 19:8). We may not have committed adultery, but we have all lusted in our

hearts, which Jesus said was the same thing (see Matt. 5:28). We may not have murdered, but we all have been angry with people, which John says is the same thing (see 1 John 3:15). So we can all identify with these people because we are in the same state: imperfect. We *"all have sinned, and come short of the glory of God"* (Rom. 3:23).

Thus we can stand as a representative of that group and pray, *"Father, forgive 'us' for the sin of _____."* There is no accusation there, no judgment, and no self-righteousness, just love, fulfilling the law, and allowing God to show mercy.

That is what Moses did when he offered himself in exchange for Israel. He was willing to be the substitute for Israel and repent for them (see Exod. 32:32). Daniel also included himself saying,

> *We have sinned and committed iniquity, we have done wickedly and rebelled, even by departing from Your precepts and Your judgments.... to us belongs shame of face, to our kings, our princes, and our fathers, because we have sinned against You* (Daniel 9:5,8).

He had not done those things that he repented of but recognized that his destiny was tied to Israel's and identified with them.

God, looking to show mercy, used Job as a priestly mediator in His dispute with Job's comforters. He declared, *"My servant Job shall pray for you: for him I will accept....And the Lord turned the captivity of Job, when he prayed for his friends"* (Job 42:8,10). Stephen stood in the gap for those stoning him, crying, *"Lord, lay not this sin to their charge"* (Acts 7:60) as he was dying.

We hold our family's destinies in our hands. God said,

> *I will give you the keys of the kingdom of heaven, and whatever you bind on earth will be bound in heaven, and whatever you loose on earth will be loosed in heaven* (Matthew 16:19 NKJV).

One of those keys is intercession. We had a friend who was having trouble dealing with her husband. He was not looking after the family needs the way she felt he should be. He thought it was her problem. This "he did/she did" impasse was bringing tension into the relationship; neither side wanted to shift their position. Since we were dealing with the wife, we suggested that she deal first with the only thing she could change: herself.

She confessed her own sins in the situation and repented to God. I (Ken) stood in proxy for her husband, and she repented to me on behalf of her husband

and asked my forgiveness for those actions. Then I stood in the gap as her husband and asked forgiveness from God for my actions. I then asked the wife for forgiveness, which she gave. It seemed rather mechanical, but forgiveness is an act of the will, not the emotions. Two weeks later, the wife phoned us and excitedly reported that everything had changed in their relationship. Jesus gave us this ministry of reconciliation, and it works, both for us and for the ones for whom we stand in proxy.

The ministry works on a simple principle: remove the right of the enemy to accuse. He is able to accuse us in the court of Heaven because we sin. "*And if any man sin, we have an advocate with the Father, Jesus Christ the righteous*" (1 John 2:1). It is Jesus' righteousness that we appeal to, not our own. Satan is always trying to drag us to this court. He is hoping to force us to try and defend our actions. You are warned to

> *...agree with your adversary quickly, while you are on the way with him, lest your adversary deliver you to the judge, the judge hand you over to the officer, and you be thrown into prison* (Matthew 5:25 NKJV).

Law or Life

There is no mention that we are not guilty; it is a foregone conclusion that we are. I (Ken) questioned God on why this is. Suppose I had done nothing wrong. Why should I agree with the accusation? I should get my day in court so that I can defend myself. That is what Job wanted—his chance to explain how right he was.

> *Oh that I knew where I might find Him, that I might come to His seat! I would present my case before Him and fill my mouth with arguments. I would learn the words which He would answer, and perceive what He would say to me. Would He contend with me by the greatness of His power? No, surely He would pay attention to me. There the upright would reason with Him; and I would be delivered forever from my Judge* (Job 23:3-7 NASB).

Satan wants us to pursue that reasoning.

We should always be suspicious when satan and our flesh agree; something is always up. It's a trap! When we are accused, the accuser is appealing to the law, saying that we did something wrong. We also are appealing to the standard of the law if we defend ourselves by saying we did it right. *"But...no man is justified by the law"* (Gal. 3:11). Moreover, *"you have been severed from Christ, you who are seeking to be justified by law; you have fallen from grace"* (Gal. 5:4 NKJV). That is where satan wants us; standing on our own merit. It doesn't matter if we are not guilty on this particular point, *"for whoever shall keep the whole law, and yet stumble in one point, he is guilty of all"* (James 2:10).

We are forgiven when we plead guilty; we are condemned when we claim innocence. The same principle stands when we intercede for others: confess their sins and they will be forgiven. The accused does not have to be in the courtroom to enter a plea; his advocate can do it for him. Giving and receiving of forgiveness, even in proxy, removes the accusation of the enemy and allows God to show mercy because *"mercy triumphs over judgment"* (James 2:13 NKJV).

Peter queried Jesus about how often he must forgive a trespass. In answer, Jesus shared a story concerning the consequences of not forgiving a debt (see Matt 18:21-35). One servant owed the king 10,000 talents in silver (approximately $262 million).[4] Unable to pay but penitent, the servant begged for time and got mercy from the king, who forgave the debt. Feeling exuberant and cocky, he went out and found a fellow servant who owed 100 denarii (approximately $220).[5] When the second servant likewise begged for more time to repay, the first servant threw him into debtor's prison.

When the king found out about the deed, he demanded to see his servant, reprimanded him, and threw him into prison till the vast debt was paid. Two men were now in prison, not for millions in debt (that had been cancelled once) but for $200. Both men could be free if the first servant would meander down the cellblock and forgive the small debt the second owed. Refuse to forgive, demand payment, and both stay in prison.

Jesus said, *"So My heavenly Father also will do to you if each of you, from his heart, does not forgive his brother his trespasses"* (Matt. 18:35). Our hearts, not our actions, dictate our level of freedom. Our sins (our debts) will not keep us from our destiny, but our lack of repentance and forgiveness will. Thus we must expose and tear down all the strongholds and hard spots in our hearts that keep us locked up.

Standing in Proxy

My (Jeanne's) two aunts had a major falling out over a minor incident concerning some eggs. They refused to talk to each other for over 20 years. I stood in proxy for the one aunt and asked my other aunt to forgive me. She was willing, forgave me, and asked for forgiveness from me, as if from her sister. Her sister knew nothing of what transpired between the two of us. Now the accuser had no more rights to accuse and harass because I had stood in the gap and asked for forgiveness of the sins committed. Both sides had asked for forgiveness, one in the flesh, the other by proxy. Within a week, without any explanation, the absent aunt phoned, reconciled, and remained friends until the older sister died.

With the success of that reconciliation, my aunt and I decided to do the same exercise with one of her brothers. He also had broken communication with the same aunt. Again I stood in the gap for my uncle, and my aunt and I exchanged prayers of forgiveness and reconciliation. Shortly afterward, he also contacted his sister and resolved the rift that was between the two of them.

The resentment stayed in place as long as the enemy had the right to accuse. When I asked for forgiveness, that right was dissolved, and the accusations ceased, which allowed reconciliation to proceed unhindered. Jesus is *"at the right hand of God…mak*[ing] *intercession for us"* (Rom. 8:34).

These strongholds are built from lies, each like a brick, which we use as a fortress to protect ourselves. They prevent others from getting too close and injuring us. They also wall us in from any intimacy or interaction. The more isolated we are, the more selfish we become. If we are not corporate, we are selfish and will go to extraordinary means to protect ourselves. We are not relevant unless we are corporate. The more people you touch, the more relevant you are; the fewer you touch, the more selfish you are.

Paul said, *"we who live are always delivered to death for Jesus' sake, that the life of Jesus also may be manifested in our mortal flesh. So then death is working in us, but life in you"* (2 Cor. 4:11-12 NKJV). All we need to do to bring life to others is to die to ourselves. Our cross is our self-life, our ambitions, our pride, and our independence. Close these doors, and satan will gain no access, no areas to put a hook into us.

We can close these doors as we repent and renounce our judgments against others and ourselves, for we do what we judge (see Rom. 2:1). We must also repent and break off our vows, oaths, and covenants that bind us to wrong thought patterns. Our words have power: *"death and life are in the power of the tongue: and they that love it shall eat the fruit thereof"* (Prov. 18:21). We must make positive declarations over our lives and the lives of our families to counteract all the negative structures that we have in our minds.

As we behold *"as in a mirror the glory of the Lord,* [we] *are being transformed into the same image from glory to glory, just as by the Spirit of the Lord"* (2 Cor. 3:18 NKJV). His glory is transforming our minds and hearts to be like His. That glory shining through us will change us, allow us to intercede, with new insights, for our families. If we set the pattern right, our children shall follow in our footsteps. Then,

> *...those from among you shall build the old waste places; you shall raise up the foundations of many generations; and you shall be called the repairer of the breach, the restorer of streets to dwell in* (Isaiah 58:12 NKJV).

Then our families will be whole and our destinies sure.

Section B

GENERATIONAL CURSES

Chapter 6

ILLEGITIMACY

No one of illegitimate birth shall enter the assembly of the Lord;
none of his descendants, even to the tenth generation
(Deuteronomy 23:2 NASB).

I (Ken) used to think that curses were just a series of bad things happening. There was no rhyme or reason to them and certainly nothing to get concerned about; things would eventually shift. I have learned the opposite is true. Curses are specific in their source and application, and they will not go away unless they are addressed. Thus, we address the first curse that Moses pronounced:

> *One of illegitimate birth shall not enter the assembly of the Lord;*
> *even to the tenth generation none of his descendants shall enter the*
> *assembly of the Lord* (Deuteronomy 23:2 NKJV).

Ten generations is a long time, in the range of three to four hundred years. That time frame encompasses 1,024 ancestors! If even one was born out of wedlock, the curse will continue down the family line. In a list that long, I would speculate that every family on earth has come under the influence of this curse that God instituted.

God wants to bless families, but satan is trying to destroy them by blocking the blessings and anointings that flow down the family lines. Historically most couples that conceived their first child outside the marriage covenant eventually married; the trend today is shifting away from that old norm. The institution of marriage, which God ordained for the loving and nurturing of the next generation, is under serious attack.

Marriage was designed for a man and a woman to become *"one flesh"* (Gen. 2:24). It is the physical example to both angels and demons of the relationship between *"Christ and the church"* (Eph. 5:32). Any attack on marriage is then designed to destroy God's working model of Kingdom love and harmony. If marriage doesn't work, neither does the covenant Jesus made with His Church: *"For we are members of His body, of His flesh, and of His bones"* (Eph. 5:30). If the type can be proven unreliable, then the reality loses its impact.

And the institution is definitely under attack.

The table below shows the *percentage* of births to unmarried mothers in the U.S. by race and ethnicity for years 1990 through 2006.[1]

Year	All Races	NH-White	NH-Black	Hispanic	Native American	Asian/PI
2006	38.5	26.6	70.7	49.9	64.6	16.5
2002	34.0	23.0	68.4	43.5	59.7	14.9
1990	28.0	16.9	66.7	36.7	53.6	13.2

*NH (non-Hispanic)

This trend is like an infectious disease that is growing and spreading as families become less cohesive. The key is the father! *"Fathers, provoke not your children to wrath: but bring them up in the nurture and admonition of the Lord"* (Eph. 6:4). It is the task of a father to awaken the child's spirit and call him forth to greet the world. John and Paula Sanford observed, "the Word does not say, 'mothers...bring them up...' Nor does it say, 'Parents...' The command is given specifically to fathers."[2]

This restoration of *"the hearts of the fathers to their children and the hearts of the children to their fathers"* is vital at this time as the return of the Lord approaches (Mal. 4:6 NKJV). God is sending Elijah's prophetic ministry to accomplish this task *"before the coming of the great and dreadful day of the Lord...lest...[He] come and strike the earth with a curse"* (Mal. 4:4-6 NKJV).

We have seen this curse in action, running down family lines. Several years ago we were invited to a house for coffee after a conference. There were five other guests there, three being pastors. The conversation came around to this curse on illegitimacy. As we spoke about the alienation and the blockage of our prayers that the curse causes, they excitedly started talking to each other.

"That is just how we feel," they said.

So I (Jeanne) asked, "Is there illegitimacy in your families?"

As it turned out, between the three pastors, their parents, and their children, there were seven instances of illegitimate children. As we started to pray for them and to get them to repent and ask forgiveness for entering into this sin, power was released. They all ended up on the floor, slain in the Spirit, and started speaking in tongues and crying. It was a long time before they recovered enough to tell us what happened.

They had all gotten a release and felt a burden and an accusation lift off of them. They were ecstatic with the presence of God they had just encountered. If a curse is able to block us from God's presence, there is a cause, for *"a curse without cause shall not alight"* (Prov. 26:2 NKJV). Our job is to recognize that something is amiss, for God will *"conceal a thing: but the honour of kings is to search out a matter"* (Prov. 25:2).

He is establishing our rule with Him by allowing us to expose the darkness to the light. God is on our side. He is looking *"throughout the earth to strengthen those whose hearts are fully committed to Him"* (2 Chron. 16:9 NIV). Most people curse the darkness by complaining about their lot in life. God wants us to shine the light, the truth, into that darkness or lie through repentance. Avoidance is not our protection from hurt; healing is. We must not hide our sins but rather *"confess your faults one to another, and pray for one another, that ye may be healed"* (James 5:16).

Signs of Illegitimacy

As mentioned earlier, if we are not walking in blessing, then we are walking under a curse. The evidence or result of being under this curse is that we cannot *"enter into the congregation of the Lord"* (Deut. 23:2). One of the effects of not being able to enter the congregation is that we are not able to draw near to the Lord. Those in the assembly of the Lord could access His court around the tent of meeting and draw near to Him (see Lev. 9:5). If we are not allowed into that assembly, then we are not allowed to be close to God. If we are experiencing a distant relationship with God, if we are unable to come into His throne room and feel His presence surround us, this curse is likely affecting us.

Jesus' sacrifice allowed us to *"enter into the holiest…by a new and living way… through the veil…*[that we may]*…draw near with a true heart in full assurance of faith…*[free] *from an evil conscience"* (Heb. 10:19-22). That is our blood-bought right (see Heb. 10:19). Yet many of us cannot access that place of intimacy. There seems to be a wall blocking us from coming into God's presence. We stand like children with our faces pressed against a window, observing rather than partaking of the love that is present within the house.

We cannot even enjoy God's people as we know we should because we are excluded from the congregation. We may have relationships, but we don't have that close family feeling that we long for. This situation is not because God is punishing you for something your parents, or in this case parents ten generations back, did. Rather, He is allowing darkness to remain that we might seek out the cause and bring forgiveness into the situation.

A friend of ours, Cheri, told us her family story.

Nine years ago I went through the "Curses to Blessings," and after asking forgiveness for illegitimacy down the family line, I was told to expect a miracle in my relationships. Our family is dysfunctional, allowing extreme alienation to operate; two of my brothers hadn't spoken to me in approximately ten years due to little misunderstandings. The week after "Curses to Blessings" was my birthday. I'm usually a little sad on my birthday because my family usually does not recognize it. That is why I was surprised when I received a phone call from one of my brothers (first time in my life)! He wished me a happy birthday, and we had a nice visit. About an hour later, another call came from my other brother. He asked me why we didn't talk anymore, and I honestly couldn't remember (it was so little). He said he loved me (he's never said those words to me before) and could we start again. I cried. It was one of my very favorite birthdays. We've been close ever since. I expected a miracle, and God came through!

Shame keeps us from coming boldly into Daddy's presence, shame that we were born illegitimate. The very word suggests that we have no right to be here. Even the world slings the slur, "you bastard" at those they despise. Jesus also endured insults and innuendoes about His birth (see John 8:41), yet as with all the other sins which He bore, He *"endured the cross, despising the shame"* (Heb. 12:2). He aggressively distained the shame that everyone was trying to put on Him and declared, *"I and My Father are one"* (John 10:30).

We must take this posture if we are to break the shame off of ourselves. If we are illegitimate, the shame did not initiate with us, but with our parents. They committed the sin of having sex outside of marriage, and the child that resulted is the constant reminder of that sin. Shame is the painful sense of guilt caused by the consciousness of guilt or of anything degrading, unworthy, or immodest.[3] If our parents are under shame because of their actions, they will transfer that shame to us, the child of their sin. We grow up thinking our feelings are normal and that everyone feels the same way.

Our friend David thought that way.

My wife, Michelle had told me about "Curses to Blessings" and I had dissed it, thinking I had already done lots of those deliverance/redemption types of things. She persevered, suggesting it was somehow different, or more thorough, and that she just *knew* I had to go through it. If I would just give her one hour of my time, she would take me through it…so I said, OK, OK.

I had always felt inadequate and that I was somehow excluded and rejected when I went to church meetings. After going through breaking off the curses with my wife, I went to church the next day and noticed an immediate and tangible change in how I felt there. When I approached a group of men, they did not turn their backs on me and exclude me. I felt part of the "tribe" and sensed no rejection whatsoever. Later in the week I went to a different church where my sons were going to Boys Brigade, and I felt the same noticeable shift to inclusion and acceptance. That feeling of inadequacy and rejection had disappeared and has never returned since. The curse had been completely broken.

We grow up with this shame-based nature and constant guilt, not about our actions, but about ourselves. We disqualify ourselves from so many things because we know that we are not worthy to be accepted by God or to do anything for Him. We know that people won't like us because we are tainted and dirty. We are like "Pigpen" in the comic Charlie Brown with this cloud following

us around. It is interesting that the creator, Charles Schultz, tied Pigpen's cloud to his past generations. Pigpen said, "I have affixed to me the dirt and dust of countless ages. Who am I to disturb history?" Science has discovered that every kid really does have their own "pollution cloud"; they have termed that cloud the "Pigpen effect."[4]

Though the science deals only with the actual dirt cloud, there is a spiritual dirt cloud that follows us around unless we clean it off.

I (Jeanne) was conceived before my parents were married. They denied the truth and claimed that I was conceived on their wedding night and born two months premature. This twisting of the timing of my birth threw my own sense of time off. It was like I was always out of sync with what was going on. It seemed like I was never in my time.

I could with great joy anticipate the future, and with happy reflections remember the past, but the present seemed to elude me. "Now" seemed like a no-man's-land. I would often fill my time with mindless activities so the "now" would pass until I came to that something special in the future. I loved life and anticipated things I would be doing next week, next month, or in the holidays, but today was harder to find joy in.

On a walk one day, God said to me that my time was out of sync. I asked forgiveness on behalf of my parents and the former generations for conceiving children out of wedlock. I asked God to forgive me for receiving shame, and broke it off. I had never realized that I was trying to live in the future. I broke off the lie that I couldn't really live until later and asked the Lord to reset my idea of time. I immediately experienced a shift over me. I began to experience joy in the day. I still look forward to future events, but today is equally important. I didn't have to live for what was coming; I could live life now!

Illegitimacy also causes us to lose our inheritance.

> *Jephthah…was a mighty man of valor, but he was the son of a harlot… and…when his* [half-brothers]*…grew up, they drove Jephthah out, and said to him, "You shall have no inheritance in our father's house…"* (Judges 11:1-2 NKJV).

It is always the accusation, "You don't really belong; you have no rights here; you are illegitimate." Even if it is not spoken directly, there are always innuendos designed to invalidate your worth.

Such was the case when the Pharisees tried to nullify the miracle of the healing of the blind man by casting doubt on Jesus' origins. They said, *"We know that God spoke to Moses; as for this fellow, we do not know where He is from"* (John 9:29 NKJV). When the formerly blind man incredulously challenged their stubborn unbelief, they lashed out at him, not with arguments, but with an allusion to sin surrounding his birth: *"'You were completely born in sins, and are you teaching us?' And they cast him out"* (John 9:34 NKJV). Illegitimacy always separates you from the assembly of the Lord.

Healing the Wound

If we take on illegitimacy, the constant lie is that we don't have a right to exist, let alone operate at any level of authority. The truth is that God said, *"Before I formed you in the womb I knew you; before you were born I sanctified you"* (Jer.

1:5 NKJV). You are no mistake; you are no accident. This must be our stance whenever we are assailed with accusation concerning our legitimacy.

I declare, "I have a right to be here because God *'formed me from the womb to be His servant'* (Isa. 49:5). God does not make mistakes. I am not a mistake, and I am not an accident."

Part of the healing process is to forgive all those who have hurt you. In this case we must forgive our parents who conceived us out of wedlock. We must forgive and release them from any judgments we have against them. This is about the family destiny that has come under a curse for conceiving children out of wedlock.

If you are illegitimate, pray for a healing of your own heart. Speak to the child within, which felt the shame and the condemnation, to be free, to come back into full relationship with the Body of Christ (the Church) and with the Lord.

Because this curse affects the whole family for ten generations, we need to be proactive in declaring the family's release into the heavenlies. When the slaves were set free, there was a proclamation to declare that fact. We also must proclaim the family's release and command the demonic forces to back off. We have authority because of God's forgiveness, and we must act like it in order to step into our freedom.

Call back the children affected by this curse. We had friends whose grown children were not serving the Lord. After they repented and broke the curse, they spoke into the heavens and called back their children. Within a week, both their son and daughter reconciled with them and started coming back to church. Our words have the authority to change the course of history, especially in our own families.

Prayer:

Lord, I stand in the gap for the generations before me on both my mother and father's side for the sin of conceiving children out of wedlock. I ask forgiveness for the 10th generation, the 9th, the 8th, the 7th, the 6th, the 5th, the 4th, the 3rd, the 2nd, and for myself. Now I take my authority, on the basis of my asking forgiveness, and I break this curse in the name of Jesus off my children and myself.

Lord, I pray for sexual purity in marriage, joy in my sexuality in marriage, and cleansing for all shame of illegitimacy. Lord, I pray for our family line to be restored to the right order under God, displaying before the angels the model of Christ and the Church.

Chapter 7

IDOLATRY

Cursed is the man who makes an idol
(Deuteronomy 27:15 NASB).

An idol is anything that occupies inordinate amounts of time, effort, finances, or affections beyond its proper due and ahead of God. When idols become obsessive or addictive, and we sacrifice for them, they will attract demonic activity. I (Ken) knew a man who suffered delirium tremens, also known as the DTs, as he was withdrawing from alcohol. He confided with me that demons attacked him along with the usual jerks and incoherency that accompanies a session of DTs. This man drank at least a 26 oz. bottle of rum every day for over 20 years. The sacrifice of his family was immense. Paul said,

> *...the things which the Gentiles sacrifice, they sacrifice to demons and not to God, and I don't want you to have fellowship with demons* (1 Corinthians 10:20 NKJV).

Jesus said to *"love the Lord your God with all your heart, with all your soul, with all your mind, and with all your strength"* (Mark 12:30 NKJV). When we shift our affections to other things, those things become a substitute for God. They may give us comfort or hope, or security and safety. They often define our purpose for living; they frame our view of success and determine our relationships. We know a lady who loved her horses so much that she fed them rather than her children. She was forced to live in a decrepit trailer, which often didn't have heat or water, so that she could keep her horses. They were attached to significant childhood memories that gave her comfort. They became the substitute for the comfort of the Holy Spirit (see John 14:16).

We use our idols to explain the highs and lows of our existence, as they demand our loyalties, affections, and commitments. Jesus warned us that *"one's life does not consist in the abundance of the things he possesses"* (Luke 12:15 NKJV). If we have a worldview centered on things, it will distort our view of the reality of the Kingdom. Jesus is Lord of all, or He is not Lord at all.

We often relegate the domain of idols to eastern religions such as Buddhism, Hinduism, or Shintoism. "Only the unsophisticated, the deluded, or the simple could worship an idol," we declare, all the while being trapped in the same sin in a different form. Paul said, *"Do you not know that to whom you present yourselves slaves to obey, you are that one's slaves whom you obey"* (Rom. 6:16 NKJV). Idols are the masks behind which demons hide. They usually are not made of stone or wood.

The following grouping has been garnered from the over two thousand individuals who have gone through the "Curses to Blessings" seminar:[1]

Natural / Physical The love of:		Spiritual The love of:	Self / Emotional The love of:
Approval of People	Sports	Cults / False Religions— Voodoo, etc.	Stubbornness
Humanistic Thinking	Rebellion	Superstitions (including Christian superstitions)	Religious Spirit
Position	Intellect		Unteachable
Power	Food		Self-comfort
Work	Things (ie., cars)	New Age and Occult Practices	Fear
Family	Computers	Meditation/ Transcendental Meditation	
Children	People		
Movie Stars / Ministry Stars	Freemasonry	Martial arts	
Religions (instead of Jesus)	Selfishness	Divination	
Country	Education	Astrology / Horoscopes / Signs	
Church	Money	Divination	
Drugs	Alcohol		
Gambling	Tarot cards		
Sexual Addiction	Doubt / Worry		
Ouija board	Worldly Doctrines		
Gangs			

Natural Idols

Loving the Approval of People

This is a substitute for seeking God's approval. It opens the door for manipulation by those you are seeking to please. This perverse way of thinking usually stems from a lack of approval from parents, older siblings, teachers, or friends. Indications that this idol exists can include feelings of being bad when others don't approve. There may be accusations that you are evil, or rebellious, or not a true friend if you don't yield to other's demands.

We become obsessed with what others think about us. There is even a saying, "What will the neighbors think?" The phrase was used in German communities to ensure that things were done properly. In ancient times, if an animal was not properly looked after according to the neighbors' collective opinion, it could be confiscated. This phrase became a manipulation tool that caused people to obsess on the approval of others.

If we are bound under an approval curse, we become subject to the whims of others. We are actually slaves of approval and cannot be our own person or "swim against the tide." Even in Jesus' day,

> *...many...of the rulers believed in Him, but because of the Pharisees they were not confessing Him, for fear that they would be put out of the synagogue; for they loved the approval of men rather than the approval of God* (John 12:42-43 NASB).

Humanistic Thinking

Humanistic thinking removes God from the center of everything and substitutes man, as the center, in His place. In that state, the Bible ceases to be the source of truth and becomes just an allegory or a book of platitudes. Philosophy becomes the preeminent source of right and wrong with no absolutes on which to base actions.

The former Soviet Union made the state the only religion in that country. By removing property rights, which had been expanded in 1910, long before the revolution, the Bolsheviks dragged the country into poverty. Between 1928 and 1934, agricultural production fell by almost 70 percent. This was due, almost in its entirety, to the removal of the land from the kulak farmers.[2] Central planning seemed like a good idea, but it wasn't a God idea. God gave each tribe of Israel a possession that they were forbidden to remove from their family's inheritance (see 1 Kings 21:2-3). That would ensure that there was never any permanent poverty in Israel. It was too good an idea, and Israel reneged on their promise to obey. Any time we reject God's ideas, we suffer the consequences.

As evolution became the dominant scientific explanation for the universe around us, nature became the substitute for God. Under this thinking, people *"exchanged the truth of God for a lie, and worshiped and served created things rather than the Creator"* (Rom. 1:25 NIV). We become subject to nature, being just another animal on the evolutionary chain, rather than nature being subject to us. We are viewed as exploiters rather than stewards and become the enemy of "mother earth." This Gaia philosophy (named after Gaia, Greek goddess of the earth) is actually a false religion and is predisposed to demonic influence.

An ancient precursor to the worship of Gaia was the animistic practice of worshiping various components of nature: trees, fire, water, earth, the sun, the moon, and the stars. Even today, though it is not called a religion, extreme environmentalism takes on many aspects of that kind of worship, exalting nature far above man. The lie is that all mining, and many manufacturing practices, are destructive.

God said He gave Israel *"a land whose stones are iron and out of whose hills you can dig copper"* (Deut. 8:9 NKJV). In the first mention of the Garden of Eden, God stated that *"the gold of that land is good: there is bdellium and the onyx stone"* (Gen. 2:12). The truth is that everything on the earth was put there for man's use. We are called to be good stewards of God's gifts, which we have not been, but not to make the gifts our gods.

God also intended man to

> *...be fruitful, and multiply, and replenish the earth, and subdue it: and have dominion over the fish of the sea, and over the fowl of the*

air, and over every living thing that moveth upon the earth (Genesis 1:28).

God was not worried about limited resources because He operated out of the heavenly realms where there is no lack. A humanistic worldview incorporates lack and limited resources, which engender fear and hoarding.

Loving Position

Position is all about striving to climb the ladder, any ladder. If there is someone on a rung above you, you must step on some fingers to go higher. Position is "all about me"—my place, my preeminence, my power.

Jesus said that in the Kingdom, *"he that is greatest among you shall be your servant"* (Matt. 23:11), which is upside down to seeking position. We don't need position; we need favor! Our position in the Kingdom is as *"sons of God, and... when He shall appear; we shall be like Him"* (1 John 3:2). No striving here, just a posture of rest in Him.

If your father owns a large corporation, you don't have to "climb the ladder" to get recognition; you are already loved as a son or daughter. You don't have to strive to rise to the top so you can reap the perks of position; you have the company as an inheritance. Jesus said, *"Fear not...for it is your Father's good pleasure to give you the kingdom"* (Luke 12:32).

Striving to maintain a position drove the Pharisees to condemn Jesus. They said, *"If we let Him...alone...the Romans shall come and take away both our place and nation"* (John 11:48). Their paranoia was so obvious that even Pilate was aware *"that the chief priests had delivered* [Jesus] *for envy"* (Mark 15:10). They occupied a privileged place, and He was threatening it. Striving for position always forces us to subjugate others' freedoms to our desires.

Self occupies the top spot and relegates others—God, spouse, children, friends, and co-workers—to lower positions. Satan desired the same high place, boasting,

> *I will ascend into heaven, I will exalt my throne above the stars of God: I will sit also upon the mount of the congregation...I will ascend*

above the heights of the clouds; I will be like the most High (Isaiah 14:13-14).

If we are seeking a higher position, we are emulating satan; if we are taking a lower posture, we are emulating Jesus (see Phil. 2:8).

Whatever method is used to obtain a position is the method required to maintain that position. If the initial push to the top took self-effort, then that same effort must be continually exerted to stay in the desired position. Saul was exalted because the people wanted a king, demanding, *"that we also may be like all the nations, and that our king may judge us, and go out before us, and fight our battles"* (1 Sam. 8:20).

The people's opinions became the main impetus dictating Saul's actions rather than God's word. Saul failed to obey the first instructions that Samuel gave him. He allowed the people's actions to overrule God's instructions. Saul protested to Samuel that he could not wait because

> *...I saw that the people were scattered from me, and that you did not come within the days appointed, and that the Philistines gathered together at Michmash...therefore I felt compelled, and offered a burnt offering* (1 Samuel 13:11-12 NKJV).

He was equally controlled when Jonathan broke Saul's vow concerning fasting. It was *"the people [who] rescued Jonathan, that he died not"* (1 Samuel 14:45).

Saul continually refused to take responsibility for his disobedience, choosing rather to blame the people. When Samuel challenged him concerning his unwillingness to completely destroy Amalek, he protested, *"I have obeyed the voice of the Lord...but the people took of the spoil"* (1 Sam. 15:20-21).

Saul revealed his heart when Samuel said,

> *"...you have rejected the word of the Lord, and the Lord has rejected you from being king over Israel." And as Samuel turned around to go away, Saul seized the edge of his robe, and it tore. So Samuel said to him, "The Lord has torn the kingdom of Israel from you today, and has given it to a neighbor of yours, who is better than you. And also*

the Strength of Israel will not lie nor repent. For He is not a man, that He should repent." Then [Saul] *said, "I have sinned; yet honor me now, please, before the elders of my people and before Israel, and return with me, that I may worship the Lord your God"* (1 Samuel 15:26-30 NKJV).

He had just lost the kingdom and destroyed the destiny of his family, yet Saul's only concern was to be honored before the people. Their honor was more important than God's. Such is the power of an idol in our hearts; it must receive homage.

Solomon declared, *"He who is slow to anger is better than the mighty, and he who rules his spirit than he who takes a city"* (Prov. 16:32 NKJV). God is more concerned with who we are than what we accomplish or what position we hold. In fact, He *"resists the proud, but gives grace to the humble"* (James 4:6). Seeking a position is a self-defeating exercise. When we open ourselves to this curse, we open ourselves to spirits of envy, competition, selfishness, and ambition.

Love of Intellect

The degree to which we are enamored with our own intellect is the degree to which we are impressed with ourselves and make idols of ourselves. Paul said,

I warn everyone among you not to estimate and think of himself more highly than he ought [not to have an exaggerated opinion of his own importance], but to rate his ability with sober judgment, each according to the degree of faith apportioned by God to him (Romans 12:3 AMP).

Kingdom function is dependent on our degree of faith, not of intellect. *"Wisdom is the principal thing; therefore get wisdom: and with all thy getting get understanding"* (Prov. 4:7). Intellect is not wisdom *"because the foolish thing [that has its source in] God is wiser than men"* (1 Cor. 1:25 AMP). The smartest man in history is a *"fool [if he] has said in his heart, 'There is no God' "* (Ps. 53:1 NKJV).

The following schematic shows the difference between how we process facts and how we process truth.[3]

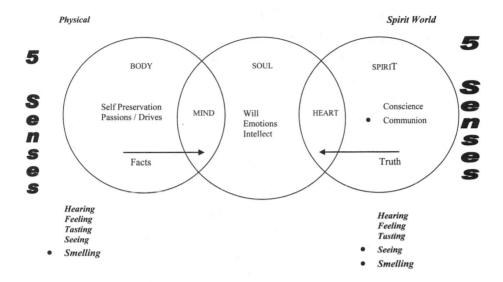

Facts flow from the senses through the mind. The bigger the interface (the mind), the greater the intelligence. A greater intellect allows the mind to interpret the facts and properly respond to them.

Truth flows from the spiritual senses through the heart. The bigger the heart interface, the greater the wisdom. The heart grows bigger as the spirit man overlays the soul. The love, resident in the spirit, allows the heart to enlarge, receive truth, and properly respond to it.

Facts are not the truth. Facts describe an event or a situation; the truth resides in a Person. Jesus said, *"I am the way, the truth, and the life"* (John 14:6 NKJV). He did not say, "I know the way, the truth, and the life." Jesus *is* the truth. The facts were that in the city of Nain, the widow's son was dead. They had already had the funeral and were carrying him out to bury him. He was dead—that was the fact. The truth was that Jesus said, *"Weep not...Young man, I say unto thee, Arise. And he that was dead sat up"* (Luke 7:13-15).

Jonah learned this lesson in the belly of the whale. The facts in his case were overwhelming.

Jonah prayed...out of the fish's belly, and said, I cried by reason of mine affliction unto the Lord, and He heard me; out of the belly of hell cried I...For Thou...cast me into the deep, in the midst of the seas; and the floods compassed me about: all Thy billows and Thy waves passed over me. Then I said, I am cast out of Thy sight; yet I will look again toward Thy holy temple. The waters compassed me about, even to the soul: the depth closed me round about; the weeds were wrapped about my head. I went down to the bottoms of the mountains; the earth with her bars was about me... (Jonah 2:1-6).

Then he said the most amazing thing: *"They that observe lying vanities forsake their own mercy"* (Jon. 2:8). He was calling the facts lies. The facts were the following: he was in the belly of the whale; seaweed was around his head; he went to the bottom of the sea. But the truth was he was going to Nineveh. When he acknowledged the truth, *"the fish...vomited out Jonah upon the dry land"* (Jon. 2:10). He would have been the epitome of the Old Testament prophet as he marched through Nineveh proclaiming judgment: wild-eyed, disheveled, skin bleached white by the fish's stomach acids, and dead sure of whom he was representing. No wonder the whole city *"turned from their evil way"* (Jon. 3:10), allowing God to turn from His judgment.

The facts of the situation refer to a particular alignment of molecules at a specific time. For example, let's examine the book that is in your hands. Is it real? What was it a hundred years ago? Possibly a tree, or soil, or air, or water. The molecules that make up this book could have been arranged very differently. What will it be in another hundred years? What we call real or the facts are only real in a moment of time. They are, in fact, in transition and will change.

The truth never changes. *"Jesus Christ the same yesterday, and to day, and for ever"* (Heb. 13:8). *"...For the things which are seen, are temporal; but the things which are not seen are eternal"* (2 Cor. 4:18). If temporal things that we see are actually in a state of transition, then the eternal things we can't see are more real and reliable. Trusting our intellect voids the *"word [which] is settled in heaven"* (Ps. 119:89).

Our actions over time become our habits, which, over generations, become our traditions. Our family's veneration of intelligence makes *"the word of God of no effect through* [the] *tradition which* [we] *have handed down"* (Mark 7:13 NKJV). God said that He would

> *...baffle and render useless and destroy the learning of the learned and the philosophy of the philosophers and the cleverness of the clever and the discernment of the discerning; I will frustrate and nullify* [them] *and bring* [them] *to nothing. Where is the wise man (the philosopher)? Where is the scribe (the scholar)? Where is the investigator (the logician, the debater) of this present time and age? Has not God shown up the nonsense and the folly of this world's wisdom?* (1 Corinthians 1:19-20 AMP)

We need to repent when we place our worldview above that of God. True wisdom is based on placing God and His thoughts above all our own. Paul noted that

> *...when they knew and recognized Him as God, they did not honor and glorify Him as God or give Him thanks. But instead they became futile and godless in their thinking [with vain imaginings, foolish reasoning, and stupid speculations] and their senseless minds were darkened. Claiming to be wise, they became fools [professing to be smart, they made simpletons of themselves]* (Romans 1:21-22 AMP).

One of the biggest stock scams ever involved Bre-X Minerals, a company with a $4.4 billion capitalization at its peak. When its mine was proven to be bogus, the stock plummeted to zero in a matter of months. The major losers were the Quebec public sector pension fund, which lost $70 million; the Ontario Teachers' Pension Plan, which lost $100 million; and the Ontario Municipal Employees' Retirement Board, which lost $45 million.[4] The experts proved to be the fools.

Love of Power

We love power because it is a method of protection. It allows us to control people and situations, squeezing them to conform to our viewpoint. It places us in the position of acting like God, though only God has the character, love, and wisdom to be God. He is designed to be God, having unlimited power; we are not.

Power corrupts; absolute power corrupts absolutely.[5] *"God is the Judge: He puts down one, and exalts another"* (Ps. 75:7 NKJV). Our pride is promoting us if God isn't. It is God's mercy that we aren't promoted before we are ready, for *"pride goes before destruction, and a haughty spirit before a fall"* (Prov. 16:18 AMP). We need God to reveal our hearts because *"the heart is more deceitful than all else and is desperately sick; who can understand it? I, the Lord, search the heart, I test the mind"* (Jer. 17:9-10 NASB).

This lust for power is an inordinate desire or pleasure that consumes and takes precedence over all other affections.[6] When present in a king, it results in war. It manifests in equal manner in us.

> *Where do wars and fights come from among you? Do they not come from your desires for pleasure that war in your members? You lust and do not have. You murder and covet and cannot obtain. You fight and war. Yet you do not have because you do not ask* (James 4:1-2 NKJV).

The pride of power is taking, not asking, and God declares, *"I will break the pride of your power...and your strength shall be spent in vain"* (Lev. 26:19-20).

We need to *"be clothed with humility, for...God resists the proud, but gives grace to the humble"* (1 Pet. 5:5 NKJV). This principle was demonstrated in God's dealings with Pharaoh. Pharaoh's fleshly pride opened the door for demonic activity. God responded,

> *...I will go through the land of Egypt...and will strike down all the firstborn in the land of Egypt, both man and beast; and against all the gods of Egypt I will execute judgments...* (Exodus 12:12 NASB).

We are called to be *"children of God, and it has not appeared as yet what we will be. We know that when He appears, we will be like Him, because we will see Him just as He is"* (1 John 3:2 NASB).

Because ultimately we will be like Him, each can *"abide in that calling in which he has been called"* (1 Cor. 7:20 Darby).

Let this mind be in you, which was also in Christ Jesus: who...made Himself of no reputation, and took upon Him the form of a servant (Philippians 2:5-7).

Love of Work

This is my (Ken's) biggest idol. It is a demonic structure stating that hard work is a requirement of piety and acceptance. As a child, my praise for working and thus my self-worth was predicated on working hard and doing it right. If I didn't, I was being lazy and I was bad. A good boy does his work! We *"train up a child in the way he should go: and when he is old, he will not depart from it"* (Prov. 22:6). I started driving a tractor on our farm at the age of nine. It required all the strength that I had in both legs just to push in the clutch.

By the time I went to university, I had amassed a fortune of $1,500. My hourly wage had averaged 25 cents per hour: that works out to 6,000 hours in eight years. I am retired, and I still feel guilty if I goof off or relax. I was trained that hard work is equivalent to being good, and now that I am old, I still have that structure embedded in my brain.

It is a lie! It is *"Christ Jesus, who...is made unto us wisdom, and righteousness, and sanctification, and redemption"* (1 Cor. 1:30). I work so I can eat, not so I can be righteous (see 2 Thess. 3:10). It is foolish to burn the candle at both ends.

Unless the Lord builds the house, they labor in vain who build it; unless the Lord guards the city, the watchman stays awake in vain. It is vain for you to rise up early, to sit up late, to eat the bread of sorrows; for so He gives His beloved sleep (Psalm 127:1-2 NKJV).

We are to be

...servants...obedient to those who are [our bosses]*...in singleness of...heart, as* [service] *to Christ; not in the way of eye-service...and only to please men, but as the servants...of Christ, doing the will of God heartily and with your whole soul; rendering service readily with goodwill, as to the Lord and not to men* (Ephesians 6:5-7 AMP).

We need to be diligent, but balanced.

God and His Word must be first in our affections. After God, come spouse, children, work, and ministry. If things are kept in that order, our lives will be in balance. I remember talking to God about this very thing. I was trying to justify my crazy work schedule by claiming it was for the good of the Kingdom and the family.

God responded, "You work hard for you. You get your self-worth, your acceptance, your approval, your recognition, and your adventure from your work. You were designed to get all these from Me in the Kingdom. You are out of order."

I was performance oriented. I was investing too much into the job. Jeanne would often joke in disgust, as I dragged myself through the door, "I see you gave at the office today." I had nothing left for the items higher on the priority list.

That attitude of venerating work had permeated my whole life. After high school, I left the farm and came to Edmonton to play junior football. I recognized that I was not the biggest, the fastest, the strongest, or the smartest player trying out for the team. Some players could kick the ball better, throw further, and were just plain tougher than I was. One hundred and thirty guys were going after 30 roster spots.

I needed some point of recognition if I was going to make the team because most of the guys had been scouted and were known to the coaching staff. So I relied on my demonic structure to get noticed: I could outwork everyone. I did every drill with the maximum effort. I ran every wind sprint full out. I did extra push-ups and took extra reps. I was eager and tireless. The result: I made the team.

Extreme work habits allowed me to achieve many things but were useless where the Kingdom and family were concerned. The Kingdom is not about work or things: *"For the kingdom of God is not meat and drink; but righteousness, and peace, and joy in the Holy Ghost"* (Rom. 14:17). You do not get ahead in the Kingdom by working harder but by loving, believing, and walking in faith.

Work then is a substitute for what Jesus accomplished on the cross. It is a form of self-sufficiency and independence. We will often make the statement, "If you need something done, you have to do it yourself." The four-year-old, tying his shoelaces, demands his independence, saying, "I'll do it myself, I'll do it myself." It is good to grow up, but independence does not develop unity.

Performance orientation and work are obsessed with production and results; Kingdom orientation delights in growth. Jesus told this parable about the Kingdom of God:

> *So is the kingdom of God, as if a man should cast seed into the ground; and should sleep, and rise night and day, and the seed should spring and grow up, he knoweth not how. For the earth bringeth forth fruit of herself; first the blade, then the ear, after that the full corn in the ear* (Mark 4:26-28).

Sleeping does not usually translate into a productive activity if you are results driven. Rest is not doing nothing; it is doing our part and letting others do theirs. Paul said,

> *I planted, Apollos watered, but God gave the increase. So then neither he who plants is anything, nor he who waters, but God who gives the increase* (1 Corinthians 3:6-7 NKJV).

Adam was *"put…in the garden of Eden to dress it and to keep it"* (Gen. 2:15). *Dress* means to work or till the garden.[7] Keep means to guard or hedge the garden.[8] There was to be a spiritual aspect to his work, not just a physical. When

Adam ignored the spiritual aspect, he allowed satan to come in and destroy the garden.

When we promote physical work as the key ingredient, we open the door to self-reliant spirits, self-important spirits, spirits of isolation, self-effort, and independence. These will come in and destroy the garden that God wants our lives to be.

Excessive Love of Family

One of the earliest rebellions in the Bible was with an extended family striving to make a name for themselves by building the tower of Babel. They said, *"let us build us a city and a tower…and let us make us a name for ourselves"* (Gen. 11:4 AMP). God had commanded them to *"be fruitful and multiply and fill the earth"* (Gen. 9:1 AMP), but they didn't want to be *"scattered abroad upon the face of the whole earth"* (Gen. 11:4). Their determination to make an idol to their own greatness forced God to come down and *"confuse their language"* (Gen. 11:7 NASB).

God wanted them to be fruitful, but they wanted to rest on the family's laurels.

A family's past should not dictate its future; the Word of God and faith should bring us to our destiny. Our families are not the expression of who we are. We have a new family: the family of God. God, the Father, has no grandchildren; we are all children of God. We bless *"the Father…from whom the whole family in heaven and earth is named"* (Eph. 3:14-15 NKJV).

We must not view our families through warped lenses. Every family has a glory and a shame. We can't exalt one and hide the other. We are told to honor, not to worship or despise our ancestors. God desires this cross-generational unity to expedite the flow of the blessing and the breaking of the curses. We will accomplish this if we repent, and then forgive and honor our ancestors, calling forth the destiny that God ordained for the family.

Inordinate Love of Children

"Children are a heritage from the Lord" (Ps. 127:3 NKJV); they are not the Lord. Modern society has promoted the child to a place of preeminence that God never intended. They rank below our spouse in order of consideration. God said that *"foolishness is bound up in the heart of a child"* (Prov. 22:15 NKJV), and they need correction.

Today, children are taught all about their rights, but not their obligations. This has warped their sense of self-importance and made them too self-aware. Parents have bought into the lie that children are their equals and that families are democracies. It is not true on either account. With the destruction of the nuclear family, confusion has come into the understanding of authority, but children are not designed to be the head in any household situation. Society has been so intent on producing self-esteem that we have produced a generation of narcissistic egomaniacs. We have made them think that freedom is a right and not a responsibility.

Jacob was taught a distorted view of a child's place in the family. He was prompted to usurp authority and lie to his father (see Gen. 27:5-30). Later he confused his own family structure by marrying multiple wives and favoring one over the others (see Gen. 29:20-35). He further exacerbated the tension in the family because he *"loved Joseph more than all his children"* (Gen. 37:3).

When Joseph was lost, Jacob switched his adoration to Benjamin. He became so attached to Benjamin that Judah was afraid to leave him in Egypt. He told Joseph that it would kill their father, *"seeing that his life is bound up in the lad's life"* (Gen. 44:30). That uncurbed favor twisted Benjamin's thinking that, in generations to come, blocked this tribe's ability to discern right from wrong. They thought they could do no wrong and were unable to receive any correction. In the end, it almost destroyed them (see Judg. 20–21).

Eli, the high priest, would not discipline his sons even though they were *"seducing the young women who assisted at the entrance of the Tabernacle"* (1 Sam. 2:22 NLT). Things were so out of order in his family that he did nothing more than mildly rebuke them. They were also taking sacrifices that belonged to

God (see 1 Sam. 2:12-17). Eli did nothing at all about that sin, even participating in it. God finally sent an angel, who pronounced a curse on the family, saying to Eli, "You *'honor your sons more than Me'* " (1 Sam. 2:29 NKJV). The Lord summed up Eli's sin for Samuel: *"His sons made themselves vile, and he restrained them not"* (1 Sam. 3:13).

That lack of restraint opens the door for rebellion. David continually failed to address his son's sins, resulting in family chaos. He *"was very wroth"* (2 Sam. 13:21) with Amnon when he raped his half-sister Tamar, but failed to deal with him for over two years (see 2 Sam. 13:1-23). This lack of action from dad prompted Tamar's brother, Absalom, to kill Amnon. Again, David did nothing to deal with the deteriorating family situation. David would not even speak to him for another two years when he was allowed to return.

No communication, no correction or resolution. Absalom finally rebelled against the father he felt he did not have (see 2 Sam. 15). Even then, David did not want to deal with him. He told his commanders to *"deal gently for my sake with...Absalom"* (2 Sam. 18:5). David was so out of order that Joab chided him:

> *...in that you love your enemies and hate your friends...for today I perceive that if Absalom had lived and all of us had died today, then it would have pleased you well* (2 Samuel 19:6 NKJV).

David continued that pattern through his whole reign. Even at the very end, Adonijah felt jusitified to exalt himself, *"saying, 'I will be king'"* (1 Kings 1:5). He did this because his father, David *"had not rebuked him at any time by saying, 'Why have you done so?'"* (1 Kings 1:6 NKJV). It is not love to fail to discipline our children; that is twisted, selfish love.

> *For those whom the Lord loves He disciplines...But if you are without discipline, of which all have become partakers, then you are illegitimate children and not sons* (Hebrews 12:6,8 NASB).

Discipline is necessary both for making children feel loved and for teaching honor.

God is the source of our life, not our children. They are to be taught to respect and honor their parents so that they will respect and honor all authority, especially God's. Under the law, *"a stubborn and rebellious son, which will not obey the voice of his father or...mother"* (Deut. 21:18) was to be stoned (see Deut. 21:21). Moses said that a son who *"strikes [or]...curses his father or his mother shall surely be put to death"* (Exod. 21:15,17 NKJV).

Even the Ten Commandments included *"honor your father and your mother, that your days may be long upon the land which the Lord your God is giving you"* (Exod. 20:12 NKJV). We as parents have tried to live vicariously through our children and avoid any discipline that would potentially harm that relationship. But our children are not our life. Our *"life is hid with Christ in God"* (Col. 3:3). The future of our families depends on us teaching our children honor. We need to repent.

Gangs

Gangs thrive where families fail. They offer young people a place within a group that will respect them, give them a sense of belonging, and offer a form of love. God designed families, including extended families, to offer that nurturing. The church family is an extension of the nuclear family and enhances the sense of community that everyone needs.

A gang is a perversion of the family structure that operates where God's original form is dysfunctional or physically not present. Gangs demand loyalty; the family gives loyalty to each other. Gangs control through fear of rejection or retaliation; the family accepts you as you are, even if they differ with you, with no strings attached. The gang forces you to be part of a whole; the family allows you to be an individual who contributes to the whole. The gang forces the members to invest in the gang; the family invests in the individuals. Gangs establish a code of conduct that may subvert the individual's morals or conscience; families help to define the truths that will form morals and conscience. Gangs are a perversion of God's order of government.

Unreasonable Love of Country

Nations in the Bible are considered extended families. When Noah's family went their separate ways after the flood they were *"divided in their lands; every one after his tongue, after their families, in their nations"* (Gen. 10:5). This definition of nations as extended families is predominant in the Old Testament, with over 360 references.[9] In the New Testament, the dominant word for nation is *ethnos,* from which we get our word *ethnic,* meaning a foreign, non-Jewish tribe or race.[10]

Today, modern nations are not well connected to family destinies but still have an ordained connection to the land. Part of a nation's destiny is determined by their response to Christians within their midst. Jesus states that *"whatever you did for one of the least of these brothers of Mine, you did for Me"* (Matt. 25:40 NIV), and then called them into their reward. National response to the Jews, as children of Abraham, will also determine a nation's ultimate destiny (see Gen. 12:3).

God said He raised up the god-king, Pharaoh, in Egypt *"that I might show you My power, and that My name may be declared throughout all the earth"* (Exod. 9:16 AMP). Persia's rise was ordained to free the Jews from their Babylonian captivity and rebuild the temple. King Cyrus declared, *"The Lord God of heaven hath given me all the kingdoms of the earth; and He hath charged me to build Him an house at Jerusalem, which is in Judah"* (Ezra 1:1-2). Rome was ordained to rule the world at the time of Christ in order that He might die by crucifixion rather than by stoning (see John 3:14). The Greek culture was adapted by Rome that the New Testament might be written in that universal, expressive language.

In modern times, God still uses the nations to accomplish His purposes. Britain championed the freedom of religion and gained an empire to facilitate the spread of the Gospel. The U.S.A. was used to bring freedom to the downtrodden. Part of the inscription on the Statue of Liberty reads,

> Give me your tired, your poor, your huddled masses yearning to breathe free, the wretched refuse of your teeming shore. Send these, the homeless, tempest-tost to me....[11]

Lincoln emphasized this message with the introduction to his Gettysburg address:

Four score and seven years ago our fathers brought forth on this continent a new nation, conceived in Liberty, and dedicated to the proposition that all men were created equal.[12]

All nations will ultimately come under the authority of God's Kingdom (see Dan. 2). Only one Kingdom will last, and it is to that Kingdom that we owe our allegiance. Abraham modeled this as he

...lived as an alien in the land of promise, as in a foreign land, dwelling in tents with Isaac and Jacob, fellow heirs of the same promise; for he was looking for the city...whose architect and builder is God (Hebrews 11:9-10 NASB).

...if they had been thinking of that country from which they went out, they would have had opportunity to return. But as it is, they desire a better country, that is, a heavenly one (Hebrews 11:15-16 NASB).

We then *"are no more strangers and foreigners, but fellow citizens with the saints"* (Eph. 2:19) if we are able to let go of our country of origin or adoption. Our first allegiance must be to King Jesus and then to the countries that He has placed us within. The Bible is clear; in the future, *"the kingdoms of this world are become the kingdoms of our Lord, and of His Christ"* (Rev. 11:15). We need to repent, ask forgiveness for our families, and get our priorities straight concerning our allegiances.

Veneration of Church or Denomination

Denominations usually begin from zeal to establish a revelation, a doctrine, or to restore a lost truth. Noble causes, but the denominational approach ultimately divides the Church. Part of the definition of denominationalism is the following:

1. A disposition to divide into or form denominations.

2. Rigid adherence or devotion to a denomination or sect; sectarianism. [13]

Neither of those appears designed to bring the unity that Christ prayed for. Concerning the division in the Corinthian church, Paul asked, *"Is Christ divided?"* (1 Cor. 1:13). Yet wars have been fought over doctrines and denominations.

I recall a joke concerning the doctrinal arguments surrounding baptism. One preacher believed in full immersion, while a bishop friend from a different denomination believed in only sprinkling the head. The bishop decided to try and reason with his friend:

"If I got someone up to his or her knees, would that not constitute baptism?" he asked.

"No," was the curt reply.

"How about up to the neck?"

"No."

"What about if he or she had everything under except the top of the head?"

"The top of the head must be covered with water to be baptized," the preacher insisted.

"So the top of the head must have water on it for baptism to be official?" the bishop queried.

"Yes."

"Well then, we both agree. As long as the top of the head gets wet, they are baptized."

We have many such foolish arguments over things that will not get us into Heaven or keep us out. Jesus prayed to the Father that Christians *"may be one, as We are"* (John 17:11). He is the basis of our unity.

Coalescing (growing together) around a doctrine is counterproductive because the revelation of God is not static but fluid and progressive. Though the truth and God never change, our understanding of it does as we mature. Truths are always connected to blessings; that is why people embrace them. Isaiah cried, *"He who blesseth himself in the earth shall bless himself in the God of truth"* (Isa. 65:16). The truth is the next revelation on this journey, not the destination. The blessing was never designed to be an invitation to camp, but an encouragement to keep going.

Israel camped 38 times in 40 years after coming through the Red Sea (see Num. 33). Some of those encampments lasted for several years. During that time God supplied them with everything they needed: protection, shade by day, heat and light at night, food, and water. Their shoes and clothing didn't wear out (see Deut. 8:4). They had all been baptized in water and the Spirit (see 1 Cor. 10:1-6). They had divine guidance, divine revelation, and apostolic authority; the very writers of the Scriptures, miracles, and the visible presence of God. They were *"the church in the wilderness"* (Acts 7:38), yet *"the Lord was angry with* [them]" (Deut. 9:8) because they didn't honor God by obeying Him.

Knowing human nature, I am sure that they would have set up their tents as comfortably as they could. They would have put up the chicken coop, accessorized the front yard, and made the kitchen functional.

"No more living out of a suitcase."

"This is where the blessings are flowing."

"Let's camp here."

But the prosperity and comfort were present because the Spirit of the Lord was present. When the Spirit moved, as He always does, all the benefits moved with Him.

If any had stayed behind, they would have been in a dry, desert place with no protection, food, water, or guidance. Such is the state of a church that camps on a truth and does not move with the Spirit. Even today, many such isolated, lifeless camps are fighting to maintain their dry, unproductive ground. The leaders of the last move of God are often the biggest resistors to the next move. Our loyalty to a doctrine or a church will keep us from depending on Jesus.

Doctrines do not promote relationship. It is through intimacy with God that we get to know Him. Jesus is the truth, not the doctrines. The doctrines are designed to give us a revelation of Jesus and to lead us to Him. "*The law* [doctrine] *was given by Moses, but grace and truth came by Jesus Christ*" (John 1:17). In this equation, grace is on the side of Jesus, not on the side of the law or the doctrines. We are out of order if we depend on doctrines to give us the truth. Jesus said, "*If you abide in My Word…you shall know the truth, and the truth shall make you free*" (John 8:32).

Idolizing a church, a doctrine, or a denomination leads to pride, legalism, and a traditional, inadaptable way of thinking. "*New wine* [new thoughts] *must be put into new wineskins; and both are preserved*" (see Luke 5:38). God does not want to destroy the denominations; therefore, He takes new moves of the Spirit and new ideas to where there is enough flexibility to accommodate them. Worship God, not doctrines or institutions.

Drugs

Though the term *drug* does not appear in the Bible, the concept does. Drugs, even illicit street drugs, are generally thought of as some chemical substance with an active ingredient. Our terms *druggist* and *pharmacist* are derived from the Greek *pharmekeus,*[14] which means spellbinding potion. It is also the word translated magician or sorcerer. The Bible severely warns that, along with many other abominations, "*sorcerers…shall have their part in the lake of fire…which is the second death*" (Rev. 21:8).

The oracle at Delphi, whom the ancient Greeks sought for direction, was drugged on laurel leaves and hallucinogenic vapors that arose from a fissure in the temple floor, to prognosticate future events.[15] She was called the *pythia,* or python. That same term is connected to the slave girl who was "*possessed with a spirit of divination* [python][16]*…which brought her masters much gain by soothsaying*" (Acts 16:16). By interfering with the proper chemical balance in the body, drugs alter many of the cognitive functions of the brain. Drugs remove the protection that the will usually exercises and opens the door to demonic activity in the user's life.

They alter the state of the mind and open it up to second heaven revelation, which is the realm of satan. Even here the devil has overplayed his hand. Many of the hippies that started the Jesus Movement in the early '70s gave their hearts to Jesus because of the demonic fear they encountered while on drugs. They literally had "the hell scared out of them."

Drugs affect the nervous system, releasing euphoric chemicals into the bloodstream that are designed to create a high. They become a poor substitute for the Holy Spirit because *"if you continually surrender yourselves to anyone to do his will, you are the slaves of him whom you obey"* (Rom. 6:16 AMP). This connection to the demonic makes drug addiction extremely difficult to break free from. A slave cannot just walk away from his master, but he can be *"bought with a price"* (1 Cor. 6:20) as Jesus did for us. Some of the demonic spirits that may need to be dealt with after involvement with drugs or drug addiction include the following:

- Spirit of Fear
- Spirit of Pharmacy
- Spirit of Witchcraft
- Spirit of Sorcery

Gambling

Legalized gambling consumes more entertainment dollars than most other forms of entertainment combined. In 1997 Americans collectively wagered more than half a trillion dollars. The gambling affects not only gamblers, but also their spouse, their children, crime rates, and society as a whole.[17] Gambling addiction, like alcohol addiction, puts the need to gamble above everything else, making it an idol.

I heard an anecdote about a man who went into a tattoo parlor in Macau. He came across a strange script as he looked over the patterns catalogue. One tattoo pattern read, "Born to Lose."

He asked the owner of the shop, "Have you ever done one of these tattoos?"

"Yes, I have done a few of them."

"Why would anyone want to stick that statement on their body?"

The owner spoke solemnly as he leaned forward and tapped his head, "Tattooed in mind before tattooed on body."

The gambling addiction is fueled by the mindset that God will not supply all of my needs and that I don't deserve to win in life. Because the odds are always in favor of the house, the more you play, the more guaranteed you are to lose. Every gambler knows that, yet continues to gamble even after winning. Gambling isn't about the money. If it was, winning big would end the need to gamble.

It seems even the winners lose. According to *Milwaukee Magazine,* national statistics show that one-third of lottery winners end up in financial ruin.[18] Money, like power, is an amplifier. If you were good with a little money, you will be better with lots. If you were reckless with a little money (the typical gambler), you will be even more reckless with riches. *"He who has an evil and covetous eye hastens to be rich and knows not that want will come upon him"* (Prov. 28:22 AMP). We need to repent of not using God's money wisely and not trusting God to supply. Some of the demonic spirits that may need to be dealt with include the following:

- Spirit of Gambling
- Spirit of Self-Pity
- Spirit of Self-Hatred
- Spirit of Greed

Fanatical Love of Sports

A sports fan is living life vicariously through the players engaged in the sport. Even though fans are passive in their actions, they can display excessive excitement, pride, and an undeserved sense of accomplishment when their team scores or wins.

They feel a sense of acceptance and camaraderie, respect, adventure, and even love for other fans. God designed the church to supply these needs, not an athlete or a team. With such great expectations also comes great disappointment. The most avid fan can become the loudest heckler when "the bum" drops the ball or completely misses the shot.

I witnessed Wayne Gretzky score his 50th goal in 39 hockey games, shattering the old record of 50 goals in 50 games. The entire Northlands Coliseum, in Edmonton, erupted into a roar of praise that would make any church pastor envious. The arena went nuts. People went into frenzy, cheering, whistling, hugging total strangers, and shouting his name. The chant of "Gretsky, Gretsky, Gretsky," that rolled through the arena eerily grew to a worship fever for their hero.

You could feel the power of that offering of praise going up. The hair on the back of my neck rose as I listened to the chorus echo repeatedly. Wayne Gretsky is a humble, gracious man, but the fans made him their idol that day. No man should occupy that place in our hearts that is reserved for God.

The term *fan* is an abbreviation of the word *fanatic*. The word *fanatic* is derived from the Latin *fanaticus,* meaning inspired by a deity; frenzied; marked by excessive enthusiasm and often, intense uncritical devotion.[19] The huge salaries that athletes garner exemplify this adoration, as do the commercial endorsements.

According to Fortune 500, Tiger Woods made 93 percent of his $100 million income on endorsements. Even though he was involved in a scandal, as of the end of December 2009, only a few of his endorsements have been lost, though his ads have not been on television for over a month.[20] Accenture Plc, the consulting company that built its marketing around Tiger Woods, removed him from its Website, while Procter & Gamble Co. said it will begin phasing the athlete out of promotions for its Gillette brand.

AT&T Inc., also a sponsor, is evaluating its relationship with Woods, the company said in an emailed statement. The No. 1 golfer has plunged to 24th from 6th in the Davie Brown Index of celebrity endorsers, which marketers and ad agencies use to gauge the ability of personalities to influence shoppers.[21] Tying ourselves too closely with fallible people will lead to disappointment.

Making sports stars heroes does not transform them or us. Sports operate in a fantasy world designed to produce pseudo emotions and victories. Unlike the real world, we can venture at daring feats without the fear of suffering loss. It is a poor substitute for God's Kingdom where *"the people who know their God shall be strong, and* [actually]...*carry out great exploits"* (Dan. 11:32 NKJV).

In God's Kingdom,

> ...*our struggle is not against flesh and blood, but against the rulers, against the powers, against the world forces of this darkness, against the spiritual forces of wickedness in the heavenly places* (Ephesians 6:12 NASB).

Unlike the world of sports, this battle forces us to fully engage and radically change. We no longer live in a fantasy world, but

> ...*have had that veil* [that blindness to reality] *removed so that we can be mirrors that brightly reflect the glory of the Lord. And as the Spirit of the Lord works within us, we become more and more like Him and reflect His glory even more* (2 Corinthians 3:18 NLT).

Some of the demonic spirits or strongholds that may need to be dealt with include the following:

- Spirit of Sports (Ken's addiction)
- False Worship
- False gods or demigods

Lust for Food

We get attached to food because it is offered at an early age as a reward or for comfort. *"Food [is intended] for the stomach, and the stomach for food, but God will finally end [the functions of] both and bring them to nothing"* (1 Cor. 6:13 AMP). They were made for the Lord, and the Lord cares about our bodies.

About two-thirds of adults in the United States are overweight, and almost one-third are obese, according to data from the National Health and Nutrition Examination Survey (NHANES) 2001 to 2004.[22]

We have elevated food from a physical necessity to an enhancer of self-worth. The Catholic Church included gluttony in its list of the "seven deadly sins."[23] Obesity is one of the leading factors for diabetes, high cholesterol, high blood pressure, joint problems, kidney problems, and heart disease. The modern church has shrugged this sin off as an inconsequential lifestyle choice when in reality it has huge consequences.

I (Ken) include myself in this group and have just begun to recognize the nature of this sin. Paul said,

> *For many walk, of whom I have told you often, and now tell you even weeping, that they are the enemies of the cross of Christ: whose end is destruction, whose god is their belly, and whose glory is in their shame* (Philippians 3:18-19 NKJV).

This is a hard saying that addiction to food makes us an enemy of the cross. Jesus told us that

> *...he who does not take his cross and follow after Me is not worthy of Me. He who finds his life will lose it, and he who loses his life for My sake will find it* (Matthew 10:38-39 NKJV).

If excessive eating has been part of "what I want to do," then that represents the thing we must put on the cross.

I repeat what Paul said:

> *All things are lawful for me, but all things are not helpful. All things are lawful for me, but I will not be brought under the power of any. Foods for the stomach and the stomach for foods, but God will destroy both it and them. Now the body is...for the Lord, and the Lord for the body* (1 Corinthians 6:12-13 NKJV).

Some of the demonic spirits or strongholds that may need to be dealt with include the following:

- Spirit of Gluttony
- Repent of operating in the flesh

Love of Things

The comical quip the world uses for success says, "He who has the most toys at the end, wins." But that is pure greed. Paul warns us against being *"men of corrupt minds, and destitute of the truth, supposing that gain is godliness"* (1 Tim. 6:5). Jesus said, *"Life is more than food, and the body is more than clothing"* (Luke 12:23 NKJV).

We are told not to

> *...seek what you should eat or what you should drink, nor have an anxious mind. For all these things the nations of the world seek after, and your Father knows that you need these things. But seek the kingdom of God, and all these things shall be added to you* (Luke 12:29-31).

> *For the kingdom of God is not meat and drink; but righteousness, and peace, and joy in the Holy Ghost* (Romans 14:17).

Our hearts will always go after the things that we value the most. That is why Jesus urged us to

> *...lay up for yourselves treasures in heaven, where neither moth nor rust destroys and where thieves do not break in and steal. For where your treasure is, there your heart will be also* (Matthew 6:20-21 NKJV).

If our treasures have our hearts, we need to beware. For no *"covetous man, who is an idolater, hath any inheritance in the kingdom of Christ and of God"* (Eph. 5:5).

Things often occupy a place in our hearts that is out of order. If we get a scratch on the new car, or tear the new dress, or break the toy, our reactions will tell us how much value we place on the thing that got wrecked. The early Christians were commended for taking *"joyfully the spoiling of your goods, knowing... that ye have in heaven a better and an enduring substance"* (Heb. 10:34).

I (Ken) used to yell and scream at my kids when they would break something that I held dear. What was more important: the thing or the kids? You could tell from my reaction that at that moment it wasn't the kids. The fact that I could lose my temper so easily alerted me to my heart's condition. God will allow our things to be desecrated until we repent of our idolatry of them.

> *So kill (deaden, deprive of power) the evil desire lurking in your members…*
> *all greed and covetousness, for that is idolatry* (Colossians 3:5 AMP).

Some of the demonic spirits or strongholds that may need to be dealt with include the following:

- Greed
- Lust

Computers (Internet)

Though computers have taken technology to incredible heights, they have also created diversion, isolation, and distraction in unforeseen ways. By 2010, Gen Y will outnumber the baby boomers, and 96 percent will have joined a social network. It took radio 38 years to reach a million users; television—just 13 years; Internet—4 years; iPod—3 years. But it only took 9 months for Facebook to add 100 million users; iPod had 1 billion hits in just 9 months.

If Facebook were a country, it would be the world's fourth largest. Add to that Twitter, Orkut, Bebo, Digg, MySpace, and YouTube, and you have a whole new way of communicating. As of December 2009, there were over 200,000 blogging sites on the Net, and 54 percent of the users post content or tweet daily. More than 1.5 million pieces of content are shared on Facebook *daily* (even 15 of my endnotes in this section are from the Web).[24]

Social networks are here to stay, but people may not be as connected as they think. I heard a radio interview concerning Facebook. The gentleman commenting said he had 600 "friends" on Facebook in the Toronto area. He thought it would be nice to have a face-to-face get-together. He invited all his "friends," and 100 replied that they would be coming. To his surprise, on the appointed night, only one person physically showed up. Though the networks make contact easy, they do not increase intimacy. In fact, they allow people to hide in anonymity.

Much of the chatter is sharing of frivolous facts and feelings. People share stuff from their lives that are of no consequence, yet the pressure to stay connected forces others to respond to the foolishness. People who have little or no connection to one another end up sharing intimate details about each other's thoughts and lives. We have created a generation of busybodies. Peter warned against being *"a murderer...a thief...an evildoer, or a busybody in other men's matters"* (1 Pet. 4:15).

I (Ken) find I can spend endless hours checking out the vast quantity of information available on the Net. Once I get online, one thing leads to another, and several hours are consumed with no profit to show for the time invested. We are to *"walk circumspectly, not as fools, but as wise, redeeming the time, because the days are evil"* (Eph. 5:15-16).

Your time belongs to God because *"you are not your own...For you were bought at a price; therefore glorify God in your body and in your spirit, which are God's"* (1 Cor. 6:19-20 NKJV). We need to repent of idle conversations. Jesus said,

> *...for every idle word men may speak, they will give account of it in the day of judgment. For by your words you will be justified, and by your words you will be condemned* (Matthew 12:36-37 NKJV).

Some of the demonic spirits or strongholds that may need to be dealt with include the following:

- Spirit of Addiction
- Stronghold of being a busybody

Idolizing People (Movie Stars, Music Stars, Ministry Stars)

Today's movie stars, music stars, media stars, and ministry stars are idolized to the point that their every thought and rumination is regarded as an expert's opinion. Putting their opinions above the Word is paramount to creating an idol.

Stars, in any field, are often egotistical, arrogant, selfish, and of low moral character. We have helped develop those characteristics by giving them praise in their area of expertise while ignoring or even sanctioning their excesses. God, however, *"without partiality judges according to each one's work"* (1 Pet. 1:17 NKJV). Jesus said, *"By their fruits ye shall know them"* (Matt. 7:20).

Celebrities have become a vicarious expression of our own desires, allowing us to share their experiences without facing any of our own consequences. We want them to be free of chastisement for their actions because we also secretly desire to live free with no restraints.

We devour pulp magazines and tune into celebrity gossip shows that exaggerate and revel in their latest escapades. We create fan clubs to feed a desire to be intimate with our heroes, yet the Word says, *"If you favor some people over others, you are committing a sin"* (James 2:9 NLT). Some Hollywood stars have more Twitter followers than the entire population of Ireland, Norway, and Panama.[25] Even the newscasts report celebrity escapades as if they are news and not just gossip. It is no accident that there are many lusting for that acclaim as they compete in "American Idol" or "Canadian Idol." Many artists perform for just "the gold, the girls, and the glory."

We have created a whole pop culture replete with various awards and honors, blogs, groupies, and adoring, envious, slavish entourages. The paparazzi flash, film, and record their every utterance and appearance. A new look, style, or mate fascinates their envious followers. They are rewarded with outrageous advertising dollars that emphasize how seriously their endorsements are taken by an idolizing public.

Christians can have the same misplaced idolization of prophets, teachers, and healers, or workers of miracles. Just because a man has a gift does not indicate he has character, as many have found out to their own hurt and disappointment. Jesus said,

> ...*Do not be called "Rabbi"; for One is your Teacher, the Christ, and you are all brethren. Do not call anyone on earth your father; for One is your Father, He who is in heaven. And do not be called teachers; for One is your Teacher, the Christ. But he who is greatest among you shall be your servant* (Matthew 23:8-11 NKJV).

Honor and *"obey them that have the rule over you, and submit yourselves"* (Heb. 13:17), but do not idolize them. John once encountered a powerful angel that revealed many things to him. John said,

> *...I fell at his feet to worship him. And he said unto me, See thou do it not: I am thy fellow servant, and of thy brethren that have the testimony of Jesus: worship God* (Revelation 19:10).

All other worship is idolatry.

Repent of making idols of people.

Worldly Doctrines

We have received many philosophies, doctrines, and

> *...irreverent babble and godless chatter, with the vain and empty and worldly phrases, and the subtleties and the contradictions in what is falsely called knowledge and spiritual illumination* (1 Timothy 6:20 AMP).

In fact, the apostle Paul said that *"in the latter times some shall depart from the faith, giving heed to seducing spirits, and doctrines of devils"* (1 Tim. 4:1). Jesus challenged the religious rulers, saying,

> *...you reject the commandment of God, that you may keep your tradition....making the word of God of no effect through your tradition which you have handed down* (Mark 7:9,13 NKJV).

Satan is always suggesting to us subtle lies that oppose the Word of God, lies designed to create doubt about what God has declared. That was his technique when he queried Eve:

> *... "Indeed, has God said, 'You shall not eat from any tree of the garden'?" The woman said to the serpent, "From the fruit of the trees of the garden we may eat; but from the fruit of the tree which is in the middle of the garden, God has said, 'You shall not eat from it or touch it, or you will die.' " The serpent said to the woman, "You surely will*

not die! For God knows that in the day you eat from it your eyes will be opened, and you will be like God, knowing good and evil" (Genesis 3:1-5 NASB).

When the woman misquoted what God had said, satan knew that she would succumb to his lies. Jesus said, *"If any man will do his will, he shall know of the doctrine, whether it be of God"* (John 7:17). If we do not know what the Word says, we will be vulnerable to satan's lies. Things like evolution and theories on the origin of man will seem plausible if we don't know what the Bible says. *"The words that I* [Jesus] *speak unto you, they are spirit, and they are life"* (John 6:63). Those words will keep us from coming under the idolatry of men's philosophies.

Some of the demonic spirits or strongholds that may need to be dealt with include the following:

- Spirit of this age
- Humanistic thinking

Education

"Knowledge puffs up, but love edifies" (1 Cor. 8:1 NKJV). Many are *"ever learning, and never able to come to the knowledge of the truth"* (2 Tim. 3:7). That is because they erroneously believe that the facts are the truth. Facts are not the truth; Jesus is *"the way, the truth, and the life"* (John 14:6). Any "truth" acquired outside of the Truth will result in error: *"For the wisdom of this world is foolishness with God"* (1 Cor. 3:19).

Education is valuable, but when it is exalted above the wisdom that comes from God, it becomes an idol. Some worldly wise people,

> *...when they knew God, they glorified Him not as God, neither were thankful; but became vain in their imaginations, and their foolish heart was darkened. Professing themselves to be wise, they became fools* (Romans 1:21-22).

True wisdom is spoken,

...not in words which man's wisdom teaches but which the Holy Spirit teaches, comparing spiritual things with spiritual. But the natural man does not receive the things of the Spirit of God, for they are foolishness to him; nor can he know them, because they are spiritually discerned (1 Corinthians 2:13-14 NKJV).

Education without the spiritual component exalts the education, not the Creator, and is idolatry.

Alcohol

As with all substance abuse, the cravings of the body overrule the dictates of the will, resulting in a type of slavery. Paul said,

Do you not know that to whom you present yourselves slaves to obey, you are that one's slaves whom you obey, whether of sin leading to death, or of obedience leading to righteousness? (Romans 6:16 NKJV)

Most often, alcohol abuse is a form of self-medication to ease the pain that life brings. God ordained Jesus to heal *"every sickness and every disease among the people"* (Matt. 9:35).

Using alcohol as a substitute for Jesus is tantamount to making it an idol. God wants us to *"be not drunk with wine, wherein is excess; but to be filled with the Spirit"* (Eph. 5:18). The psalmist thanked God because

...He causes the grass to grow for the cattle, and vegetation for the service of man, that he may bring forth food from the earth, and wine that makes glad the heart of man, oil to make his face shine, and bread which strengthens man's heart (Psalm 104:14-15 NKJV).

Paul said, *"Let your moderation be known unto all men"* (Phil. 4:5), not your abstinence. God gave alcohol to be a benefit, not a detriment. Paul told Timothy to *"use a little wine for your stomach's sake and your frequent infirmities"* (1 Tim. 5:23 NKJV). When it is abused, *"wine is a mocker, strong drink is raging: and whoever is deceived thereby is not wise"* (Prov. 20:1). When alcohol occupies the primary place, it has replaced God and become an idol.

Sexual Addictions

Sexual drives are a part of the makeup of our body and are designed by God to increase intimacy and ensure the procreation of the species. The flesh makes a great servant but a lousy master. Like all other addictions, sexual addictions are substitutes for a lack in our lives. This addiction results from the increasing need for feel-good endorphins to comfort the addict and compensate for the lack of intimacy. An in-depth study will appear later, in the section on sexual sins.

Prayer:

Lord, I acknowledge the sin of idolatry in all its forms of everything that I love more than You. I stand in proxy on behalf of myself and the generations before me, on both my mother and father's side, and ask forgiveness for the sin of idolatry of things, specifically for making idols of _____. I ask forgiveness back to the 4th generation, the 3rd, the 2nd, and for myself. On the basis of the authority gained through receiving forgiveness, I now break this curse over my children and myself in Jesus' name.

Spirits associated with idolatry that may need to be dealt with include the following:

- Spirits of the Fear of Man
- Spirits of Humanistic Thinking
- Spirits of Lust
- Spirits of Addiction

Lord, make me pure in worship toward You. Smash every false idol in my life. I declare, "as for me and my house, we will serve the Lord" (Josh. 24:15). I will not put idols before my God, and I will submit to His authority in Jesus' name.

Chapter 8

SPIRITUAL IDOLATRY

Satan is not a creator; he is a counterfeiter. All counterfeits have the appearance of the original but are false because they lack the authorization of the Creator. The closer to the original design, the better the counterfeit. False religions have many of the truths, but they still lack the power or the life that God endued the Kingdom truths with. False religious truths may not be false in themselves, but they become just laws, which ultimately produce death (see Rom. 7:5).

"The sting of death is sin; and the strength of sin is the law" (1 Cor. 15:56). Jesus is *"the way, the truth, and the life: no man cometh unto the Father, but by [Him]"* (John 14:6). He is *"the door...all that ever came before...are thieves and robbers"* (John 10:7-8). If Jesus is not the center of worship, then an idol has replaced Him, and it will bring death and bondage. The following is a representative list of false religious practices that we have encountered; it is not intended to be comprehensive.

Cults

"Christian" Cults

This may sound like a contradiction in terms, but the Romans called Christianity a cult in the first century. The word *cult* is derived from the Latin *colere,* which is also the root for culture, meaning to cultivate or worship.[1] Where the culture of an organization is restrictive, abusive, manipulative, or controlling, it would be considered cultish.

Cults derive their attraction from either a form of worship or the object of that worship. Idolatry occurs when the cult leader, their writings, their miracles, or the organization itself dominates the central focus rather than Jesus. This is why they seem eccentric or out of balance. If Jesus is not the center, then everything revolves around something else, and that something else becomes an idol.

The cult may have much of their doctrine right, but they become the final authority rather than the Word of God. Some cults will hold up the Word as the final authority yet demand that the only correct interpretation of Scripture lies with them. They set themselves up as the doorway to God. Jesus said, *"I am the door: by Me if any man enter in, he shall be saved"* (John 10:9). *"He who does not enter the sheepfold by the door, but climbs up some other way, the same is a thief and a robber"* (John 10:1 NKJV). *"There is one God, and one mediator between God and men, the man Christ Jesus"* (1 Tim. 2:5).

As long as we get to Jesus and enter through Him, we are in the right Kingdom. It is not the mandate, or within the scope, of this book to designate what organizations constitute a cult; rather, it is to bring forth repentance from those who feel either they or their families were involved in a cult.

Voodoo or Witchcraft Cults

White magic or black magic is still magic. The word *magic* is derived from "Magi," who were Persian priests. It is defined as any occult practice, especially those putting into action the power of spirits by the use of sorcery or enchantments.[2] Two of *"the works of the flesh are manifest, which are these…idolatry, witchcraft….they which do these things shall not inherit the Kingdom of God"* (Gal. 5:19-20). Moses agrees, saying, *"Thou shalt not suffer a witch to live"* (Exod. 22:18).

During King Saul's reign, the witch at Endor knew the penalty for dallying in witchcraft. When asked to conjure up Samuel's spirit, she lamented,

*"Are you trying to get me killed?" the woman demanded. "You know
that Saul has outlawed all the mediums and all who consult the spirits
of the dead. Why are you setting a trap for me?"* (1 Samuel 28:9 NLT)

Jehovah's Witnesses

Though they acknowledge God and the Bible, they do not place Jesus in His
proper place as God.[3] Jesus allowed Himself to be worshiped when Thomas fell
down at His feet and declared, *"My Lord and my God"* (John 20:28). God makes
*"His angels spirits, and His ministers a flame of fire. But unto the Son, He saith,
'Thy throne, O God, is for ever and ever…' "* (Heb. 1:7-8). Moving Jesus out of the
center allows the church to become an idol.

Mormons (The Church of Jesus Christ of Latter Day Saints)

Mormons try to sound like Christians but their own theology says that they
are different and the only true church. They also believe that there are many gods
on other planets and that God was once in the form of man.[4] These doctrines
set them outside the scope of what all other denominations consider Christian.
Like all cults, only those that adhere to their doctrine and are members of their
sect will go to Heaven. This puts the church between God and man, making
them the door instead of Jesus.

Christian Science

Though Christian Scientists acknowledge the Bible as the inspired Word
of God, they interpret it according to the writings of Mary Baker Eddy, chiefly
her book, *Science and Health With Key to the Scriptures* (S&H). They view
God as more impersonal: "God is incorporeal, divine, supreme, infinite Mind,
Spirit, Soul, Principle, Life, Truth, Love."[5] In their doctrines, the material world
does not really exist: "Spirit is immortal Truth; matter is mortal error. Spirit is
the real and eternal; matter is the unreal and temporal."[6] A Christian Scien-
tist believes that sin and death are false notions (illusions). Therefore, salvation
comes through understanding and overcoming these false beliefs and recognizing that humans are divine spirit and mind. They believe that since matter, sin,

disease, and death are illusions and are unreal, then people are not subject to them. "Through immortal Mind, or Truth, we can destroy all ills which proceed from mortal mind."[7]

The essence of Christian Science is that through knowledge and the proper view of God and the universe, man can connect with the truth. This denies the fact that evil is real, the devil is real, and sin is real. With no reality we do not have to *"overcome evil with good"* (Rom. 12:21), *"resist the devil"* (James 4:7), or repent of sin; all of which the Bible commands us to do.

Kabbalah

The Kabbalah's view of evil is that it originated with God and is part of His universal plan. Kabbalah's philosophy does not include the sinful nature of man; therefore, there is no need for the redeeming qualities of a Messiah. According to the ideals of Kabbalah, there are ten parts to God, which are called *emanations*.

Some Kabbalahists utilize divination and clairvoyance to foretell events or to know occult events, and some deal with potions and curses. Practical Kabbalah is termed for use in referring to secret sciences (ESP, psychic readings, Ouija boards, tarot cards, reading tea leaves, reading bones, numerology, mediums, spirit guides, channeling, mysticism, etc.), mystic art, or sorcery. God forbids all of these practices (see Deut. 18:9-13). Kabbalahism is a mixture of mysticism, Jewish oral traditions, occultic and ancient deities, Hinduism, and Buddhist traditions, and is in no way Christian.

Superstitions

There are almost as many superstitions as there are people—things like not crossing the path of a black cat, or walking under a ladder, breaking a mirror, stepping on a door sill, or spilling salt or milk, etc. The word *superstition* comes from the Latin *super-* meaning above or over, and *stare* to stare or stand.[8]

Superstitious people believe that something spiritual or above us, on another plane, is affecting our lives. This gives the object of the superstition a veneration or regard that it doesn't deserve, creating an idol. This worship embodies a dread or evil foreboding that demons or gods will inflict dire consequences if not appeased.

Paul said, *"What shall we then say to these things? If God be for us, who can be against us?"* (Rom. 8:31). We are told many times to *"fear not, nor be dismayed, be strong and of good courage"* (Josh. 10:25). We need to be *"nourished up in the words of faith and of good doctrine...but refuse profane and old wives' fables, and exercise...*[ourselves] *rather unto godliness"* (1 Tim. 4:6-7). We need to repent if we give more credence to things than God does.

New Age Activities

Satan is a counterfeiter, not a creator. Everything that New Agers attempt to do is either deception or an aberration of the truth. The closer to the truth, the better a counterfeit appears and the harder it becomes to detect. The following list was assembled during the course of several years from Christians who took the "Curses to Blessings" seminar. It is not intended to be anything more than a sample of what families can get into:

- Numerology—Occult significance of numbers.

- Feng Shui—Chinese system of aesthetics based around directional orientation to receive positive "chi" or energy flow.

- Channeling—Use of a medium as a channel for spirits. May involve trances.

- Tarot Cards—A set of 78 cards used in fortune telling.

- Teacup Reading—Tasseography, divination, using patterns in tea leaves.

- Ouija Board—Spirit Board used during a séance to contact spirits.

- Divination—Foretelling future events or discovering hidden knowledge by interpreting omens, aided by supernatural powers.

- Water Witching—Dowsing, using divining rods to locate water or metallic objects.

- Astrology—Divination derived from the positions of celestial bodies.

- Horoscopes—Astrological chart used to divine events. Often used to determine one's actions based on birth date or sign.

- Fortune Telling—Practice of predicting life events through mystical means.

All divination and occult practices are designed to garner information and knowledge outside of God's ordained pattern. James said, *"If any of you lacks wisdom, let him ask of God, who gives to all liberally and without reproach, and it will be given to him"* (James 1:5 NKJV).

The Bible warns that

> *...there shall not be found among you anyone who makes his son or his daughter pass through the fire, or one who practices witchcraft, or a soothsayer, or one who interprets omens, or a sorcerer, or one who conjures spells, or a medium, or a spiritist, or one who calls up the dead. For all who do these things are an abomination to the Lord* (Deuteronomy 18:10-12).

Many families dabbled with what seemed to be harmless parlor games and ended up cursed and under demonic influences without being aware of it.

My (Ken's) brother Rod and his wife, Marge, were led to burn our old Ouija board after reading the above Scripture. They were staying in a small cabin by a lake that had a pot-bellied stove for heat. It was cool outside, so they had a small fire going. They prayed over the Ouija board and threw it in the stove. Immediately the temperature soared, forcing them outside. There was definitely some anger released because they destroyed it.

As a child, I (Jeanne) had played with a Ouija board. After I became a Christian, I realized my sin and repented of dabbling in the occult, including playing with the Ouija board. Some time later I drove out to visit my mother in our old house. The Ouija board was still there. I explained to her the significance of the occult involvement that the Ouija board had. With her permission, I took it, asked forgiveness again for using it, and broke it under the authority of Jesus' name.

Immediately after I had left to drive home, my mother heard a tremendous crash, like the breaking of glass, echo through the house. She thought a mirror or a window had shattered. My younger sister, Laura, thought a wardrobe and the ornaments on it had toppled over and smashed. They searched throughout the house but could find nothing broken or out of place. They had heard, in the spirit, the sound of the power of divination, working through the Ouija board, being broken.

Satan's power is real, but only if we give our authority to him. He has none of his own by reason of origin: he is not from earth. We have the authority because Jesus redeemed it after Adam lost it. Lucifer threatens that he will destroy us, but the truth is he needs to ask permission from our heavenly Father who only allows what will profit us in the end.

Operating in the occult removes us from God's covering and puts us in satan's hand. God wants to bless, but He states of the wicked, *"As he loved cursing, so let it come unto him: as he delighted not in blessing, so let it be far from him"* (Ps. 109:17).

Transcendental Meditation

TM was declared a religion in 1977 by the United States District Court.[9] This removed it from schools, access to public monies, and eliminated the government from propagating its beliefs, teachings, and theories. Maharishi Mahesh Yogi, who was the founder of TM, had claimed it was only a self-help methodology. It is a form of Hinduism, not a scientific form of tension release. All the mantras they use are not meaningless sounds but names of Hindu gods:

For our practice, we select only the suitable mantras of personal gods. Such mantras fetch to us the grace of personal gods and make us happier in every walk of life. [Maharishi Mahesh Yogi in "Beacon Light of the Himalayas," 1955.][10]

In fact the mantras were designed to summon up the gods whose name the initiate was chanting. The following is a discussion by a former teacher of TM:

> We saw tapes of Maharishi where he repeatedly explained that the sounds of the mantras, especially as one approaches transcendence, had the effect of summoning very refined "impulses of creative intelligence." In other tapes, he explained that the "impulses of creative intelligence" or "laws of nature" were devas (*Hindu deities*) such as Indra, Agni, and so forth. He also explicitly said that in the proper state of consciousness, that repeating the name of "impulses of creative intelligence" in Sanskrit had the effect of creating or summoning the "form."[11]

> And what did Maharishi procure for? The Vedic gods. He sold us a meaningless word that was supposed to guide our minds to transcend superficial consciousness. Later we learned those meaningless words, our mantras, were names of deities. He taught us advanced techniques with the Sanskrit word "namah" at their core: "I bow down." Mantra meditation is a form of paying worship to those who call themselves gods. When you scrape away all the fancy and misleading explanations—like "meaningless sounds" and "impulses of creative intelligence," what you get very simply is people with their eyes closed bowing down in their minds to an assigned Hindu deity.[12]

> There is no doubt here that the Maharishi is indicating that chanting Vedas and mantras while performing yajnas (yagyas) are for the express purpose of summoning the Vedic Gods. ...it is straightforward Hinduism, after all.[13]

Meditation is not designed to be a passive action. God says, *"You will call upon Me and go and pray to Me, and I will listen to you. And you will seek Me and find Me, when you search for Me with all your heart"* (Jer. 29:12-13 NKJV).

TM is idolatry that uses mantras to call up demonic forces. It teaches passivity that lets down the filter of the will and allows these demons access into our lives.

Paul says, "[Is]...*that which is offered in sacrifice to idols...anything? But I say, that the things...*[or the worship] which *the Gentiles sacrifice, they sacrifice to devils, and not to God*" (1 Cor. 10:19-20). If we, or our family, have practiced TM, we need to repent of worshiping demons and command them to leave our lives.

Martial Arts

Martial arts are not evil in themselves. Only when passive meditation or mantras are employed do they touch onto the occult.

Freemasonry

Freemasonry began in the Middle Ages with stonemasons who were "free to travel" as they plied their trade building cathedrals, mosques, and temples. Many of these projects would take decades to complete, and the bond of common language or ancestry drew these artisans to form fraternities in these foreign lands. Over time, these close-knit communities developed into more than just social gatherings.

Because their work was mainly centered on religious structures, the conversations frequently dealt with the aspects of various religions. Being often far removed from priest or pastor, the craftsmen developed their own style of worship that was influenced by the multiple beliefs and practices of the people associating in that particular lodge. These loose-knit, but strongly fraternal, connections slowly took on structure until they formally incorporated them into the first Grand Lodge of England in 1717.

Though Masonic Lodges advertise themselves as fraternal, social, and civic service organizations, they take on all the trappings of a religion. The following is a quotation from Albert Pike's *Morals and Dogma*, published by the authority of the "Supreme Council of the Thirty-Third Degree for the Southern Jurisdiction of the United States" in 1871:

Masonry, like all the Religions, all the Mysteries...conceals its secrets from all except the Adepts and Sages, or the Elect, and uses false explanations and misinterpretations of its symbols to mislead those who deserve only to be misled...Truth is not for those who are unworthy or unable to receive it, or would pervert it.[14]

Masonic truth is not based on the Bible but on a mixed bag of "truths." Harold J. Berry writes,

Masons refer to the Bible as the "Volume of the Sacred Law" (V.S.L.), and it is considered an indispensable part of what is called "the furniture" in a Masonic Lodge. But the Bible is used *only* in a so-called "Christian" lodge—the Hebrew Pentateuch is used in a Hebrew lodge, the Koran in a Mohammedan lodge, the Vedas in a Brahmin lodge, etc. Jim Shaw, a former 33rd degree Mason, says that Masonry is not based on the Bible (referred to as "The Great Light"), but on the Kabala (Cabala), a medieval book of mysticism and magic. Masonic authority Henry Wilson Coil also admits that the Kabala's teachings can be seen in some of the mystical and philosophical degrees of Masonry. Albert Pike...the man responsible for virtually rewriting the Scottish Rite degrees into their present form, said that the Masonic "search after light" leads directly back to the Kabala, the ultimate source of Masonic beliefs (*Morals and Dogma*).[15]

One of the great authorities on Masonry was Albert Pike (1809–1901), Sovereign Grand Commander of the Southern Supreme Council of Scottish Right Freemasonry in the U.S.A. Pike authored *Morals and Dogma of the Ancient and Accepted Scottish Rite of Freemasonry for the Supreme Council of the 33rd Degree*, which was published by its authority. This compendium of official Masonic lore clearly traces Masonry to Hinduism, Buddhism, Zoroastrianism, and other Eastern religions. Albert G. Mackey, co-author of *Encyclopedia of Freemasonry*, is also one of Masonry's highest authorities. In his *Manual of the Lodge*, he traces Masonic teaching back to "the ancient rites and mysteries practiced in the very bosom of pagan darkness...."[16]

Each level of Masonic initiation is sealed with specific curses that the initiate places upon himself and his offspring. Masonic generational curses are too extensive to deal with here, but there are good resources for breaking them found on the Internet.[17]

False Religions

This list would be as long as my arm if I were to mention them all. We will include only those false religions that have been rejected by Christians to whom we have personally ministered.

- Buddhism

- Islam

- Confucianism

- Taoism

- Shintoism

- Hinduism

- Sikhism

- Animism

- Humanism

- Paganism

All of these religious efforts are vain attempts by man to make himself acceptable to God. The reality is that every religion just exposes our sinful nature. In all places of worship, including temples and mosques,

> *...both gifts and sacrifices are offered which cannot make the worshiper perfect in conscience, since they relate only to food and drink and various washings, regulations for the body imposed until a time of reformation* (Hebrews 9:9-10 NASB).

How much more will the blood of Christ, who through the eternal Spirit offered Himself without blemish to God, cleanse your conscience from dead works to serve the living God? (Hebrews 9:14)

We need to repent of any affiliation with any religion that does not present Christ as the only answer to the world's sin and sickness.

Prayer:

Lord, I acknowledge the sin of spiritual idolatry and the worship of other gods or belief systems. I stand in proxy on behalf of myself and the generations before me, on both my mother and father's side, and ask forgiveness for the sin of idolatry, specifically for making idols of _____. I ask forgiveness back to the 4th generation, the 3rd, the 2nd, and for myself. On the basis of the authority gained through receiving forgiveness, I now break this curse over my children and myself.

Here are some demonic spirits associated with spiritual idolatry that may need to be dealt with:

- Religious Spirits
- Divination
- Lying Spirits
- Occult Spirits
- Fear

Break off any involvement in cults or false religions. Repent for and break off the vows or curses associated with any religious rights. Command any demonic spirits to leave your life.

Lord, make me pure in worship toward You. Smash every false idol in my life. I break off the bondage to "fate" and move into the liberty of destiny in You. I ask that You would perfect my love of the truth. I declare, "as for me and my house, we will serve the Lord" (Josh. 24:15). I will not put idols before my God, and I will submit to His authority in Jesus' name.

Chapter 9

IDOLS OF SELF

Idols of self are the hardest to recognize, and the hardest to remove, as they often comprise our self-image. It is hard to repent of those things that are part of our nature. The demonic spirits associated with these types of idols hide behind the activity of our flesh and thus mask their identity. Our confusion becomes their best defense. We try to cast out a spirit when we should discipline our flesh, and attempt to starve the flesh when we should be removing a demon. We have identified the most common forms of self-idolatry.

Rebellion

"Rebellion is as the sin of witchcraft" (1 Sam. 15:23a). God created us to fulfill a destiny. He knows the beginning from the end and is able to use all of the events in our lives to mold our character to reach that destiny. God had us born at the right time, in the right place, into the right family, with the right personalities to help form us. Many of the things God chose for us do not seem right.

We may not like the stern father He gave us, or the nagging mother. We may not appreciate the financial, social, or racial situation we discover ourselves in. We may not like our own body, our face, our mind, or our personality. But God *"who made you and formed you from the womb...will help you"* (Isa. 44:2 NKJV).

The Hebrew root of rebellious is *marah,*[1] which literally means to be or make bitter or unpleasant (see Num. 20:24). It usually relays the idea of provocation or defiance. If we are rebellious, bitterness against our situation has taken root and defiled us (see Heb. 12:15). To the degree that we do not accept God's good plan for us, we are in spiritual rebellion.

Joseph learned that God had a plan, and even those who tried to destroy him assisted in bringing that plan to fruition. He could say to his brothers who sold him into slavery, *"You meant evil against me, but God meant it for good in order to bring about this present result, to preserve many people alive"* (Gen. 50:20 NASB). Even our enemies will work the will of God in our lives as we submit to His authority.

The demonic forces arrayed against Jesus saw a chance to destroy Jesus when He was on this earth in a weak human body. They said, *"This is the heir; come, let us kill him, and let us seize on his inheritance"* (Matt. 21:38). They were looking through natural eyes, but

> *…we speak the wisdom of God in a mystery, even the hidden wisdom, which God ordained before the world unto our glory: which none of the princes of this world knew: for had they known it, they would not have crucified the Lord of glory* (1 Corinthians 2:7-8).

God is for us! We must not allow bitterness and rebellion to separate us from God and our destinies. Jesus is *"able also to save forever those who draw near to God through Him, since He always lives to make intercession for them"* (Heb. 7:25 NASB).

Repent, change your mind, and *"in every thing give thanks: for this* [your life] *is the will of God in Christ Jesus concerning you"* (1 Thess. 5:18).

Stubbornness

"Stubbornness is as iniquity and idolatry" (1 Sam. 15:23b). The word *stubborn* comes from the Anglo-Saxon word *styb,* meaning like a stub, stockish, or blockish, thus obstinate.[2] Stubbornness is tied to rebellion—where we refuse to listen to anyone or anything that does not agree with our own thoughts. It makes an idol of what I think, what I feel, and what I want.

Israel did that in the wilderness. Moses chastened them, saying,

> *...understand that the Lord your God is not giving you this good land to possess because of your righteousness, for you are a stiff-necked people* (Deuteronomy 9:6 NKJV).

They had *"again and again...tempted God, and limited the Holy One of Israel"* (Ps. 78:41 NKJV). They had literally drawn a line in the sand and said, "This far and no farther." That is what the Hebrew word *tavah* translated "limit" means: mark out or scratch a line.[3]

Stubbornness stops or limits God's grace from reaching us. Ken and I had an argument once, and he quickly brushed it off and was ready to make up. I was not quite at that stage when he reached over to turn my head to get a kiss. He encountered a stiff neck. I would not turn to receive love, as I was still hurting from our fight. That is how we all are with God when we are stubborn and stiff-necked. He wants to give us grace, but we want things our way. God said,

> *"My thoughts are not your thoughts, nor are your ways My ways," says the Lord. "For as the heavens are higher than the earth, so are My ways higher than your ways, and My thoughts than your thoughts"* (Isaiah 55:8-9 NKJV).

We must learn to be pliable and think outside of our small boxes. Jesus cried,

> *O Jerusalem, Jerusalem...How often I wanted to gather your children together, as a hen gathers her chicks under her wings, but you were not willing! See! Your house is left to you desolate* (Matthew 23:37-38 NKJV).

Their stubbornness resulted in their destruction; so will ours if we don't repent and allow God to change the way we think.

Religious Spirit

A religious spirit is not about being holy; it is about being right and doing things right. The obsessive, anal-retentive type of personality, where everything has to be proper and in order, is the outcome of this mindset. Anyone who does it differently is wrong and an irritant to this type of people. There is no freedom to have things out of order or out of their control. This is the main problem for a religious spirit; we are not in control—God is.

Anything worth doing is worth doing poorly. Babies will never learn to talk if they are not allowed to talk poorly; they will never learn to walk if they don't walk poorly. The religious spirit shuts people down and never lets them learn by making mistakes. It is a form of legalism that Paul called the *"ministration of death* [and]...*the ministration of condemnation"* (2 Cor. 3:7,9). Repent of following a religious spirit and *"stand fast...in the liberty wherewith Christ hath made us free, and be not entangled again with the yoke of bondage"* (Gal. 5:1).

Being Unteachable

Isaac Asimov joked that "those people who think they know everything are a great annoyance to those of us who do."[4]

Jesus said, *"They that are whole have no need of the physician, but they that are sick: I came not to call the righteous, but sinners to repentance"* (Mark 2:17).

You can't help people who don't think they need help. I (Jeanne) had a lady tell me that she could only think of one sin that she had ever committed. It is hard to present Jesus as the answer when there is no question.

The Holy Spirit comes to *"convict the world concerning sin, and of righteousness, and of judgment"* (John 16:8 NKJV). It is not our job to convince anyone that he or she needs to deal with sin. It is our job to be *"blameless and harmless, children of God without fault in the midst of a crooked and perverse generation,* [shining]...*as lights in the world"* (Phil. 2:15 NKJV). Satan *"has blinded the minds of the unbelieving so that they might not see the light of the gospel of the glory of Christ, who is the image of God"* (2 Cor. 4:4 NASB).

People may be blind to their sins, but they can still recognize light.

> God who commanded light to shine out of darkness, who has shone in our hearts to give the light of the knowledge of the glory of God in the face of Jesus Christ (2 Corinthians 4:6 NKJV).

We develop a stronghold in our thought patterns. Strongholds are built by believing a series of lies that we stack like bricks around our mind. It is an actual structure and not the person. You cannot argue or reason with a brick wall and you cannot argue or reason with a stronghold in a person's mind, but you can shine a light into it.

Being unteachable is being full of you. If you are full, you won't be able to eat even if a banquet is set for you. Proverbs says, *"the full soul loatheth a honeycomb; but to the hungry soul every bitter thing is sweet"* (Prov. 27:7). Jesus said, *"Blessed are they which do hunger, and thirst after righteousness: for they shall be filled"* (Matt. 5:6). God *"filled the hungry with good things; and the rich He hath sent away empty"* (Luke 1:53).

When we feel we have "been there, done that," there is little or nothing that shakes our confidence in our own worldview. Pride prevents us from learning anything new. Once we put on the guise of being the expert, we must maintain that façade even if we have to bluff or lie in order not to appear ignorant. But God *"will destroy the wisdom of the wise, and will bring to nothing the understanding of the prudent"* (1 Cor. 1:19). Real wisdom is to know Jesus and the value of the cross (see 1 Cor. 2:2). Everything else we need to repent of.

Selfishness

It's all about me: how I feel, what I think, how I look. When the world revolves around me, my universe becomes very small, too small for God. If we take the position in the center of everything, we push Jesus to the side. However, Jesus actually is the center of our world; He has the real weight, not us. If we put the real weight of a tire off center, it becomes unbalanced and creates a rough ride in our car. When we do that, we become eccentric in our opinions and actions, and will experience a rough ride in our life. God recently told me (Ken) that I was no longer allowed any opinions. It was not how *I* saw things but how *He* saw things that counted. I was no longer allowed to assign motives to other people's actions, or else I would judge them rather than love them. You cannot be selfish and loving at the same time.

Loving others is not thinking less of yourself; it's thinking about yourself less. Have you ever had a talk with someone who was willing to answer all your questions about himself, but who never asked any questions about you or your situation? Or had someone who wanted to dump all her problems on you, but started looking at her watch when the conversation swung around to you? Body language is a good key to spot self-absorption.

Eve's temptation was to disobey God by valuing her opinions above the Word, which they had received. She looked at the tree of the knowledge of good and evil, and

> *...when [she]...saw that the tree was good for food, and that it was pleasant to the eyes, and a tree to be desired to make one wise, she took of the fruit thereof, and did eat* (Genesis 3:6).

Her self-absorption with what she thought was good for her plunged her family into death and destruction.

Self is the biggest idol that we must deal with. It is the most difficult to avoid because it is always speaking to us. "Love me, listen to me, value me, protect me, obey me, bless me, honor me, entertain me...." There is no end to the demands of the flesh. But *"it is the Spirit Who gives life [He is the Life-giver]; the flesh conveys no benefit whatever [there is no profit in it]"* (John 6:63 AMP). *"So then indeed I, of myself with the mind and heart, serve the Law of God, but with the flesh the law of sin"* (Rom. 7:25 AMP).

> *Little children, keep yourselves from idols (false gods)—[from anything and everything that would occupy the place in your heart due to God, from any sort of substitute for Him that would take first place]* (1 John 5:21 AMP).

Self-Comfort

We all have a comfort zone that can set the boundaries of where we allow God to take us. God said to Abram, *"Get out of your country, from your family and from your father's house, to a land that I will show you"* (Gen. 12:1 NKJV).

That would be a big stretch for anyone, but that is what faith is: a stretch. If we could do it by ourselves, we wouldn't need God or faith. Comfort zones are faith killers.

They cause us to avoid certain people, or subjects, or situations. They make us inadaptable to change or conflict. All satan has to do is to throw an uncomfortable obstacle in our way, and we will stop in our tracks rather than deciding to push through the roadblock.

If we are addicted to comfort, we will try and get everyone to accommodate us. We will try and manipulate them to go out of their way to make our life more comfortable. We say things like, "Do you mind if I take that seat? I don't like sitting by the window." Or, "Would you start my car? I don't like the cold." Our desire for others to make our life comfortable will turn us into users.

The lone clerk at a jewelry counter was waiting on me (Jeanne) when another lady rushed in and demanded service. She snapped at the clerk and announced, "I have an important meeting to get to. I need service right now." There were two other ladies in line after me, waiting to be served. The young clerk was flustered by the intimidating way the woman demanded service, and she looked at me, hoping I would give permission for her to serve this self-important lady and get her out of an awkward situation.

I decided that I could not submit to this attack from this Jezebel spirit (controlling spirit), and I addressed the lady. "You will have to wait your turn. She is serving me, and these other ladies are before you." Indignantly, she backed down and waited her turn. I could have shown her mercy and let her in, but felt a compulsion in my spirit to resist her attempt to control the clerk for her personal convenience. Her lack of planning was not my emergency. Later the young clerk thanked me for standing up to that lady. If we come from a family that enjoys its comforts to the detriment of others, we need to stand in the gap and repent.

Fear

Fear is a spirit: *"God has not given us a spirit of fear, but of power and of love and of a sound mind"* (2 Tim. 1:7 NKJV). Fear will rob us of power, love, and a sound mind. Fear screams that we can't trust God to look after us, or our situations, or those we love. It destroys faith. Jesus marveled, *"Why are you fearful, O ye of little faith?"* (Matt. 8:26), when a storm arose and frightened His disciples.

The main cause of fear comes because we don't know that we are loved.

> *...There is no fear in love [dread does not exist], but full-grown (complete, perfect) love turns fear out of doors and expels every trace of terror! For fear brings with it the thought of punishment, and [so] he who is afraid has not reached the full maturity of love [is not yet grown into love's complete perfection]* (1 John 4:18 AMP).

> *For I am persuaded, that neither death, nor life, nor angels, nor principalities, nor powers, nor things present, nor things to come, nor height, nor depth, nor any other creature, shall be able to separate us from the love of God, which is in Christ Jesus our Lord* (Romans 8:38-39).

No demon, no history, and no situation can remove us out of God's hand. If we really believe that, we will not fear.

Though fear is a spirit, it taps into wounds in our character and stirs up our feelings. Feelings are our responses to stimuli; they are not the reality, and they need not dictate out responses. Fear should be treated like any other feeling. Though I may be hungry, I don't have to eat. Though I am tired, I don't have to sleep. Though I am afraid, I can do it afraid. Feelings are signals to be observed, not necessarily obeyed.

Anger is often the mask that fear hides behind. Most men only allow themselves one emotion: anger. If fear shows up, it must put on that mask and manifest as anger. I (Ken) remember when Jeanne scalded herself, and I had to rush her to the hospital. My first response was anger. I barked at her, "What were you thinking, opening that pressure cooker! You knew better!" Here my wife is crying and suffering in pain, and I ooze with empathy—not! I was afraid, and the situation was out of my control. That is the receipt for anger. Men, be honest with yourself. Most of your anger comes from those two sources, and, in the end, control is also an expression of fear.

That is why we women try to control situations; we are afraid. Afraid someone will do something stupid and get hurt. Afraid someone will hurt us. Afraid things will get out of control, my control. Fear is a spirit that demands control. It is all control and all motivated by our fears because we don't trust the love and care of God. It is idolatry of self.

Doubt and Worry

Paul said, *"Be anxious for nothing, but in everything by prayer and supplication with thanksgiving let your requests be made known to God"* (Phil. 4:6 NASB).

Jesus said,

Stop being perpetually uneasy (anxious and worried) about your life, what you shall eat or what you shall drink; or about your body, what you shall put on. Is not life greater [in quality] than food, and the body [far above and more excellent] than clothing?…And who of you by worrying and being anxious can add one unit of measure (cubit) to his stature or to the span of his life?…So do not worry or be anxious about tomorrow, for tomorrow will have worries and anxieties of its own. Sufficient for each day is its own trouble (Matthew 6:25,27,34 AMP).

Paul said, *"Above all, [take]…the shield of faith with which you will be able to quench all the fiery darts of the wicked one"* (Eph. 6:16 NKJV).

We have substituted the shield of mistrust and worry for the shield of faith. Faith says, "If God said it; that settles it." Mistrust and worry says, "God may have said it, but I need to proceed with caution." It is putting more stock in what satan whispers than what God declares.

Worry comes from not having peace within. If we can't control our doubts inside, then we attempt to control the situations outside. We keep all agitations at a distance and try to control everything so that it doesn't affect us. If we worry enough, we will be able to identify any potential problem and cut it off before it impacts us. Worry becomes our safety net; it protects all we love. God's design is that *"your righteousness will go before you; the glory of the Lord will be your rear guard"* (Isa. 58:8 NASB). Trust God, not your ability to worry. Give God all your burdens, and He *"will give you rest"* (Matt. 11:28).

Prayer:

Lord, I acknowledge the sin of self-idolatry in all its forms. I stand in proxy on behalf of myself and the generations before me, on both my mother and father's side, and ask forgiveness for the sin of idolatry, specifically for making idols of _____. I ask forgiveness back to the 4th generation, the 3rd, the 2nd, and for myself. On the basis of the authority gained through receiving forgiveness, I now break this curse over my children and myself.

Some of the demonic spirits associated with self-idolatry that may need to be dealt with include the following:

- Spirit of Rebellion
- Spirit of Stubbornness
- Religious Spirit
- Unteachable Spirit
- Spirit of Fear
- Spirits of Doubt and Worry

I declare, "as for me and my house, we will serve the Lord" (Josh. 24:15). *I will not put myself as an idol before my God, and I will submit to His authority and His will in my life in Jesus' name.*

Chapter 10

HONORING FATHERS AND MOTHERS

Cursed is he who dishonors his father or mother...
(Deuteronomy 27:16 NASB).

Honor in the Godhead

Hear, O Israel! The Lord is our God; the Lord is one! You shall love the Lord your God with all your heart and with all your soul and with all your might (Deuteronomy 6:4-5 NASB).

The Kingdom of God is a society of honor. The Godhead models the proper love, honor, and respect that They want to reproduce when it comes to relating to authority. They are mutually submissive and honoring of each other.

The Father is honored by the Son:

When everything is subjected to Him, then the Son Himself will also subject Himself to [the Father] Who put all things under Him, so that God may be all in all [be everything to everyone, supreme, the indwelling and controlling factor of life] (1 Corinthians 15:28 AMP).

Real honoring comes when we prefer another above ourselves even when he or she is our equal.

Let this same attitude and purpose and [humble] mind be in you which was in Christ Jesus: [Let Him be your example in humility:] who, although being essentially one with God and in the form of God [possessing the fullness of the attributes which make God God], did not think this equality with God was a thing to be eagerly grasped or retained, but stripped Himself [of all privileges and rightful dignity], so as to assume the guise of a servant (slave)... (Philippians 2:5-7 AMP).

The Son is honored by the Father:

Therefore [because He stooped so low] God has highly exalted Him and has freely bestowed on Him the name that is above every name that in (at) the name of Jesus every knee should (must) bow, in heaven and on earth and under the earth, and every tongue [frankly and openly] confess and acknowledge that Jesus Christ is Lord, to the glory of God the Father... (Philippians 2:9-11 AMP).

Both honor the Spirit by defending His reputation:

Everyone who makes a statement or speaks a word against the Son of Man, it will be forgiven him; but he who blasphemes against the Holy Spirit [that is, whoever intentionally comes short of the reverence due the Holy Spirit], it will not be forgiven him [for him there is no forgiveness] (Luke 12:10 AMP).

All are placed on an equal footing, being equally credited with creation: "*In the beginning God created the heaven and the earth*" (Gen. 1:1). But we see that "*the earth was without form, and void; and darkness was upon the face of the deep. And the Spirit of God moved upon the face of the waters*" (Gen. 1:2).

Jesus is also credited with creation:

For by Him were all things created, that are in heaven, and that are in earth, visible and invisible, whether they be thrones, or dominions, or principalities, or powers: all things were created by Him and for Him: and He is before all things, and by Him all things consist. And He is the head of the body, the church: who is the beginning, the firstborn from the dead; that in all things He might have the preeminence (Colossians 1:16-18).

All three are credited with raising Jesus from the dead. Peter said that *"Jesus Christ of Nazareth, whom ye crucified…God raised from the dead"* (Acts 4:10). Paul testified that *"if the Spirit of Him that raised up Jesus from the dead dwell in you, He that raised up Christ from the dead shall also quicken your mortal bodies"* (Rom. 8:11). Jesus said, *"I lay down My life, that I might take it again. No man takes it from Me, but I lay it down of Myself. I have power to lay it down, and I have power to take it again"* (John 10:17-18).

That is how God manifests Himself on this earth, with mutual submission and honor. That is to be the posture of the Church to God and each other. *"Though you might have ten thousand instructors in Christ, yet you do not have many fathers"* (1 Cor. 4:15 NKJV). We need to honor the ones who are.

Honoring Earthly Authority

Children, obey your parents in the Lord, for this is right. "Honor your father and mother," which is the first commandment with promise: "that it may be well with you and you may live long on the earth" (Ephesians 6:1-3 NKJV).

The Bible emphasizes that honoring parents is a prerequisite for long life and prosperity. In the verse quoted, Paul expands this promise to include those in authority over us. We are to honor, not just good authority, but all authority.

David wrote, *"Touch not Mine anointed, and do My prophets no harm"* (1 Chron. 16:22), concerning Abraham. But David understood that it referred to all of God's anointed leaders. David warned Abishi to *"not destroy* [Saul], *for who can stretch out his hand against the Lord's anointed, and be guiltless?"* (1 Sam. 26:9 NKJV). God anoints leaders in every area of life.

Paul included the political field:

Everyone must submit to governing authorities. For all authority comes from God, and those in positions of authority have been placed there by God. So anyone who rebels against authority is rebelling against what God has instituted, and they will be punished (Romans 13:1-2 NLT).

Also in the workplace, he said,

Servants, be obedient to them that are your masters according to the flesh, with fear and trembling, in singleness of your heart, as unto Christ; not with eyeservice, as menpleasers; but as the servants of Christ (Ephesians 6:5-6).

The greatest model of submission is in the home. Though there is equality in position, there is a hierarchy in function. In marriage, we are equal: *"submitting* [ourselves] *one to another in the fear of the God"* (Eph. 5:21).

Wives, submit yourselves unto your own husbands, as unto the Lord....Husbands, love your wives, even as Christ also loved the church, and gave Himself for it....Children, obey your parents in the Lord: for this is right. Honor thy father and mother; which is the first commandment with promise (Ephesians 5:22,25; 6:1-2).

The promise *"that your days may be long upon the land which the Lord your God is giving you"* (Exod. 20:12 NKJV) is a result of God *"showing mercy and steadfast love to a thousand generations of those who love [Him]"* (Exod. 20:6 AMP).

The family blessing flows down the family line to those who, in faith, pick it up. As we choose to honor those generations that came before us, we can, in faith, claim a long peaceful life that is connected to that honoring.

Dishonoring authorities annuls the blessing and opens the door for the visitation of *"the iniquity of the fathers upon the children and the children's children to the third and fourth generation"* (Num. 14:18 NKJV). The Pharisees said to Jesus, *"If we had lived in the days of our fathers, we would not have been partakers with them in the blood of the prophets"* (Matt. 23:30 NKJV). They were accusing their forefathers of murder. Jesus responded to their accusations: *"Thus you are witnesses against yourselves that you are sons of those who murdered the prophets"* (Matt. 23: 31 NKJV).

Paul said that *"you have no excuse, everyone of you who passes judgment, for in that which you judge another, you condemn yourself; for you who judge practice the same things"* (Rom. 2:1 NASB). Jesus went on to say,

> *Because of this, take notice: I am sending you prophets and wise men...and scribes...some of them you will kill...and some you will flog...and pursue and persecute from town to town, so that upon your heads may come all the blood of the righteous...shed on earth, from the blood of the righteous Abel to the blood of Zechariah...Truly I declare to you, all these [evil, calamitous times] will come upon this generation* (Matthew 23:34-36 AMP).

The judgment that came upon Jerusalem was a consequence of their choice to accuse, instead of honoring their forefathers. It didn't matter that they killed the prophets. Jesus *"wanted to gather...[Jerusalem's] children together, as a hen gathers her chicks under her wings, [but they]...were not willing"* (Matt. 23:37 NKJV). They were unwilling to admit their family's mistakes and repent for themselves and in proxy for the family.

God is always displaying *"unto the principalities and powers in heavenly places...the manifold wisdom of God"* (Eph. 3:10). We do the same thing in our families, which has a far greater effect than we can imagine. When discussing family authority, Paul noted, *"because the angels are watching, a woman should wear a covering on her head* [her father or husband's covering, not just a physical covering] *as a sign of authority"* (1 Cor. 11:10 NLT). We are playing out a cosmic drama that both demons and angels observe. Our position also influences other people.

In Persia, Queen Vashti was summoned before her husband, but she refused to come. By this act, the king's advisors told him,

> *Queen Vashti...wronged not only the king but also all the princes and all the peoples who are in all the provinces of King Ahasuerus. For the queen's conduct* [would]*...become known to all the women causing them to look with contempt on their husbands* (Esther 1:16-17 NASB).

The higher the position and power we hold, the greater the effect of the decisions we make.

Absalom's rebellion against his father, King David, affected the whole nation. He announced, *"Absalom reigns in Hebron"* (2 Sam. 15:10 NKJV). *"So Absalom stole the hearts of the men of Israel"* (2 Sam. 15:6 NKJV) that were due to the king. His lack of honor for his father resulted in a civil war and the loss of many lives.

How We Dishonor

Speaking Against

This does not have to be an "in your face" type of confrontation. Satan spoke against God by subtly suggesting to Eve that God didn't want her to be able to discern like Him. He also insinuated that God's agenda was hidden beneath false concern for Eve. Hints and innuendoes are often more destructive to a relationship than outright opposition: *"Faithful are the wounds of a friend; but the kisses of an enemy are deceitful"* (Prov. 27:6).

Similarly, Absalom subtly spoke against King David. He told

> *...anyone who...came to the king for a decision..."Look, your case is good and right; but there is no deputy of the king to hear you." Moreover Absalom would say, "Oh, that I were made judge in the land, and everyone who has any suit or cause would come to me; then I would give him justice"* (2 Samuel 15:2-4 NKJV).

Disobeying

Jesus said, *"If ye love Me, keep My commandments"* (John 14:15). The antithesis is that those who disobey don't love or honor. Jesus honored the Father when He said, *"The Son can do nothing of Himself, unless it is something He sees the Father doing"* (John 5:19 NASB). He added, *"I have glorified You down here on the earth by completing the work that You gave Me to do"* (John 17:4 AMP). When we do what God asks us, we glorify Him. If we disobey as Eli's sons did, we are despising Him (see 1 Sam. 2:29-30).

When we don't want to obey, we often use sacrifice as a substitute for obedience. Samuel asked, *"Has the Lord as great delight in burnt offerings and sacrifices, as in obeying the voice of the Lord? Behold, to obey is better than sacrifice"* (1 Sam. 15:22). Disobedience demonstrates independence and is dishonoring to those in authority over us.

Most of our "better way" substitutes interfere with the intentions of God. The Lord would not allow an exchange made for the animal tithes. The tither

> *...must not pick out the good from the bad or make any substitution. If he does make a substitution, both the animal and its substitute become holy and cannot be redeemed* (Leviticus 27:33 NIV).

Harboring Resentments and Judgments

Resentment is anger and ill will toward real or perceived injury or wrong. If left unforgiven, it will escalate into bitterness. Bitterness, even in food, prevents us from partaking of it. The children of Israel *"could not drink of the waters of Marah, for they were bitter"* (Exod. 15:23). They were craving water, but the bitterness of the situation shut them out of the benefit. If we are resentful of authority, we will not come under the covering and protection that they could supply.

We will either get bitter or better. So many people are locked *"in the gall of bitterness"* (Acts 8:23). There are two ways people age: they become sweet and gentle or bitter and caustic. Either they tap into the root of forgiveness and grow kinder, or they bring to fruit the *"root of bitterness...and...become defiled"* (Heb. 12:15 NKJV). To prevent bitterness, we must *"pursue peace with all people... looking carefully lest anyone fall short of the grace of God"* (Heb. 12:14 NKJV).

Forgiveness is an act, not a feeling or a condoning of actions. We can know someone is totally at fault and still forgive him or her. Jesus did it for us! Everybody fails and will disappoint us. We must always be *"bearing with one another, and forgiving one another...even as Christ forgave you, so you also must do"* (Col. 3:13 NKJV).

Judgments

"In whatever you judge another you condemn yourself; for you who judge practice the same things" (Rom. 2:1 NKJV). Judgments are like seeds; if we plant them, they will grow.

> *Do not be deceived, God is not mocked; for whatever a man sows, this he will also reap. For the one who sows to his own flesh will from the flesh reap corruption* (Galatians 6:7-8 NASB).

God told me (Ken) that He didn't want me judging people's actions. A judgment makes assumptions about motives as I decide why I think people do things. We seldom have enough information to make an informed decision, and we usually are filtering those actions through our own distorted lenses. The Scriptures agree: *"To the pure all things are pure; but to those who are defiled and unbelieving, nothing is pure"* (Titus 1:15 NKJV). We only consider what we would do in their shoes. We are not in their shoes and don't understand how God is dealing with them individually. Pride alone causes us to say that we would have done it better.

Rebellion

We dishonor those over us by being insubordinate and rebellious. Our charge is to *"obey your leaders and submit to them, for they keep watch over your souls as those who will give an account"* (Heb. 13:17 NASB).

> *Every person is to be in subjection to the governing authorities. For there is no authority except from God, and those which exist are established by God. Therefore whoever resists authority has opposed the ordinance of God; and they who have opposed will receive condemnation upon themselves* (Romans 13:1-2 NASB).

Rebellion is self-will, in opposition to being *"filled with the knowledge of His will in all spiritual wisdom and understanding"* (Col. 1:9 NASB).

Prayers of Agreement

We come into prayers of agreement simply by agreeing with two or three who are speaking. If they are complaining about the government or other leadership, our agreement adds strength to their words. King David had power because *"the heart of all the men of Judah,* [became]...*even as the heart of one man"* (2 Sam. 19:14). All their swords became his swords. With dishonoring prayers of agreement, all our authority becomes satan's authority.

Our unity has power both for good or evil. As the tower of Babel was rising, God said,

> *Behold, they are one people, and they all have the same language. And this is what they began to do, and now nothing which they purpose to do will be impossible for them* (Genesis 11:6 NASB).

To break this power we must actively resist lending our agreement to complaints or rebellion.

Mocking and Belittling

In jest there is truth. We often use humor to hide behind when we want to criticize people. It can be a form of mocking and is often driven by a spirit. As Elisha *"was going up the road, some youths came from the city and mocked him, and said to him, 'Go up, you baldhead; go up, you baldhead!' So he turned around and looked at them and pronounced a curse on them in the name of the Lord"* (2 Kings 2:23-24 NKJV). Elisha was responding to the spirit, not the youths.

Accusation

Satan is *"the accuser of our brethren...which accused them before our God day and night"* (Rev. 12:10). If we are an accuser or faultfinder, we are doing satan's work. It is more than being negative; it is resisting whatever decisions have been made by or for a person (see Zech. 3:1). Accusers use perverse innuendoes and such, rather than speaking to the person directly. It is *"a whisperer* [who] *separates the best of friends"* (Prov. 16:28 NKJV). Satan is often that whisperer.

An accusation assigns motives to actions. We can see the actions but totally misinterpret the motives. Our opinions that assign those motives indicate that we are walking by sight and not by faith. We are reacting to what we see and not responding to what we have heard from God. Likely we don't even ask God because we "know what's going on."

I (Jeanne) just had a situation occur that illustrated the folly of accusing. While we were away, writing this book, I had a birthday. Ken did some things for my birthday, but never really made it special. I got some emails of congratulations but no cards or presents from my friends. I was devastated and couldn't get any peace. My expectations were shattered, and I felt that nobody cared. God was bringing a death to the culture of appreciation that I had grown up with, and it was hard.

What I didn't know was that all of my friends had ignored my birthday on purpose. I was to speak at a women's retreat, and they had planned a big surprise party with a cake and everything for the retreat. They wanted to honor me in a bigger way than normal. Their action of ignoring my birthday had triggered an accusation in me that assigned false motives to them. I had dishonored my friends by accusing them in my mind. We don't know what is in people's hearts; God does. Trust Him.

Some of the individuals we may dishonor:

- Natural Parents (including in-laws)
- Spiritual Fathers and Mothers (including past spiritual leaders)
- Government Leaders
- Teachers
- Police and Military
- Spouses
- God
- First Peoples (First Nations, Native Americans, Aboriginals)

- Bosses and Authority Structures

Some of the demonic spirits that we may need to deal with include the following:

- Spirit of Rebellion
- Spirit of Independence

Prayer:

Lord, I stand in proxy on behalf of myself and the generations before me, on both my mother and father's side, and ask forgiveness for the sin of dishonoring parents, specifically dishonoring _____. I ask forgiveness back to the 4th generation, the 3rd, the 2nd, and for myself. On the basis of the authority gained through receiving forgiveness, I now break this curse over myself and my children. I declare long life for my children and myself.

Chapter 11

MOVING BOUNDARIES

Cursed is he who moves his neighbor's boundary mark
(Deuteronomy 27:17 NASB).

Realms of Authority

Legitimate Authority

God establishes all authority on the basis of origin. You are a citizen of your country because you were born there. You are a member of a family because you were born into it. You may get adopted in, but it is not your choice; it is the choice of those with authority whether to include you or not. Once you are accepted into a family, a country, or as a partner in a company, you have the privileges of ownership. You cannot be deported if you are a citizen, no matter what citizenship you previously held. Your adopted family cannot change their minds and strip you of their name.

Paul understood realms of authority. He said,

> *...we will not boast beyond our measure, but within the measure of the sphere which God apportioned to us as a measure, to reach even as far as you. For we are not overextending ourselves, as if we did not reach to you...not boasting beyond our measure...we will be, within our sphere, enlarged even more by you* (2 Corinthians 10:13-15 NASB).

Within your spheres, you can function with legitimate authority.

We all have spheres of authority that God has assigned to us. These spheres are like concentric circles emanating from the splash of a pebble thrown into a pond. If you are the authority in a realm, those expanding circles of influence expand your authority as it did Paul's. He said, *"we will be, within our sphere, enlarged by you"* (2 Cor 10:15 NASB). If you are only an influencer and not the authority, the bigger realms lessen your influence. Problems arise when influencers try to take authority that is not theirs to take. *"...The earth is disquieted, and...cannot bear...a servant when he reigneth...."* (Prov. 30:21–22).

Within our own lives we are the absolute authority: the kings and queens of our personal realms. Within our families, we have influence over more people, but we are not the authority or dictator of every thought or action that they may have. The same applies to our jobs, churches, and the government. The bigger the realm, the smaller our influence. In a big arena, when my realm of influence is small, my comments on the government will not elicit much of a response. However, if the authority, the Prime Minister or President, speaks, it is in all the papers. Influencers can speak into a realm; authorities speak for a realm.

Proper boundaries and order are maintained when we, with our smaller, more absolute realms of authority, participate in the larger realms but are not dictated to by those realms. For example, my personal thoughts may influence government policy, but the government policy cannot control my thoughts. My family values will impact my action on a job, but my job cannot overrule my family values.

Illegitimate Authority

Where the reverse is true, illegitimate authority is fostered. Paul was ministering in Ephesus with great authority *"so that even* [when] *handkerchiefs or aprons were brought from his body to the sick...the diseases left them and the evil spirits went out of them"* (Acts 19:12 NKJV). That prompted a great deal of excitement and joy but also stirred up some envy.

Then some of the itinerant Jewish exorcists took it upon themselves to call the name of the Lord Jesus over those who had evil spirits, saying, "We exorcise you by the Jesus whom Paul preaches" (Acts 19:13 NKJV).

The problem was they had no authority to use the name because they were not Christians. Illegitimate authority will always attract demonic activity.

The demon recognized their lack of authority:

And the evil spirit answered and said, "Jesus I know, and Paul I know; but who are you?" Then the man in whom the evil spirit was leaped on them, overpowered them, and prevailed against them, so that they fled out of that house naked and wounded (Acts 19:15-16 NKJV).

We knew a woman who fought against some sexual teachings at her daughter's school. She was successful and decided to take the fight to the next level. She won there as well and felt empowered to go international with the fight. Now she was way beyond her realm of authority and was easy pickings for demonic retaliation. In the end she lost her marriage and the reputation she created earlier. She was a needless casualty because she went past the realm God had placed her in.

The Philistines took the Ark of the Covenant to Ashdod when Israel lost a battle to them. They set it up in their temple as they would any other idol. They were shocked the next morning when they found

...Dagon [their god] *fallen upon his face...before the ark of the Lord. And they took Dagon, and set him in his place again...when they arose...behold, Dagon was fallen on his face...before the ark of the Lord; and the head of Dagon and both the palms of his hands were cut off* (1 Samuel 5:3-5).

When the Ark was in Israel, Israel was blessed. "*But the hand of the Lord was heavy upon them of Ashdod, and He destroyed them*" (1 Sam. 5:6). The Philistines were "*aliens from the commonwealth of Israel, and strangers from the covenants of promise, having no hope, and without God in the world*" (Eph. 2:12). They had no authority, by reason of origin, to approach the Ark and suffered the consequences of their ignorance.

Factors Allowing Illegitimate Authority

- A Man-Pleasing Spirit

- Allowing the Moving of Our Boundaries

If we are under the control of a man-pleasing spirit, we can't say no to any request, no matter how much it moves our boundaries. It becomes impossible to disappoint anyone except us. We continually say "yes"—only to regret it later—but refuse to cancel our commitments, even when we know things are out of order.

That type of bondage makes us a slave to everybody else's whims and wants. We need to deal with the man-pleasing spirit, not with someone else's strong personality. Acquiescing to another's demands, when our spirit says no, is tantamount to giving that person the status of God in our lives.

Saying "No!" is not selfishness; it is the lawful exercise of our personal authority. Another's wish becomes my command only if I am his or her slave! *"You were bought at a price; do not become slaves of men"* (1 Cor. 7:23 NKJV). Rather than submit to men, we need to submit to God.

I (Jeanne) often agreed to do things I didn't have the time to do. I became overwhelmed and often felt dread of the task ahead, rather than joy. Once, when our children were small, we all came down with the flu. I was already exhausted when I received a call asking me to make a meal for another mother sick with the flu, who had five children. I should have said no! My family was sick also. That family had three teens who were able to cook. I succumbed to the man-pleasing spirit and resentfully did my duty because I couldn't say, "No." Today, I would properly assess the situation and not allow anyone to force me beyond my proper boundaries.

Fear

Our fear of rejection or of a reaction to our saying no, enables others to dominate us. If we will yield our personal authority at the first sign of a conflict, others will use that weakness to intimidate us. We must repent of selling our birthright—our authority and liberty in the Kingdom—for peace. Jesus said, *"Blessed are the peacemakers* [not the peacekeepers]: *for they shall be called the children of God"* (Matt. 5:9).

Peace is not the absence of conflict but our restful attitude in the midst of conflict. *"Looking diligently lest any man fail of the grace of God...Lest there be any...profane person, as Esau, who for one morsel of meat sold his birthright"* (Heb. 12:15-16). *"Thus Esau despised his birthright"* (Gen. 25:34). Adam's birthright, and ours, was to have dominion in this realm. If we sell that for peace, we also will be as Esau and despise *"the liberty by which Christ has made us free"* (Gal. 5:1).

Power rests with the one who has the least to lose. If we do not love our lives, we have power to overcome anything (see Rev. 12:11). But if we are desperate to be in someone's "good books," we open ourselves to all kinds of manipulation. Fear is a spirit; we must resist because it's designed to rob us of power: *"For God hath not given us the spirit of fear; but of power, and of love, and of a sound mind"* (2 Tim. 1:7).

During his teen years, our middle son would always threaten to leave home as a power play to get his own way. I (Jeanne) was afraid of him leaving and usually gave in to the manipulation. I suffered through this time *"because fear hath torment"* (1 John 4:18). When he got into his 20s, the threat had no more power because I would have been happy to see him out on his own. The one with the least to lose has the most power. In the end we encouraged him to buy a house of his own, and he happily left at age 25.

Low Self-Esteem

We must love ourselves and believe we are worthy of being loved. Otherwise we will be treated as we feel we deserve: poorly. Our poor self-image sends out a signal that we are unworthy. The unnatural walk of a wounded animal will attract the attention of vultures. So the unhealthy actions of a person overwhelmed by self-pity will attract the attention of demons.

Joyce Meyer often says we can be pitiful or powerful, but we can't be both. Things are worth what someone is willing to pay: *"[You were purchased] with the precious blood of Christ"* (1 Pet. 1:18-19 AMP). God paid the highest price possible for you. You may think you are worthless, but God has put inestimable value on you. He sees in you what you can't see: He sees the image of His Son in you. Truth can only be seen from God's perspective.

I (Jeanne) have a friend with low self-esteem who goes above and beyond for her boss. She is busy with her family but will often work evenings and even holidays to please him. Her job is interfering with her life, but she can't let go because her self-esteem comes from her job. She is easily manipulated to do more than she wants, even though there is no benefit for her. Healing the wounds that make us demean ourselves is the only solution to low self-esteem.

Moving Boundaries

When we are selfish and self-centered, we move others' boundaries. Their opinions and views are discounted as irrelevant. They become a means to an end—our desired end. This need to control exposes our independence and immaturity and is always motivated by fear.

If we are out of control within ourselves, if we don't have peace, then we attempt to control all the situations around us. We feel that if we can control every exterior circumstance, then we won't be disturbed, and we will be able to maintain our interior peace.

> *What causes fights and quarrels among you? Don't they come from your desires that battle within you? You want something but don't get it. You kill and covet, but you cannot have what you want. You quarrel and fight. You do not have, because you do not ask God* (James 4:1-2 NIV).

We try and get what we want from people instead of God. To do this we push into other people's realms, exercising illegitimate authority over them. This attracts demonic activity, and a spirit of Jezebel joins us to control those people. This will manifest differently depending on our character.

- We can quietly manipulate people by tricking them to do it "my way."

- We can strongly dominate people by forcing them to do it "my way."

- We can aggressively intimidate people by scaring them to do it "my way."

But it is all control and all evidence of walking in the flesh.

The sweet manipulation is just as demonic as the fearful intimidation. Most families use all three at various times. Guilt, shame, and condemnation are often the tools used by a Jezebel spirit to exercise her control. If we trust God, we won't control people. Our friend Drew had an interesting mother who had troubles with boundaries, in both directions.

My father began to "take off," as my mother would put it, early on in their relationship. So, by the time I was in my early teens, they were divorced. My mother and I, however, developed a very close relationship, and we would spend hours and hours talking about life, mostly mine; working out the problems and challenges that I faced growing up. And she was quite candid too, often asking my opinion about situations. I believed our relationship was rooted in love and mutual respect and faith in God.

So it came as a huge shock to me that three days before my wedding my mother organized my kidnapping. She had enlisted the help of a deprogrammer because she believed that I was in a cult. The fact of the matter was, however, that I was in a very Christian church, and I was very passionate about my faith in Christ and a new depth of relationship with the Holy Spirit.

I came to understand that I had become a replacement for my father in my mother's life, and the closeness that we had developed was something that she had come to depend upon. Her control, in this extreme demonstration, was her effort to avoid another major rejection in her life. I had not heeded her fears about the church, or my conviction that I wanted to marry Julia, my current wife of 25 years. Though she failed, mom attempted the ultimate moving of boundaries—controlling my mind, and my thoughts.

But she wasn't always controlling. In fact, in some respects she allowed me to operate with no boundaries. I always remember my mother saying to me, "You're only young once. Try everything. Do it with all your heart and enjoy what you do." So I did…and did…and did, everything.

By the time I was eighteen, I was given the "Salute to Youth Award" by the Kinsmen Club along with countless other awards because I was recognized as being one of the busiest and most successful kids in the city. I not only played soccer, hockey, football, basketball, volleyball, and curling; I refereed soccer and hockey; edited the school newspaper; was President of the Student's Council; organized the ski trips; sang in the choir; acted, debated, etc.

When I was only thirteen, my friends and I were imitating rock bands and doing shows at the local schools and hospitals. That venture turned into a mobile Disco company that I managed and would deejay for. This full-scale business, however, required that I pick up and drop off rental equipment. My mother, who drove me all over God's green earth, very willingly, to every one of my appointments (usually late), became a little overwhelmed.

When I learned to drive at 14, it was a huge relief to her. She began to let me use the car to get the equipment I needed. Driving that car made it easy for me to meet the demands of my outlandish schedule. I was the only kid in grade nine with his own car—driving illegally for the next two years of my life. It's not that Mom didn't understand boundaries; she did, but she just ignored them. She did put this caveat on my using the vehicle, "You can use the car, but I want you to be very careful!"

Controlling parents are fearful parents and manifest that fear in many ways. A fearful mother restricts her children so much that they are unable to develop in a normal fashion. The children submit to the fear and become fearful themselves. The adventure, which naturally is in them, subsides, and they become dominated by the need to be safe. Likewise, lack of control by a parent creates children with no sense of boundaries in their own lives or those of others.

We do not know what is best for our children; only God does. Making them conform to our image will not bring them to their destiny. At one point, God asked me (Jeanne) to release our children to be what He had created them to be. It was no longer my will and wants but God's for their lives. I turned my trust, for their careers and lives, over to Him.

Arenas of Boundary Moving

The people with the most control over our lives are usually the ones who abuse that trust and step into illegitimate control. This would include parents, older siblings, teachers, bosses, and governments. This control is exercised through various expressions.

Physical Moving of Boundaries

1. Being forced to walk out a role that you don't want:

    - Playing the piano when you have no natural ability and just want to play football.
    - Playing football when you want to play the piano.
    - Dressing up pretty for a tea party when you want to ride the horse.

- Riding the horse when you want to dress up pretty for a tea party.

2. Having family or personal standards set up as laws:

- We never act rough.

- We never sing in public.

- We never share our problems.

- We always maintain aloofness.

3. Using relationships as tools of control:

- If you don't do it my way, you can't be my friend.

- Do it my way, or I will take my ball and go home.

- If you want to be part of this family, you can't associate with them.

4. Sexual abuse:

- Incest

- Pornographic material in the house

- Inappropriate touching

- Lack of personal privacy

It is pure selfishness when someone uses his or her children for personal gratification. We knew a young girl who was abused by both her parents. She always felt dirty, and hid, staying in the dark, knowing she couldn't escape. She felt she was the problem and didn't matter to anyone. She developed multiple personalities to cope with her pain and shut out what was happening. For years, she experienced self-hatred, depression, and suicidal thoughts.

The truth is that victims are not responsible for abuse; they did not create the situation. She needed help to see the truth and establish her hope in God. She finally got free and is able to love herself.

5. Deprivation: Not supplying the necessities of life.

Deprivation can come through divorce, abandonment, or the death of a parent. My (Jeanne's) aunt took in a child who had been previously adopted but unwanted. When the glow of having a new baby in the house wore off for the adoptive parents, he was left in his crib, untouched and unwanted. Rarely was he changed or fed. As a two-year-old, he was small and skinny and still only being fed a bottle. It was so bad a situation that the authorities finally removed him from the home. It took a great deal of love and patience for my aunt to begin to restore him back to health.

6. Physical moving of landmarks.

There is a road in our county that veers off the straight line for half a mile and then comes back to the road allowance. When the crew was surveying the road, it was all bush, and they could only see from one marker to the next. After they laid out the boundary markers, one of the farmers came and moved them several hundred feet onto his neighbor's land. This caused the road to move and added several acres to that farmer's holdings. It wasn't until the road was built that the deception was discovered, but it was blamed on poor surveying. We always move another's boundaries for our benefit.

7. Breaking treaties.

European settlers forced Native Americans and First Nation peoples in the U.S. and Canada off their traditional lands. Eventually there were treaties signed, but even then these were often broken. The land was taken by force and manipulation. The same is true of the aboriginals in Australia and many other native cultures. We must repent of our ancestors' roles in these robberies and evictions.

8. Using drugs to control people.

Drugs such as Ritalin are used to control hyperactivity and attention deficit hyperactivity disorder (ADHD). There has often been criticism of the use of Ritalin for children because many of the symptoms, such as restlessness and lack of concentration associated with ADHD, are characteristic of young children. The other major criticism is the allegation that using this medication can lead to a life of substance abuse.[1] Some parents, teachers, and doctors prefer doping rather than training children.

Reports suggest that only 37 percent of drug abuse is recognized in the elderly and that 25 percent of prescriptions have been inappropriately prescribed.[2]

Drugs are the treatment of choice in psychiatric hospitals with hypnotic sedatives being prescribed. In a British hospital, there was clear agreement from all, that a significant motivation for the over-diagnosing of benzodiazepines prescriptions was a desire on the doctor's part not to be disturbed by nursing staff during the night. Indeed, the Royal College of Psychiatrists' statement on benzodiazepine prescribing and the Committee on Safety of Medicines have recommended that their use as hypnotics should be considered only when the condition is severe, disabling, or subjecting the individual to extreme distress. Yet this study found that they were routinely prescribed upon admission.[3]

9.   Emotional moving of boundaries.

Restricting Emotional Responses

Some families frown on anyone who cries. The favorite threat in my family (Ken) was, "If you want to cry, I'll give you something to cry about." When I first heard myself saying that to my children, I gasped, "Oh my God! I sound just like my dad." That is the fingerprint of a judgment, manifesting through a generational curse: When *"posing as judge and passing sentence on another, you condemn yourself, because you who judge are habitually practicing the very same things [that you censure and denounce]"* (Rom. 2:1 AMP).

Other families have restricted expressions of excitement, disappointment, pity, anger, or even laughter. All these are illegitimate uses of control which damage and scar children. Most of the control is exercised strictly at the convenience or the tradition of those in charge.

Sexual Confusion

Being treated as the opposite sex is another form of emotional boundary manipulation. Calling a girl "Daddy's little boy" will bring all kinds of confusion about sexual orientation. The daughter often tries to please by taking on the role the parent has designated as acceptable. I (Jeanne) was ministering in an outreach when a beautiful young lady I didn't know approached me for ministry.

She had long, gorgeous, black hair pulled back into a ponytail. She wore a baseball cap, T-shirt, jeans, and a quilted vest. She was of Asian origin, and when I saw her, I saw a boy. The Holy Spirit told me that her parents had wanted a boy, as that brought honor to the family. She was a disappointment to them.

The first thing I said as she sat down was, "You are not a disappointment. God created you and formed you in your mother's womb as a girl. You are no surprise to God. He loves you and created you as a girl." The tears streamed down as she shared that all her life she knew she was a disappointment because in her culture there is shame if the oldest is not a boy. I prayed with her and reset her boundaries. I saw a girl who, for the first time, saw herself of value as a girl.

A mother who has desired a girl often dresses up her baby boy as a girl. She may curl his hair and put in ribbons. She may dress him in a pink outfit and tell him how pretty he looks. It seems innocent and fun, but the words that are spoken will create an impression and affect his view of his sexuality, often resulting in confusion later.

We knew a family that had three boys. The mother, who was addicted to painkillers, longed for a daughter. I (Jeanne) used to go over and help her clean as she would get overwhelmed with the children. The house was always a disaster with cat feces, dirt, toys, and clothes everywhere. She liked to dress the youngest up as a girl because his hair was long and curly. She thought it was cute. I often prayed for the family after they moved away.

Parental Inversion

When one spouse is absent through divorce, death, or emotional dysfunction, the other often assigns that role to the oldest sibling. He or she becomes the confidant, being required to carry all the emotional, and often the physical, baggage that belongs to a spouse.

We had a neighbor whose child became very depressed. A teacher was concerned, and upon questioning the child, found out that he was worried about finances. This child was only in grade one! The parents had been discussing their financial woes in front of their children and had not realized the impact their conversations were having. The young boy was a burden bearer and had taken on the worry that did not belong to him.

Often parents force their children to realize their dreams. This may come in the form of what schools they must attend and degrees they must graduate with. They may be required to enter a certain fraternity or sorority and compete in certain sports. The parents' emotional needs become the child's responsibility.

But children are not designed to carry adult responsibilities. We have found that people who are denied their childhood never properly mature. Immaturity is a prerequisite for maturity. Those who are stretched too far are seldom able to return to their proper place of authority.

I (Ken) was given adult responsibilities long before I was ready. I mentioned earlier that as a nine-year-old I used to work almost full-time on the farm. We rose early, did chores, had breakfast, and then went to school or out to the fields when there was no school. I would put in 10 hours a week during the school term and 50 hours during the summer. Most nine-year-olds have an attention span of about half an hour if they are not playing a video game. I was in the field, driving a tractor for eight hours at a stretch. How I didn't kill myself I don't know. When I think of my own grandson being forced to work that way, I see how warped my thinking was.

Spiritual Moving of Boundaries

Traditions are often substituted for truth. Tremendous pressure is often exerted to maintain the family traditions. In most families, an individual choice to follow the Lord differently is met with opposition and suspicion. Often, outright threats of expulsion or, at least, loss of privilege with the family are issued. This imposition of the family's values over the individual's is illegitimate use of that authority.

We knew a young lady who chose to marry a man of a different culture. He was righteous, very mature, and well able to provide for her. His whole family embraced her as a daughter, and we were excited, knowing the Lord was in this union. Unfortunately her parents threatened to disown her if she married this man. When she could not be dissuaded, they chose not to attend the wedding, which was a great embarrassment in the groom's culture. Even when grandchildren arrived, the parents refused to get involved in their young family. Their blindness robbed them of sharing the joy that their daughter was experiencing.

Legalism is often substituted for faith, but *"the law is not of faith"* (Gal. 3:12). Legalistic families or churches do not operate in faith but in fear. Fear that you will go astray if you don't do it right (and we know what is right). Legalism is not restricted to religious beliefs but will rule every aspect of our lives. If we are legalistic, then we must wear certain types of clothes, have particular friends, speak certain ways, work certain types of jobs, and entertain a certain quality of people. We cannot have certain thoughts or speak taboo opinions. Everything is choreographed; nothing can be spontaneous. Everything must be done right. That is true bondage when we must submit to our rules rather than trust Jesus to keep us.

Amorality is the opposite of legalism; there are no absolutes, no moral or ethical considerations.[4] This type of an upbringing leaves a child with no moorings by which to make decisions. The truth is that if we *"train up a child in the way he should go: and when he is old, he will not depart from it"* (Prov. 22:6). The commission is to train, not to let them discover everything with no mentoring. Having no boundaries results in the same illegitimacy as moving boundaries: there are no fences within which to operate.

Some of the demonic spirits associated with moving boundaries that may need to be dealt with include the following:

- Jezebel (control spirit)

- Man-Pleasing Spirit

- Ahab Spirit (allows others to control them)

Prayer:

Lord, I acknowledge the sin of "Moving Boundaries" in all its forms. I stand before You for myself and in proxy on behalf of the generations before me, on both my mother and father's side. We ask forgiveness for our sin of "Moving Boundaries," specifically for moving boundaries through _____. I ask forgiveness back to the 4th generation, the 3rd, the 2nd, and for myself.

On the basis of the authority gained through receiving forgiveness, **I now break this curse** off of me and my children. Lord, set my boundaries with grace and balance. Help me to recognize and respect other people's boundaries.

Holy Spirit, I ask You to realign my boundaries. Where I have been stretched too far, beyond my natural boundaries, realign them back to their natural position. Where I was restricted and not allowed to experience my natural boundaries, I ask You to extend them back to where they belong. Bring my body, soul, and spirit back into their proper alignment.

I choose to forgive_____ for trying to control me and for not respecting my boundaries.

Lord, help me to respect others and to maintain healthy boundaries. Help me not to judge others or try to force them into my idea of what they should be. Where I have allowed manipulation or control in my life deliver me from a man-pleasing spirit.

Chapter 12

MISLEADING THE BLIND

Cursed is he who misleads a blind person on the road
(Deuteronomy 27:18 NASB).

This curse has been expanded to include all those who are blinded and don't see.

Physical Misleading

1. An actual blind person. We have only encountered one person, in the thousands we have ministered to, who admitted that his family had actually taunted a blind person and led that person into objects he or she couldn't see.

2. Many business deals have used misleading language to keep one party in the dark about the true intention of the other. Though the main deal may appear simple, the fine print often contains what would be unacceptable restrictions or limitations. If these were made clear, the deal would never be entered into. The devil is in the details—so is the deception.

I (Ken) was looking over a set of construction prints for a building I was bidding on. I felt uneasy about one aspect of the drawings when something in my spirit drew me to examine a detail in a section that did not appear to be in my scope of work. As I studied the detail, I realized there was an engineering design error that looked good on paper but which could not be physically built.

Though it was listed in another section of the contract, I saw that it fell within my bid. I decided to pull that steel out of what I was bidding on and listed the drawings and the detail numbers on an exclusion list. I noted in my contract that those sections would be done only on a time and material basis.

We were awarded the contract, and those details proved unworkable and had to be redesigned. We did that steel work off a new set of drawings, for which I charged over $80,000. Had I not sensed the problem in the details, I would have been out of pocket that amount of money.

3. Many mislead for unjust gain. One way that a merchant would get unjust gain was to have one set of weights for buying and another for selling. A quick switch would mean a fractionally better deal. But to God *"a false balance and unrighteous dealings are extremely offensive and shamefully sinful to the Lord, but a just weight is His delight"* (Prov. 11:1 AMP). Though weights and measures are regulated in most parts of the world, there are many ways to skim more profit at the expense of the uninitiated.

I (Jeanne) bought a ring in a foreign country that was guaranteed by the seller that it was sterling silver. It even had the .925 markings that normally ensure the highest quality. When I started wearing the ring at home, the silver started to wear off. I had been misled.

Deceivers are looking for the naïve who have no experience. That which is worthless is lauded as having great value by the deceiver. Conversely, for that which is valuable, he insists, *"It is worthless; it is worthless!" ...but when he goes his way, then he boasts [about his bargain]"* (Prov. 20:14 AMP). God warns that *"wealth obtained by fraud dwindles"* (Prov. 13:11 NASB).

We all know the story of the elderly lady who has a contractor come to her door and offer to install the new roof he claims she needs. He is polite, respectful, and charming as he explains the danger she is in if the roof is left to rot. They seal the deal, and she naïvely gives him a check for the job. He never returns, and she still talks about that nice young man hoping that he will show soon. The better the con, the more likable they are.

4. Charm is used in relationships to mask our true character. We can be charming with someone on the outside, while we are churning on the inside. That is why Jesus said people could come to you *"in sheep's clothing, but inwardly they are ravening wolves. Ye shall know them by their fruits"* (Matt. 7:15-16).

I (Jeanne) sensed this about a man I knew. He was very charming with women, but there was another side to him. Although he had many women friends, he was often critical toward them. He would rip women apart over trivial situations. I felt he had a woman-hating spirit and I was wary of him. Later, his wife confided to me that he used to beat her. That had stopped, but now he used words to control, and his wife, because of fear, totally submitted to him.

We need wisdom to discern people's true motives: *"Jesus, on His part, was not entrusting Himself to them...for He Himself knew what was in man"* (John 2:24-25). Jesus had discernment and knew that the same people who were praising Him would crucify Him. He said, *"I send you out as sheep in the midst of wolves. Therefore be wise as serpents and harmless as doves. But beware of men"* (Matt. 10:16-17 NKJV). We are to be aware that many will try and mislead us.

Everyone has different expectations in a relationship. A boy may say, "I love you." What he really wants is sex. A girl may say, "I love you," and want friendship, not intimacy. Someone may say, "I want to be your friend," and just want a connection.

We will only recognize the true heart motives by seeing their fruit, not by hearing their words. We are not to be paranoid that everyone is out to get us, but we are not to be naïve either. Bad actions may not be evil; they may just be immature. Likewise, good actions may not be pure; they may just be deception.

I (Jeanne) was head of a Christian organization in our town and had a friend who was very attentive to me. She was a good friend until I stepped down from my position. After that I never saw her. I thought she was a friend, but without discernment we cannot see what's in people's hearts.

Spiritual Misleading

1. **False Religion Designed to Mislead**

Many have used religion as a false form of piety in order to extract economic gain from the church. Churches are fertile ground for shysters because there is a level of trust there that is not found out in the world. The Church has a history of propagating the lie that if you are successful you must be godly. People who believe this lie have corrupt minds, *"and they have turned their backs on the truth. To them, a show of godliness is just a way to become wealthy"* (1 Tim. 6:5 NLT). "Trusted Christian friends" have sucked more than one person into a pyramid scheme or a shady investment.

The Bible says, *"Where no counsel is, the people fall: but in the multitude of counselors there is safety"* (Prov. 11:14). A man once phoned the church we were attending, looking for some assistance. Our pastor recognized it as a scam and phoned every church in town alerting them to this guy, who had done this before. Years before he had gone through town with his sob story and bilked many churches out of funds that were earmarked for real needs. Unity among the churches prevented the same thing from happening again.

Cults demand obedience and use the rebellion trump card to control and victimize their flocks. "If you don't obey us, you are being rebellious, and bad things will happen to you." Fear is the main tool of intimidation they use. Fear that only the leader can hear me. Fear that if I don't obey I will go to hell. Fear that the leader is the new manifestation of Christ and must be blindly followed. Jesus said, *"I am the way, the truth, and the life"* (John 14:6). We are told to *"take up...[our] cross daily, and follow...[Jesus]"* (Luke 9:23). Too long have we followed leaders rather than following Jesus. True leadership does not draw people to themselves but points the way to Jesus. They know that *"unto Him shall the gathering of the people be"* (Gen. 49:10).

Almost every Christian has been hurt or disappointed by leadership at one time or another. Pastors, prophets, and teachers, as they interact with people and attempt to love them, will touch wounded areas. All of these leaders have their own unhealed wounds and have often pushed people away when these areas were irritated. Some of these leaders even gave in to their weaknesses and sinned against their flocks.

Some leaders have misappropriated funds. Some have succumbed to their sexual urges and destroyed people's lives. Some have used people and their ideas for personal gain. Some have acted like kings and wanted others to serve them.

> *...The rulers of the Gentiles lord it over them...yet it shall not be so among you; but whoever desires to become great among you, let him be your servant...Just as the Son of Man did not come to be served, but to serve, and to give His life a ransom for many* (Matthew 20:24-28 NKJV).

We should not be surprised or discouraged when leadership is infected with sin. "*For all have sinned, and come short of the glory of God*" (Rom. 3:23). Leadership is not appointed because of superior righteousness; they are put in place because of an anointing. Peter was not made the leader in the early church because he was without sin; Jesus appointed him knowing he would sin. Jesus said, "*I have prayed for you, that your faith should not fail; and when you have returned to Me, strengthen your brethren*" (Luke 22:32 NKJV).

The "*righteous...falls seven times, and rises again*" (Prov. 24:16 NASB). God will restore any who come to Him for forgiveness. Leadership develops; it is not born. Leaders have more pressures and attacks than the normal person; that is why we are exhorted that

> *...first of all, supplications, prayers, intercessions, and giving of thanks, be made for...all that are in authority, that we may lead a quiet and peaceable life* (1 Timothy 2:1-2).

Jesus knows the human condition. He was immersed in flesh so that He could be "*touched with the feeling of our infirmities...tempted like as we are, yet without sin*" (Heb. 4:15). The "*kingdom of heaven is like a man who sowed good seed in his field; but...his enemy came and sowed tares among the wheat*" (Matt. 13:24-25 NKJV). Our job is to make sure those tares don't take root in us and to restore those who have "*yield*[ed]...[their] *members as instruments of unrighteousness unto sin*" (Rom. 6:13).

Pastor Richard, whose father was a Haitian voodoo witch doctor, told me (Ken) that all voodoo practitioners are in it for the money and the resulting power. It has always been about the money. The owners of the *"slave girl possessed with a spirit of divination"* (Acts 16:16 NKJV) were furious when she was delivered. The Bible says that *"when her masters saw that their hope of profit was gone, they seized Paul and Silas"* (Acts 16:19 NKJV). Some things never change.

2. Misrepresentation Designed to Mislead

Everywhere that Paul went he *"turned the world upside down"* (Acts 17:6). The silversmiths at Ephesus were incensed with Paul because he turned their world upside down. They *"made silver shrines for Diana,* [which] *brought no small gain unto the craftsmen"* (Acts 19:24). They incited a riot, couching the reasons for it in a religious cloak. Demetrius, the silversmith, said, *"Of course, I'm not just talking about the loss of public respect for our business. I'm also concerned that the temple of the great goddess Artemis will lose its influence"* (Acts 19:27 NLT). I guess it wasn't about the money.

This "shearing of the sheep" has gone on for centuries. Indulgences granted by the church for money was the final straw that motivated Luther to move at variance with the church. The Council of Trent instituted severe reforms in the practice of granting indulgences, and, because of prior abuses, "in 1567 Pope Pius V canceled all grants of indulgences involving any fees or other financial transactions."[1]

Even today, the *New York Times* reports:

According to church teaching, even after sinners are absolved in the confessional and say their Our Fathers or Hail Marys as penance, they still face punishment after death, in Purgatory, before they can enter heaven. In exchange for certain prayers, devotions, or pilgrimages in special years, a Catholic can receive an indulgence, which reduces or erases that punishment instantly, with no formal ceremony or sacrament.

There are partial indulgences, which reduce purgatorial time by a certain number of days or years, and plenary indulgences, which eliminate all of it, until another sin is committed. You can get one for yourself, or for someone who is dead. You cannot buy one—the church outlawed the sale of indulgences in 1567—but charitable contributions, combined with other acts, can help you earn one. There is a limit of one plenary indulgence per sinner per day.[2]

Many denominations and cults demand that their parishioners tithe or contribute specific percentages of their income to the church. Abraham tithed to God, not to an institution, as a part of his covenant relationship (see Heb. 7:1-8). Demanding specifically how that covenant is worked out is a form of control by leadership.

Too often we have seen much of that money funneled into exorbitant lifestyles that are an embarrassment to the Kingdom. The world knows that two things always make money: sin and religion. We personally know of situations where a prophet with a powerful ministry convinced many people to pay for his personal excesses. Illicit sex was also mixed in, *"for of this sort are those who creep into households and make captives of gullible women loaded down with sins, led away by various lusts"* (2 Tim. 3:6 NKJV).

Until that prophet went to jail, none of those involved saw the manipulation that they were under. Jesus dealt with the same spirit. He vilified the religious leaders, charging that *"they do not practice what they preach. They tie up heavy loads and put them on men's shoulders, but they themselves are not willing to lift a finger to move them"* (Matt. 23:3-4 NIV). Abuse will only disappear when the king attitude disappears and true servant-leaders emerge in the Body of Christ.

3. **Hiding/Wearing Masks to Mislead**

We all wear masks to prevent people from seeing us as we really are. I (Ken) once put on a costume and a mask to act a role in a play. I found that I could act completely differently and display an alternate personality when I was in costume. I could put on an act.

God wants us to manifest the epistle that is *"written in our hearts, known and read of all men"* (2 Cor. 3:2). He wants us to be transparent and open, not veiled and closed up.

Why do we hide?

First, we hide because shame motivates much of our action. We hide because we feel that people will not like us if they see the real us. God wants to break that shame-based nature off of us. Shame comes because we feel guilty about our inability to keep the law. Don't *"frustrate the grace of God: for if righteousness came by the law, then Christ is dead in vain"* (Gal. 2:21). *"For by grace are ye saved through faith"* (Eph. 2:8). *"And the law is not of faith"* (Gal. 3:12).

God wants us to shake off the condemnation of the law *"because the law worketh wrath: for where no law is, there is no transgression"* (Rom. 4:15).

> *For the promise, that he should be the heir of the world, was not to Abraham, or to his seed, through the law, but through the righteousness of faith. For if they which are of the law be heirs, faith is made void, and the promise made of none effect* (Romans 4:13-14).

"For the promise is unto you, and to your children...even as many as the Lord our God shall call" (Acts 2:39). What promise? The promise that if you *"repent, and* [are]*...baptized...in the name of Jesus Christ for the remission of sins...ye shall receive the gift of the Holy Ghost"* (Acts 2:38). *"His divine power has given to us all things that pertain to life and godliness"* (2 Pet. 1:3 NKJV).

Our efforts don't change us; His power does. The God of the whole universe has taken up residence in us. He has not come to visit us; He has come to indwell us. We need not be ashamed and hide if *"God is not ashamed to be called* [our]*... God"* (Heb. 11:16 NKJV).

Second, we hide because we are two-faced. We don't know who we are, so we become chameleons, shifting and changing to match the situation. We wear one hat in the church, another at home, and a third at work or school. We are afraid of people, so we shift to accommodate them.

I (Jeanne) know a woman who came to me for help because of confusion in her life. She continually adapted to whatever group she was with. She could never be true to her own feelings or opinions. Others seemed to make up her mind for her. Finally, she became so depressed that she sought help. I showed her that her need to fit in had robbed her of her own identity. Her thoughts and feelings were not consistent with her actions. She needed God's love and acceptance in order to replace the need for other's acceptance.

We need to know that we are *"wisdom, and righteousness, and sanctification, and redemption"* (1 Cor. 1:30) in Christ. *"We have this treasure in earthen vessels, that the excellency of the power may be of God, and not of us"* (2 Cor. 4:7). We are the Body of Christ, His very flesh and blood. And *"there is…no condemnation for those who are in Christ Jesus"* (Rom. 8:1 NASB). When we believe that, we can always be who we are, the beloved of God (see Song of Sol. 2:16).

Third, we hide because we want to appear more mature than we really are. We put on a spiritual mask of knowledge to disguise our immaturity as Adam and Eve mistakenly did. They assumed that if they had knowledge they would be more mature, like God (see Gen. 3:5). In reality, *"knowledge* [just] *puffs up, but love builds up"* (1 Cor. 8:1 NIV).

I (Ken) had a very low opinion of myself and thought that others felt the same way. I decided early to acquire knowledge so that people would think I was smart. Having knowledge does not make you smart; it only makes you a source of trivia. Wisdom is what makes you wise. I knew something about everything, but I didn't really know the love of God. The most important thing you will ever discover is that God truly loves you.

Knowledge does not make us mature; love does. Immaturity is actually selfishness; maturity is corporateness. Adam and Eve's immature, selfish response separated them from God and the unity that they had enjoyed. God is concerned about purity, not maturity—and maturity is not purity. They were not content to be immature and pure. So they tried to take a shortcut to maturity, but just got knowledge and impurity.

If we are content in the knowledge that we are *"approved in Christ"* (Rom. 16:10), we would not need a mask of knowledge.

Fourth, we hide to keep others in the dark about the truths in our lives. We may not have the job or the pay that matches the persona that we broadcast. Our marriage or children may not be in the order we portray. We may have some habits that, if they were known, would be frowned upon. We may even have a family history that we would rather stay hidden.

There are many reasons to stay in the dark. The strongest is to prevent our sins from being exposed. But the Word says that *"if we walk in the light, as He is in the light, we have fellowship one with another, and the blood of Jesus Christ His Son cleanses us from all sin"* (1 John 1:7 NKJV). Satan wants us to hide; God wants us to *"come boldly unto the throne of grace...and find grace to help in a time of need"* (Heb. 4:16).

I (Jeanne) worked with a very good friend of mine for over a year on her problem with fear. She would phone and relate to me her latest fear. God gave me a strategy to deal with these unreasonable fears; I laughed at them. I laughed, and then I spoke the truth. My laughter trivialized the problem and speaking the truth magnified the Lord, which allowed her to overcome fear after fear. Because of her personal victory, she is now able to help many young women through their fears.

The Problem With Hiding

Masks limit our vision. Though we may be covering up to keep others from seeing us, we end up blocking our own ability to see. We need to look in a mirror to get an accurate picture of what we look like. The Word is like a mirror (see James 1:23-25), but if we have a mask on we will not *"see* [ourselves and will]... *walk away, and forget what* [we]...*look like"* (James 1:24 NLT). If we don't see the truth, we will never change. *"But we all, with unveiled face, beholding as in a mirror the glory of the Lord, are being transformed into the same image from glory to glory"* (2 Cor. 3:18 NKJV).

That transformation allows us to see as Jesus sees, not just ourselves, but the truth as well. Prophets in the Old Testament were often called seers (see 1 Sam. 9:9). Our masks limit our ability to see in every realm we want to look into.

I (Jeanne) was pressing into God to get more love for other people, and I went to a friend and confessed my weakness. She exclaimed that she had a big heart and lots of love for others. I knew that she was deficient here as well, but she was blind to it. About a week later, she came admitting that God had lifted off the blinders and exposed her wicked heart. She had run into some difficult people and found that her love was not enough. We see what we want to see, but God wants us to see the truth.

Lying

We don't love the truth. We love our version of the truth, our opinion. When God told me (Ken) that I was not allowed an opinion anymore, I needed to learn to love the truth. The truth is not a series of facts; Jesus is *"the truth"* (John 14:6). The truth is a manifestation of the Lord, a revelation of Him.

We like to modify the truth and often misrepresent a situation to cast a more favorable light on us. I (Ken) liked to embellish the truth (lie). My stories would grow from the three fish caught to five or six within a few short months. When Jeanne would challenge me, I would get angry and try to deflect the heat away from me. The truth is the truth, not my enhanced versions of the event. We do this for protection or greed, or because we can't face the truth; it may be too painful. But if we continue lying too long, we will lose our ability to discern the truth. Paul said, *"Because they received not the love of the truth…God shall send them strong delusion, that they should believe a lie"* (2 Thess. 2:10-11).

Secrets

Keeping secrets is not lying; it's just not telling the whole truth. Leaving out some of the fact can change the whole meaning of what was said. We are very careful in this book, when excerpting a Scripture, to maintain its original intent. Words or phrases are left out only when they do not highlight or modify the point being made.

Secrets are designed to limit what others are allowed to know. We use secrets as a shield of mistrust, not a shield of faith. Our mistrust of people forces us to keep them in the dark about things that are important to us. By speaking only part of the truth, we give the impression to others that they are in our confidence when they are not. If we are the only ones who know the truth, it gives us more power.

Knowledge is power.[3] Company insiders make millions using insider trading on the stock market. Trading with their knowledge of company secrets is considered illegal. God wants us to trust Him for the knowledge that we need and not depend on keeping things in the dark to benefit. If we can love the truth, God will be able to trust us with words of knowledge that reveal the truth. With a word of knowledge, we no longer have to speculate; we know.

Some of the demonic spirits we may need to deal with include the following:

- Lying Spirit
- Deceiving Spirit
- Spirit of Flight
- Spirit of Isolation
- Spirit of Mistrust

Prayer:

Lord, I acknowledge the sin of "Misleading the Blind" in all its forms. I stand before You for myself and in proxy on behalf of the generations before me, on both my mother and father's side. We ask forgiveness for our sin of "Misleading the Blind," specifically for misleading through _____. I ask forgiveness back to the 4th generation, the 3rd, the 2nd, and for myself.

*On the basis of the authority gained through receiving forgiveness, **I now break this curse** off of me and my children. Lord, let me walk in the light and truth and not hide in the darkness. Grant that I would also give light to those who are bound in darkness.*

Prophetic acts:

- Lord, I take off the masks that I use to hide myself.

- Lord, I remove the shield of mistrust and replace it with the shield of faith.

- Lord, I receive Your forgiveness for lying to others and myself.

- Lord, I break off the fear of man.

- Lord, I break off trust in cheating and lying to obtain what I need.

Chapter 13

PERVERTING JUSTICE

Cursed is he who distorts the justice due an alien, orphan, and widow (Deuteronomy 27:19 NASB).

This curse refers to the helpless who have no ability to resist those who take advantage of them. The list of those who have the most control will also be the list of those who abuse their position of power. Parents top the list, followed by older siblings, teachers, and bosses. On a broader, less personal level, are oppressive governments and their enforcement agencies: the police, lawyers, and the military, who have done their fair share of perverting justice.

This curse usually comes to the fore when existing norms shift. Situations like divorce, death, and the breakup of a company or partnership often stir up the greed and resentments hidden beneath the surface. Personal and legal battles that ensue foster the abuse that the stronger imposes on the weaker or less aggressive.

A friend of ours completed a painting job for a contractor and presented him with the invoice. After the normal 30-day pay period passed, he phoned to see if there was a problem with the bill, and to find out why it had not been paid. He was assured that there was no problem and not to worry, the money was on the way. Our friend trusted what was said and did nothing to protect his interest. It wasn't until the lien time limit passed that he realized this man had no intention of paying.

Repeated phone calls were ignored, and our friend finally gave up. Many years later, that same contractor was bidding for a contract with a Christian school, where our friend's wife was a member of the board. She cautioned the board about dealing with a man whose ethics were questionable. When the board queried the man about this unpaid invoice, he assured them that the matter was being looked after. He got the contract, did a poor job, and still never paid the bill. Jesus is coming back to *"execute judgment and justice in the earth"* (Jer. 23:5); we need to be doing that now. Let's look at a few examples that involve the perversion of justice.

Breaking of Marriage Vows

When we marry, we vow to each other, before God and witnesses, that we will love, honor, and cherish for better or worse, through sickness and health till death do we part. *"It is better to say nothing than to make a promise and not keep it"* (Eccles. 5:5 NLT). The sin in divorce is the breaking of vows that we made.

Jesus said that *"whoever divorces his wife for any reason except sexual immorality causes her to commit adultery; and whoever marries a woman who is divorced commits adultery"* (Matt. 5:32 NKJV). Later in the Book of Matthew, we read, *"Because of your hardness of heart Moses permitted you to divorce your wives; but from the beginning it has not been this way"* (Matt. 19:8 NASB). *"Therefore what God has joined together, let not man separate"* (Matt. 19:6 NKJV).

Love is a choice, not just a feeling. Today our promises to love don't mean much. We enter marriage as we would a contract and not a covenant. In a covenant, I promise to do something for you no matter what happens. In a contract, you promise to do something for me under certain conditions. A covenant commits me to safeguard needs and obligations for you. A contract safeguards my needs and obligations from you. A covenant lasts as long as the term of the original agreement. A contract lasts until the conditions are broken.

Our daughter-in-law Suzanne ministered to a lady whose ex-husband had not been paying child support for over a year. The woman was bitter and angry about the situation. She spewed out her anger and pain while Suzy slowly brought her back to the only weapon she had to combat the injustice: forgiveness.

Suzy showed her in the Scriptures how forgiving releases God to bring justice. The woman repented for her own anger, bitterness, and hopelessness. Then she forgave her husband and with the authority gained called in the monies owed. Two weeks later, she contacted Suzy with exciting news. Her husband had decided to pay everything he owed. *"A father of the fatherless, and a judge of the widows, is God in His holy habitation"* (Ps. 68:5). Our anger only reaps bitterness; our forgiveness will produce justice.

We had friends who were having a hard time conceiving, and asked for prayer. It was not long before babies started to come, and they asked us to stop praying after they had four. The pressure of the children on the wife who worked full time was too much, and she asked her husband if she could quit. Even though she was burnt out, he didn't trust God to supply and insisted that she continue working.

It has been said that "fatigue makes cowards of us all."[1] She was burnt out and needed to get some things in order. We all need to have our lives in balance to have the strength to ward off the attacks of the enemy. This lady didn't, and in a weak moment she got involved with a family friend we'll call Bill. She looked to Bill to supply her needs that, at the time, her husband wasn't. Our friend left her husband and moved in with Bill. He was married with a new baby but chose to divorce and remarry with our friend. Her husband later became involved with another lady, in the same church, resulting in a third divorce. It was a mess.

I (Jeanne) met her some years later and asked her if she would do it differently if she had a chance. She admitted the whole thing was a mistake. Everyone suffered, especially the children. Breaking vows that we made before God invites a curse and the resulting judgment.

Prenuptial agreements are in vogue today because they are a form of contract and take away the need for a covenant. They are not a form of commitment; they are a form of protection. In the covenant of marriage, I declare that I love you and I trust you to care for my heart, my children, and my finances. If I trust you, I can commit to you. If I don't, I commit to myself and manifest my fear and my selfishness, which usually results in a divorce.

That is why Jesus said divorce was about the hardness of our hearts. If there are truly irreconcilable differences, divorce was allowed. Remarriage is still a sin, but not the unforgivable sin. The Church has a problem handling divorce and ends up shunning and condemning those who are divorced. We are to treat divorce like Jesus did.

The Pharisees wanted to stone the woman taken in adultery. Jesus said, *"I do not condemn you...Go on your way and from now on sin no more"* (John 8:11 AMP). No condemnation but no soft-pedaling of the sin. Divorce is not a problem. If you have a problem, you will have a problem all your life. If you have a sin, it can be repented of today.

We must be like God, for *"great is His mercy toward those who fear Him; as far as the east is from the west, so far has He removed our transgressions from us"* (Ps. 103:11-12 NKJV). Often when I (Jeanne) minister to women who are strangers to me, I have felt their pain and betrayal. I then listened to many sad stories about husbands of 15, 20, or 30 years who suddenly abandoned their wives and families.

God often gave me this verse to minister to them.

> *...The Lord has called you, like a wife forsaken and grieved in spirit, even like a wife of one's youth when she is rejected...for a brief moment I forsook you, but with great compassion I will gather you* (Isaiah 54:6-7 NASB).

Let's not compound the perversion of justice that divorce brings by condemning those caught in its web.

Breaking First Nation Treaties

North American governments for the most part robbed their native populations of their lands and their way of life because of superior force and selfish desires. The European immigrants with their farming and ranching techniques pushed out a culture that depended largely on hunting and fishing. They did it because they could, and any resistance was seen as rebellion against the new landlords (the settlers). All efforts to stop this wealth transfer were met with harsh reprisals.

When treaties were signed (over 750 in the U.S.A.), they were imposed on a culture that did not consider land a property. Thus they had no expertise to properly negotiate these treaties. The government's policy was one of removal coupled with compensation. It was a one-sided process with concessions, not negotiations, setting the tone. Even then, many of the conditions were changed when it was convenient for the government.

The Black Hills of Dakota are sacred to the Sioux Indians. In the 1868 treaty, signed at Fort Laramie and other military posts in Sioux country, the United States recognized the Black Hills as part of the Great Sioux Reservation, set aside for exclusive use by the Sioux people. In 1874, however, General George A. Custer led an expedition into the Black Hills accompanied by miners who were seeking gold. Once gold was found in the Black Hills, miners were soon moving into the Sioux hunting grounds and demanding protection from the United States Army. Soon, the Army was ordered to move against wandering bands of Sioux hunting on the range in accordance with their treaty rights. In 1876, Custer, leading an army detachment, encountered the encampment of Sioux and Cheyenne at the Little Bighorn River. Custer's detachment was annihilated, but the United States would continue its battle against the Sioux in the Black Hills until the government confiscated the land in 1877. To this day, ownership of the Black Hills remains the subject of a legal dispute between the U.S. government and the Sioux.[2]

The Lakota Indians, who gave the world legendary warriors Sitting Bull and Crazy Horse, have withdrawn from treaties with the United States, leaders said. ..."We are no longer citizens of the United States of America and all those who live in the five-state area that encompasses our country are free to join us." ...A delegation of Lakota leaders delivered a message to the State Department...announcing they were unilaterally withdrawing from treaties they signed with the federal government of the United States, some of them more than 150 years old. …The new country would issue its own passports and driving licenses, and living there would be tax-free—provided residents renounce their US citizenship …The treaties signed with the United States are merely "worthless words on worthless paper," the Lakota freedom activists say on their website. The treaties have been "repeatedly violated in order to steal our culture, our land and our ability to maintain our way of life," the reborn freedom movement says.[3]

The same process took place in Canada with the difference that treaties were signed and enacted without any significant battles being fought. Still the government of Canada holds the position that the First Nations, "ceded, surrendered, and yielded" all their aboriginal rights and titles to their ancestral lands through these treaties.[4]

Today, this narrow and one-sided view that these vast parcels of land were traded for small initial and continuing payments has been challenged. There have been many blockades and court challenges by the natives claiming that the intent of the original treaties has been violated.

In Australia, no treaties were ever signed. Captain Cooke claimed the entire continent for Britain in 1770. He regarded the land as "terra nullis," land belonging to no one. This concept allowed the settlers to take whatever land they wanted. The estimated 500,000 natives were ignored as ignorant savages. The resulting conflict claimed upward of 20,000 lives (18,000 Aboriginal). It wasn't until 1841 that any legal action was taken in defense of the Aborigines. The Aboriginal community today is fighting for its own recognition and treaties that would ensure some of their stolen rights.

Having seen the problems created by unjust practices with other native populations, Britain attempted to have the Treaty of Waitangi solve those problems in New Zealand. The Maori chiefs signed the Treaty of Waiangi in 1841, believing it would give the British government control over the problematic European settlements. The British believed it gave them control over the whole country.

Settlers did not abide by the treaty, and frequent skirmishes occurred. This was a betrayal in the eyes of the Maori.[5]

The Maori had acquired weapons and were more aggressive and organized than other native tribes. Several battles flared up, especially between 1860 and 1890. By that time the Maori population had decreased by 60 percent, and they lost 95 percent of their original lands. In 2006 the New Zealand government attempted to right some of the abuses by returning some large parcels of land to Maori control.[6]

Selfishness is at the center of all perversion of justice. It is part of the fallen nature and can only be redressed by repentance and asking of forgiveness.

Abandonment of Children

Withholding of love and security leaves children in a vulnerable spot. Almost two percent of children in the U.S. are abused or neglected each year.[7] These include educational neglect, physical neglect and abuse, sexual abuse, and emotional abuse. This figure does not seem high until you extrapolate it out for a child's 18 years.

In 1999, the McCreary Adolescent Health Survey II found that:

- 35% of girls and 16% of boys between grades 7-12 had been sexually and/or physically abused

- Among girls surveyed, 17-year-olds experienced the highest rate of sexual abuse at 20%[8]

University of Victoria's Sexual Assault Centre posts the following childhood sexual abuse statistics:

- 1 in 3 females and 1 in 6 males in Canada experience some form of sexual abuse before the age of 18.

- 80% of all child abusers are the father, foster father, stepfather, or another relative or close family friend of the victim.

- Incestuous relationships last 7 years on average.

- 75% of mothers are not aware of the incest in their family.

- 60-80% of offenders in a study of imprisoned rapists had been molested as children.

- 80% of prostitutes and juvenile delinquents, in another study, were sexually abused as children.[9]

The problem is large and is increasing. Saying anything beyond that seems meaningless. Every attempt to measure incidence to date has been flawed. The estimates range from less than 5 percent to more than 40 percent of all children. The National Center on Child Abuse and Neglect (NCCAN), part of the U.S. Dept. of Health and Human Services, compiles data about the number of cases reported to Child Protective Services (CPS) each year, but the fact is the number of reported cases is small compared with the number of actual cases.[10]

A study conducted at a large managed care organization in the northeast, which examined the differences in annual health care costs between women with and without histories of abuse, found that "childhood abuse and neglect histories were reported by 42.8% of the women in this HMO sample (sexual abuse: 18.4%; physical abuse: 14.2%; emotional abuse: 24.1%; emotional neglect: 21.1%; physical neglect: 12.2%), with about half of these women meeting severity criteria for more than one type of maltreatment."[11]

Family breakdown contributes to the majority of abuse and neglect with children. Satan's most effective weapon against a nation is to attack its foundation, which is the safety and sanctity of its families. "*Righteousness exalteth a nation: but sin is a reproach to any people*" (Prov. 14:34). Lord, help us protect the helpless.

Abandoned children may be cheated out of their inheritance by unscrupulous relatives or strangers. Even the death of a parent, in a child's eyes, constitutes abandonment. The results can often be the same, as the statistics show. Single-parent families create eight times the risk for abuse than do families that contain two biological parents.[12] Abandoned children have rejection issues, poor self-esteem, and are often locked up emotionally.[13]

The father of our friend Diana was robbed of his inheritance by an unscrupulous aunt. Their family emigrated from Romania, and unfortunately, the mother never learned English. Her husband had prospered and had set aside a half-section of land for each son. Diana's father was the eldest son, but was only 11 when his aunt came to the farm with a lawyer. She convinced Diana's grandmother to sign some papers, which she claimed would be beneficial to the family.

She signed, over the protests of her son, because she trusted her sister-in-law. What she couldn't read was a contract assigning the aunt title to the half-section that was the inheritance of Diana's father. For some reason, the culture of the Romanian community didn't result in the aunt being ostracized. Years later, her father bought that land back from the aunt. Diana said that the aunt's family never prospered and remained poor despite the theft.

Wars

Wars always pervert justice for the helpless victims who are caught in the conflict. People lose property, citizenship, freedom, families, possessions, and all their rights. There is a huge cost to wars:[14]

WAR	$ COST	LIVES LOST
WW1	$196.5 B	11,016,000
WW2	$2,091 T	59,028,000

No one wins, but the helpless caught in the war zones are the big losers. Wars create widows and orphans, leaving them destitute and vulnerable to all kinds of abuse.

Identity Theft, Pyramid, and Ponzi Schemes

Though the technology for these crimes is new, the schemes are not. They have been in existence in one form or another for hundreds of years. Worldwide in 2008 there were 10,000,000 victims of identity theft. The average dollar amount lost per household amounted to $1,620. An additional $1,000 and an average of 330 hours were spent resolving the problems created. Interestingly, 43 percent of the victims knew their perpetrators.

Cost to business worldwide is approximately $221 billion per year.[15] We had a credit card compromised in the last month. Even though the credit card company was informed about where we would be, who would be gone, and how long we would be gone, they still approved fraudulent purchases in another country to the tune of $3,500.

Ponzi schemes take from the new investor to pay the old investor. As long as enough people keep investing, the scam carries on. Pyramid schemes have low-level investors pay the higher-level investors. Like the Ponzi scheme, there are never the infinite numbers of new recruits required to prevent massive losses. In just one Ponzi scheme in the U.S.A., Bernie Madoff was estimated to have created $50 billion in losses for investors.[16]

An estimated 4 million Colombians, from the political elite and members of the armed forces to small businessmen and the poor, invested in pyramid scams. Some have lost their life savings. The collapse of dozens of *pyramid schemes* has left Columbia in a financial crisis with losses of over $1 billion.[17]

Albania was impacted even more by a pyramid-like Ponzi scheme. At one point, more than half of Albania's GDP was invested in the scheme. Half the population was invested when it all collapsed in 1997. The scams set Albania back in terms of economic development by at least a couple of years and precipitated a near civil war. The total value of all 16 major pyramid schemes totaled $1.2 billion.[18]

An estimated 2,000,000 Filipinos were scammed $1.1-1.4 billion, an amount that exceeded the nation's entire defense budget. The lure is always the same:

greed. To quote a Filipino senator, "There are gullible people who want to make a fast buck without sweating for it."[19]

We were some of those gullible people who invested in a scam. I (Jeanne) prayed and felt the company would overextend themselves and run into difficulties. Ken didn't want to hear it. He felt it was my fear and not the Holy Spirit speaking. We borrowed a large sum of money and invested it in this project. A year later, it all collapsed because they overextended themselves. It looked like we were going to lose the entire investment when a few men spearheaded a campaign to take over the project. They succeeded in recovering $1.6 million, then without permission reinvested it in another scheme and lost it all. We never recovered anything from that investment, but God looked after us, restoring the money through another source in under 18 months.

> There is no calamity greater than lavish desires.
> There is no greater guilt than discontentment.
> And there is no greater disaster than greed.[20]

The Bible says, *"For the love of money is the root of all evil: which while some coveted after, they have erred from the faith, and pierced themselves through with many sorrows"* (1 Tim. 6:10). To parody a famous quotation, "Grief walks on the heels of pleasure: invested (or scammed) in haste, we repent at leisure."[21]

Some of the demonic spirits we may need to deal with include the following:

- Lying Spirit
- Jezebel Spirit

Prayer:

Lord, I acknowledge the sin of "Perverting Justice Due to the Helpless" in all its forms. I stand before You for myself and in proxy on behalf of the generations before me, on both my mother and father's side. We ask forgiveness for our sin of "Perverting Justice," specifically for perverting justice through _____. I ask forgiveness back to the 4th generation, the 3rd, the 2nd, and for myself.

On the basis of the authority gained through receiving forgiveness, **I now break this curse** off of me and my children. Lord, let me walk in love and integrity toward others. Forgive me where I have hurt others by being selfish.

Forgive us for creating widows and orphans during wars.

Chapter 14

SEXUAL PERVERSION

Cursed is he who lies with his father's wife
(Deuteronomy 27:20 NASB).

Cursed is he who lies with any animal
(Deuteronomy 27:21 NASB).

Cursed is he who lies with his sister
(Deuteronomy 27:22 NASB).

Cursed is he who lies with his mother-in-law
(Deuteronomy 27:23 NASB).

We combined all the above curses under one heading of sexual perversion. According to Jesus, *"everyone who looks at a woman with lust for her has already committed adultery with her in his heart"* (Matt. 5:28 NASB). Thus all sexual activity outside of marriage, including thoughts, imaginations, and deeds are lumped together as sin. As the verses listed indicate, there are many different expressions of sexual perversions. Here are a few examples prevalent in the Body of Christ.

Adultery

Adam said, *"a man shall...be joined to his wife, and they shall become one flesh"* (Gen. 2:24 NKJV). This phraseology "one flesh" is a sexual connection as Paul pointed out: *"the one who joins himself to a prostitute is one body with her... For He says, 'The two shall become one flesh' "* (1 Cor. 6:16 NASB). Becoming one is the result of a connection in the physical, soulish, and spiritual realms. Even after the physical connection has been severed, the soul ties and spiritual bonds will remain intact.

A soul tie is an emotional connection that links two sexual partners to each other. After having a sexual union, the natural response for the woman is to come under the man and for the man to cover or protect the woman. In addition to the emotions, our brain also imprints images, visually associated with our sexual feelings, in its memory bank. These images will constantly rise to the surface whenever we engage in sexual activity.

A soul tie or soulish adultery is not strictly sexual but can also occur through unhealthy soulish connections. There is evidence that a soul tie exists if our first inclination is to connect with someone emotionally, or even intellectually, who is not our spouse. Most marriages function so far below the level that God intended that we don't believe that we can be truly one in all three realms: physically, emotionally and intellectually, and spiritually. Many are so fearful and independent that they don't even want that close of a connection. An extramarital, sexual union confuses that process even further as these other "soul mates" cloud the picture.

A spirit tie, though not as obvious, connects the partners through whatever spiritual connections they already possess. In the physical realm STDs are spread by multiple sexual contacts. One person can affect hundreds as each subsequent union passes the virus to the next partner. It is identical in the spirit realm. Paul says,

> What harmony can there be between Christ and Belial [the devil]? Or what has a believer in common with an unbeliever? What agreement [can there be between] a temple of God and idols? For we are the temple of the living God; even as God said, I will dwell in and with and among them and will walk in and with and among them (2 Corinthians 6:15-16 AMP).

Every spirit that infects a person has the potential to pass to the next sexual partner and infect him or her as the two become one. Without breaking these ties, hundreds of other people and their demons can get in bed with us. Activity in the physical realm is simply a mirror of the activity in the spirit realm. The world's increased sexual activity is designed to pollute both the genetic and spiritual health of God's people.

A study in Britain, dealing with STDs, showed that the average British male has had 9 sexual contacts; the average woman, 6.3. When this process is extrapolated for five "generations" of partners, it exposes the ordinary Briton to around 2.8 million people. Clare Kerr, head of sexual health at Lloyd's pharmacy, said, "When we sleep with someone, we are, in effect, not only sleeping with them, but also their previous partners and their partners' previous partners, and so on."[1]

These connections, physical, soulish, and spiritual, will continue until they are consciously broken. They exact a large toll on all who have been sexually engaged outside of marriage. STDs ravage the physical body. Rejection, abandonment, and betrayal all leave deep wounds in the soul. Demonic activity and the resulting depression and confusion rack the spirit.

Repentance and breaking of these ties will break the cycle and set coming generations free.

Fantasizing

God wants us to live in reality, not in a fantasy world. He wants our imaginations used to create reality. We have been duped into believing that our thoughts have no power and what we think is not relevant or important. The Bible declares that as a man *"thinks in his heart, so is he"* (Prov. 23:7 NKJV). What we think about dictates what we will accomplish.

Every invention was first a thought. Every building was first constructed in someone's mind. Moses had to see the tabernacle before he could duplicate it (see Exod. 25:40). God intended our thoughts to be like His thoughts, not some random pictures that float across our imaginations, accomplishing nothing. Our whole being is designed to create what we think, so we need to bring *"into captivity every thought to the obedience of Christ"* (2 Cor. 10:5).

The Lord saw before the flood *"the wickedness of man...and that every intent of the thoughts of his heart was only evil continually"* (Gen. 6:5-6 NASB). That is why He brought the flood: to prevent the spread of their imagined evil. That evil reappeared at the tower of Babel, where God saw that *"nothing* [would] *be restrained from them, which they have imagined to do"* (Gen. 11:6). That is the power of imagination.

Satan is still drawing men into his web through their imaginations. Sin always begins in the mind. Ezekiel was shown *"what the ancients of the house of Israel do in the dark, every man in the chambers of his imagery* [his imagination]*"* (Ezek. 8:12). Their imaginations fueled even greater abominations (see Ezek. 8:13). Satan knows that if he can flood our minds with sexual images, as the world is doing through advertisements and the Internet, he can capture our imaginations.

Fantasizing during sex causes us to be present physically while having our minds and emotions someplace else. This destroys intimacy, as there is no actual connection. This is a type of adultery, where the emotional connection, fueled by the fantasies, creates a soul tie through the imagination. That is not love, which is giving to our spouse; rather, it is lust, which uses our spouse physically to fulfill our imagination.

It is a destroyer of intimacy because we become more connected to the images in our minds than to the reality of our spouse. We become dependent on outside images to produce our emotional and physical responses. This is a perversion of the marriage bed by allowing someone or something else to occupy the spot belonging to our spouse.

Fornication

Fornication is unsanctified sexual relations outside of marriage.[2] Know *"that no person practicing sexual vice or impurity in thought or in life...has any inheritance in the kingdom of Christ and of God"* (Eph. 5:5 AMP). Habitual sexual immorality is an indication of an unrepentant lifestyle. Satan desires us to live this lifestyle, as it pollutes the land and brings in judgment (see Deut. 24:1-4).

Moses said concerning sexual sins that *"by all these the nations are defiled... for the land is defiled; therefore I visit the punishment of its iniquity upon it, and the land vomits out its inhabitants"* (Lev. 18:24-25 NKJV). Judgment comes because sexual sins and idolatry are tied together. Idolatry leads to adultery (see Num. 25). Jesus connected them in His warning to the church of Thyatira. He challenged them concerning their false prophet Jezebel who led the church into *"sexual immorality and the eating of foods sacrificed to idols"* (Rev. 2:20 NIV). These actions, unrepented of, would eventually bring sickness and tribulations to the church (see Rev. 2:22 NASB).

Fornication and idolatry are satan's best tools to take the human race out of fellowship with God and each other and bring about its ultimate destruction. It was this mixing of spiritual beings through sexual relationships that caused the initial breakdown of the uniqueness of Adam's race and brought about the flood as a corrective measure (see Gen. 6:2-13). Ultimately, the *"sexually immoral... will be in the fiery lake of burning sulfur"* (Rev. 21:8 NIV).

Bisexuality

This is just a variant form of fornication. It indicates a deeper depravity of the flesh.

Pornography

Pornography is a visual form of fantasy. Because of the increase in isolation in today's society, pornography has replaced relationships as the chief form of interaction. Unfortunately, it is addictive, as ever-increasing levels of endorphins are required to achieve the same level of pleasure. This requires more graphically erotic and violent images to ramp up the chemicals needed to get a "high."

The statistics are truly staggering. According to compiled numbers from respected news and research organizations, every second, $3,075.64 is being spent on pornography. Every second, 28,258 Internet users are viewing pornography. In that same second, 372 Internet users are typing adult search terms into search engines. Every 39 minutes, a new pornographic video is being created in the U.S.

It's big business. The pornography industry has larger revenues than Microsoft, Google, Amazon, eBay, Yahoo, Apple, and Netflix combined. Worldwide pornography revenues of 2006 ballooned to $97.06 billion.[3] Eventually the images are not enough, and various sexual outlets are employed to vent this built-up lust.

Masturbation

Masturbation has engendered much discussion about its validity as a sexual expression. Masturbation is designed to achieve orgasm without sexual intercourse. As such, it is an expression of lust and not love. Also, masturbation does not occur in a vacuum. It requires mental and/or physical stimulation. Stored images we have seen or created are used to stimulate us physically to achieve orgasm. This is another outlet for our fantasies and is just as addictive, invariably resulting in the use of pornography.

I (Ken) thought that my masturbation addiction would end when I got married; it didn't. That was because masturbation isn't another expression of love, but rather an expression of lust. The love did not replace the lust because the lust was fueled by selfishness, not unity. It wasn't until I revealed my sin to Jeanne and repented of it that I got free.

If both partners are locked into lust, their sexual union is often nothing more than mutual masturbation. They are interested in self-gratification rather than in gratifying their partner.

Homosexuality

Homosexuality is an aberration of the intimate sexual relationship that God designed for a man and a woman. It affects the mental, emotional, and physical makeup of an individual. Like all sin, homosexuality can be learned or passed down generational lines.

I (Ken) was born a thief. I would take things that I wanted. Because I had an active conscience, I would not steal from people. Because my conscience was not that active, I would steal from institutions. But I could not use the fact that I was born that way as an excuse for my actions, only as a reason. I had to repent of my sin and "...*through the power of the [Holy] Spirit...[habitually] put...to death (making extinct, deadening) the [evil] deeds prompted by the body*" (Rom. 8:13 AMP). It is the same with everything the Bible calls a sin: we must repent and turn from it.

The natural bent in homosexuals arise when they set up their own feelings and thoughts as objects of worship, bowing to them rather than submitting to God.

> *For this reason God gave them over and abandoned them to vile affections and degrading passions. For their women exchanged their natural function for an unnatural and abnormal one, and the men also turned from natural relations with women and were set ablaze (burning out, consumed) with lust for one another—men committing shameful acts with men and suffering in their own bodies and personalities the inevitable consequences and penalty of their wrongdoing and going astray, which was [their] fitting retribution* (Romans 1:26-27 AMP).

Homosexuality has such a strong demonic force driving it because homosexuals give themselves corporately to it. Demonic powers derive their authority from tapping into the legitimate authority of those who submit to them.

> *Do you not know that to whom you present yourselves slaves to obey, you are that one's slaves whom you obey, whether of sin leading to death, or of obedience leading to righteousness?* (Romans 6:16 NKJV)

The power of a homosexual arch-type demon comes from the power of unity. Most other sins are done individually and in secret: my anger is my anger; your anger is your anger. We don't celebrate an "Anger Pride Day" or a "Pride, Pride Day" or "Masturbation Pride Day." My sin is not corporate; it is individual.

Any demonic influence we come under is individual. Corporateness in sin gives the enemy more power.

The Jews allowed a corporate anti-Semitic spirit access when they corporately took the responsibility for Jesus' death. They cried, *"His blood be on us, and on our children"* (Matt. 27:25). Homosexuals have also brought on themselves a *"strong delusion, that they should believe a lie...who believed not the truth, but had pleasure in unrighteousness"* (2 Thess. 2:11-12).

If you are dealing with homosexuality, you need to understand that you are not just dealing with your individual sin or a minor demonic entity. You are dealing with a massive demonic structure and an arch-demon who draws from the power of the entire homosexual community. Without proper covering and repentance, many have foolishly attacked this structure, to their own hurt. You want and need love and a real community to counter the false love and community if you are to reach and maintain freedom. *"Lord, we pray no condemnation."* Do not allow yourself to get isolated, or you will not survive the shift to a straight world. You have lived in a world of lust; we come in the opposite spirit, open our arms to you, and welcome you into a Kingdom of true love.

Bestiality

You shall not *"lie with any beast and defile yourself with it; neither shall any woman yield herself to a beast to lie with it; it is confusion, perversion, and degradedly carnal"* (Lev. 18:23 AMP).

Those who do this have lost contact with reality and allowed a perverse spirit to deceive them. God wants you to know that He loves you and wants to clean off all the degrading lies that have trapped you in this low self-image.

Incest

God has ordained the family as the safe haven in which children may grow and flourish surrounded by love. Incest breaks this covering and brings confusion. Incest is the most common form of child abuse, amounting to 43 percent of the cases.[4] Victims are often reluctant to report the abuse for fear of family breakup and denial that there is anything wrong with the behavior that they have encountered. Many are convinced by the perpetrator that incest is just a "learning experience" that happens in every family.

Some victims even encounter biochemically-induced amnesia caused by the trauma. Incest can have serious long-term effects. In one study, 60 percent of women and 25 percent of men who had been abused through incest had eating disorders. Eighty percent of the women and all of the men had sexual problems later in life. Two-thirds of the women avoided doctors and dentists as an examination terrified them. They also suffered from guilt, shame, low self-esteem, depression, and self-destructive behaviors, such as substance abuse and prostitution.[5]

Transvestitism

The term *transvestite* refers to the habit of cross-dressing. Those caught in this form of sexual confusion use dressing as the outward symbol of internal psychological problems.[6] The Bible is clear that a *"woman shall not wear anything that pertains to a man, nor shall a man put on a woman's garment, for all who do so are an abomination to the Lord"* (Deut. 22:5 NKJV).

We cannot allow our feelings or our fetishes to overrule the Word. God will heal all the lies we receive if we let Him.

Pedophilia

Pedophilia is considered a mental disease for which, at present, there is no cure. Pedophiles are usually insecure in an adult relationship and thus seek children to avoid the conflicts. Children are confused by their abuse and only later in life are able to come to grips with their feelings.[7] As many as one-third of abused children become pedophiles in later life.[8]

It is a family-and-friends sickness with 89 percent of child sexual assault cases involving persons known to the child, such as a caretaker or family acquaintance. The typical offender is male, begins molesting by age 15, engages in a variety of deviant behavior, and molests an average of 117 youngsters, most of whom do not report the offence. It becomes addictive, with more than half of all convicted sex offenders being sent back to prison within a year. Within two years, 77.9 percent are back, according to the California Department of Corrections.[9]

Telesex/Internetsex (Cybersex)

A lack of intimacy is at the root of Telesex and Internetsex. It is interactive pornography and is very addictive.

Sex With Demons

The two demons that attack sexually at night are *incubus* (the male form) and *succubus* (the female form). The Latin name for nightmare is *incubo* (to lie upon). These familiar spirits mask themselves as just figments of our imagination as we sleep. There is usually a feeling of paralysis or of a weight pressing down on the person. Though these seem like only dreams, they are actual demonic sexual interference. As with all demonic attacks, we must *"submit to God. Resist the devil and he will flee from you"* (James 4:7 NKJV).

Rape

Rape is a traumatic sexual assault that often produces feelings of guilt, confusion, and self-recrimination for the victim. The trauma comes because your will and your body have been violated. A violent rape often allows an entrance for demonic harassment. If you have been a victim, you should break off any soul and spirit ties to your attacker. Forgiveness is necessary to be released from the control that the attacker exerted and any connection to a Jezebel (control) spirit. God will even restore a theft of your virginity (see Exod. 22:7).

Lust

Lust wants to get; love desires to give. Lust is a spirit that connects to us and infects us. It is more than just a sexual spirit; it is connected with unrestrained desires or cravings.

> *Every man is tempted, when he is drawn away of his own lust, and enticed. Then when lust hath conceived, it bringeth forth sin: and sin, when it is finished, bringeth forth death* (James 1:14-15).

I (Ken) recall the story told by a man who was a homosexual. He used his lust to fulfill his sexual desires. One day he was in a jewelry store and saw a ring that he admired. He later testified, "I don't know what came over me, but I had to have that ring, and I stole it." When I heard that story, I knew immediately what came over him: a lust spirit. Lust is always out to get. Though this man was not naturally a thief, the spirit of lust that he had given free reign to sexually took that authority, and manifested itself differently in this theft.

We think we use spirits, but they are the ones that use us. This man could easily have afforded the ring, but the pressure from that spirit of lust demanded that he take it. That one theft ruined his career. Lust produces inordinate desires within us that do not submit to simple discipline. James describes the battle that lust causes to rage within us. He says,

> *Where do wars and fights come from among you? Do they not come from your desires for pleasure that war in your members? You lust and do not have. You murder and covet and cannot obtain. You fight and war* (James 4:1-2 NKJV).

Feel the driving passions he is describing. That is why lust is so hard to control. It is the chief formulator of *"the corruption that is in the world"* (2 Pet. 1:4).

> *For all that is in the world, the lust of the flesh and the lust of the eyes and the boastful pride of life, is not from the Father, but is from the world. The world is passing away, and also its lusts; but the one who does the will of God lives forever* (1 John 2:16-17 NASB).

Prostitution

Prostitution has been a sexual trap since early times and is not fading away. It springs from the dual lusts of the flesh: sex and money. Women are often trapped into a life of prostitution through financial distress. Some use prostitution as a means to finance a drug habit. More often, a pimp induces the drug habit that ensnares them.

Seventy-nine percent of human trafficking is for sexual exploitation. The victims of sexual exploitation are predominantly women and girls. It may come as a surprise, but in one-third of the countries that provided information on the gender of the traffickers, women made up the largest proportion of those traffickers. In Central Asia and Eastern Europe, women make up more than 60 percent of those convicted of trafficking.[10]

This is not as foreign to the Church as one may think. We were ministering a "Curses to Blessings" seminar at another church when I (Ken) got to this point with a couple in their late 40s. They had been Christians for a few years but were diamonds in the rough at this time. The wife commented that they should repent of this curse. I asked if the husband had used prostitutes in the past. "Oh no," the wife piped up. "I prostitute myself when we get short of money," she nonchalantly replied. We got them to repent and cleaned off all the connections. A few years later I met them again and almost didn't recognize them; they had so much life. With the weight of their sins gone, they looked ten years younger. There is a high cost to low living.

Withholding of Sex Within Marriage

God designed marriage so that the wife would be *"a helper meet (suitable, adapted, complementary) for him"* (Gen. 2:18 AMP). They were to cleave to each other and *"be one flesh"* (Gen. 2:24): to be intimate. That intimacy was not an option; it was to be the glue in the relationship. In fact,

> *...the wife does not have authority over her own body, but the husband does. And likewise the husband does not have authority over his own body, but the wife does* (1 Corinthians 7:4 NKJV).

The lie the world tells is that "I have control over my own body." The Word says that we should

> ...*not refuse and deprive and defraud each other [of your due marital rights], except perhaps by mutual consent for a time, so that you may devote yourselves unhindered to prayer. But afterwards resume marital relations, lest Satan tempt you [to sin] through your lack of restraint of sexual desire* (1 Corinthians 7:5 AMP).

I am designed to fulfill my wife, and she is designed to fulfill me. If one of us refuses to have sex, then we are defrauding the other.

We learned early that even in marriage we needed to operate in faith; that is, to have a word from God, believe it, and declare it operational in our lives. The word God gave us was "*Be ye angry, and sin not: let not the sun go down upon your wrath*" (Eph. 4:26). We had to stay up many nights till two or three in the morning, but we never let an argument go into the next day. That way we never gave "*place to the devil*" (Eph. 4:27), and we never used sex as a manipulation tool.

Some use withholding for revenge and retaliation, which is an ungodly use of the authority we have over our bodies. It cheapens the sexual union into a form of prostitution where you must pay for sex by giving me something I want. I (Jeanne) talked to a lady who was nonchalant about the fact that she would not have sex with her husband unless he did certain household chores for her. She felt justified in using sex as a tool of manipulation.

Sex in marriage was to be the ultimate form of intimacy where we actually make love, not just function in lust. God designed our brains to receive certain hormones that increase bonding with our partners. These hormones, oxytocin and vasopressin, are released during intercourse, which increase pleasure and have lasting physical benefits. The more sex, the more bonding. We have found in our counseling that the frequency of sexual intercourse is directly relational to the health of the relationship.

Oxytocin causes the female to cuddle and show affection toward her mate, while vasopressin causes the male to protect, guard, and help in the care of offspring. Though these hormones are released whenever mating occurs, they only are absorbed if the proper receptors and neuron pathways are present in the brain.

These receptor and pathways are developed first in young children through nursing and later through affectionate touch. A "love" circuitry or neuro-pathway funnels these hormones, which promote physical, emotional, and psychological health. These pathways are formed by behaviors that promote exclusivity and intimacy of sexual bonds: monogamy.[11]

The "lust" channels are triggered by attraction and desire outside of exclu-sive intimate relations. They trigger adrenaline, dopamine, and norepinephrine, which are the passion chemicals. These chemicals are grating on the physical, emotional, and psychological dimensions of a person. The body buffers the release of these chemicals, requiring an increased presence to produce the same feelings. Oxytocin and vasopressin actually block the release of the lust chemi-cals. Though passion may fade, attachment grows.[12]

When the bonds of intimacy are broken through abandonment or divorce, the loss of the feedback systems that produced the bonding chemicals creates feelings of depression. Withholding can have the same effect, and the pain of the loss of intimacy will weaken the resolve to try one more time.

Lack of sex through withholding is a strong indicator of spiritual rebellion. We are not loving God and being intimate with Him if we are not loving and being intimate with our spouse. The Bible says that *"if we don't love people we can see, how can we love God, whom we cannot see?"* (1 John 4:20 NLT).

Marriage is a covenant, not a contract. We don't enter it to get, but to give. Sex is not designed to be a commodity to barter with. It is an expression of our intimacy for one another and part of our marriage covenant, which we give to please our partner.

Belief That Sex Is Dirty Within Marriage

Many of our upbringings warned us against sex in general. It was consid-ered dirty and evil by our parents. Society has given a different message—that any sex is good if it feels good. Both ends of the spectrum are false. God uses marriage to be a role-play of the relationship between Jesus and the Church (see Eph. 5:23-32). He declares that *"marriage is honorable in all, and the bed undefiled"* (Heb. 13:4).

Prayer:

Lord, I acknowledge the sin of "Sexual Perversion" in all its forms. I stand before You for myself and in proxy on behalf of the generations before me, on both my mother and father's side. We ask forgiveness for our sin of "Sexual Perversion," specifically for sexual perversion through _____. I ask forgiveness back to the 4th generation, the 3rd, the 2nd, and for myself.

*On the basis of the authority gained through receiving forgiveness, **I now break this curse** off of my children and me.*

Lord, make me pure sexually. Cleanse me from all sexual defilement. Realign my sexual boundaries to enjoy sex within marriage.

Lord, I ask you to spiritually cleanse my reproductive organs from any defilement.

Lord, realign my sexuality that I might use this gift in Your preordained way.

Lord, cleanse my mind from all the unholy sexual images that I have stored up.

Lord, as a single, help me to resist temptations and keep my virginity for my mate.

Some demonic spirits associated with sexual perversion that we may need to deal with include the following:

- Pornography
- Lust

- Adultery

- Unclean Spirits

- Fantasy

- Perversion

- Homosexual Spirits

- Incestuous Spirits

- Incubus and Succubus

- Guilt, Shame, and Condemnation

These last three spirits follow sexual sins like relatives who move in when the sexual spirits moved in. Even when the sexual spirits are cast out, these will remain if not dealt with. The person will be drawn back into sex for comfort from the guilt, shame, and condemnation.

Lord, forgive me for allowing guilt, shame, and condemnation to affect me. I now wrap you all up together and command you out of my life in Jesus' name.

Prophetic Acts:

- List all sexual contacts on a sheet of paper.

- Ask God to forgive you and to help you forget all these people.

- Break all soul and spiritual ties to these people.

- Then tear up the list as a prophetic act that connections are severed.

- Pray a cleansing over your reproductive organs.

- Realign your sexuality to the order that God intended.

- Cleanse the mind from memories.

Chapter 15

SLAYING YOUR NEIGHBOR

Cursed is he who slays his neighbor secretly
(Deuteronomy 27:24 AMP).

This curse has been expanded to include all methods of slaying or destroying people's lives—through thoughts, words, or deeds. Our words are containers of power, for *"death and life are in the power of the tongue, and they who indulge in it shall eat the fruit of it [for death or life]"* (Prov. 18:21 AMP).

Jesus confirmed that

> *...the mouth speaks out of that which fills the heart. The good man brings out of his good treasure what is good; and the evil man brings out of his evil treasure what is evil. But I tell you that every careless word that people speak, they shall give an accounting for it in the day of judgment. For by your words you will be justified, and by your words you will be condemned* (Matthew 12:34-37 NASB).

We may not have shot someone or stuck a knife into him or her, but we have all thought or spoken negative things about people. We have all given voice to some of those destructive thoughts. We may have even done some harmful deeds out of our anger. It doesn't matter which path we took; the verdict is the same: we are guilty of murder (see Matt. 5:21-22). God judges *"righteously, testing the mind and the heart"* (Jer. 11:20 NKJV). We may be able to stifle some of our words and actions, but God is not interested in our performance; He is interested in us, and in the health of our hearts. Here are some ways in which we slay our neighbors.

Slander and Gossip

Slander and gossip are cutting knives that can destroy a reputation. Paul said to tighten *"the belt of truth around your loins"* (Eph. 6:14 AMP). We must not spread rumors; rather *"speak...the truth in love"* (Eph. 4:15), if we are to *"speak as the oracles of God"* (1 Pet. 4:11). God does not want *"out of the same mouth* [to proceed both] *blessing and cursing"* (James 3:10 NKJV). He wants you to *"bless, and curse not"* (Rom. 12:14). If we want to be used of God, we must speak like God: *"A perverse man spreads strife, and a slanderer separates intimate friends"* (Prov. 16:28 NASB).

> *...Let none of you think or imagine or devise evil or injury in your hearts against his neighbor, and love no false oath, for all these things I hate, says the Lord...The fast*[s]*...shall be to the house of Judah times of joy and gladness and cheerful, appointed seasons; therefore [in order that this may happen to you, as the condition of fulfilling the promise] love truth and peace* (Zechariah 8:17-19 AMP).

Slander and gossip are usually based on rumors, and all rumors are lies. I (Ken) was hired as a maintenance mechanic to work on mining equipment. The superintendent personally asked me to take this job, as they needed someone with experience rigging heavy gears and shafts. When I took the job, rumors immediately circulated that I was not qualified and the job should have gone to someone already working at the mine. Until a meeting was called to deal with this issue, I was ostracized and harassed.

I finally got a chance to share the truth and prove the rumors to be lies. I had built most of the equipment at the mine and had both a university education and a journeyman ironworker's certificate. The truth put a stop to the harassment and ended the hard feelings. All lies have a demonic source, satan, who *"is a liar, and the father of it"* (John 8:44).

Slander and gossip always bring contention and strife because they are expressions of our wicked pride.

To the wicked God says: "...You give your mouth to evil, and your tongue frames deceit. You sit and speak against your brother, you slander your own mother's son...I will rebuke you" (Psalm 50:16; 19-21 NKJV).

God desires to have us walk in unity with Him and each other. He calls into His presence the one *"who does not slander with his tongue, nor does evil to his neighbor, nor takes up a reproach against his friend"* (Ps. 15:3 NASB). God will answer our prayers if we take away *"the pointing of the finger and speaking wickedness"* (Isa. 58:9 NASB).

Maligning

Malign comes from an Old English root meaning to attack.[1] It means we make evil, harmful, and often untrue statements about people. Our intention is to wound and hurt them by casting doubt on their character or their intentions. Many bitter political campaigns resort to "mudslinging" and speaking innuendoes to malign an opponent's name or cause.

Hatred

Hatred is a strong loathing for another person. We may despise them so much that we have wished them dead.

Anger

Anger is a strong emotion, and in itself is not a sin. However, our acceptance of that feeling and the resulting actions move us into the realm of sin. Paul says, *"'Be angry, and do not sin'...nor give place to the devil"* (Eph. 4:26-27 NKJV). Jesus also tied our anger to murder. He said,

> *It was said to those of old, "You shall not murder, and whoever murders will be in danger of the judgment." But I say to you that*

whoever is angry with his brother without a cause shall be in danger of the judgment (Matthew 5:21-22 NKJV).

Jacob was so upset at Simeon and Levi's outburst of anger that he dissociated himself from their actions. He said,

May I never be a party to their plans. For in their anger they murdered men, and they crippled oxen just for sport. A curse on their anger, for it is fierce; a curse on their wrath, for it is cruel (Genesis 49:6-7 NLT).

I (Ken) was always angry—not that I walked around with a chip on my shoulder, but I always flared up when things didn't go my way. I flared up when I made a mistake. I flared up when something broke. I yelled at cars, tools, and people. I could be charming for a few hours, but eventually the anger came out. I was taught that anger is the only emotion men are allowed to express.

I couldn't cry, feel empathy, or really love; it wasn't manly. Jeanne was always on pins and needles wondering whether I would be in a good mood. I couldn't watch sports without turning ugly. She couldn't cheer right, comment correctly, or even bless me during a game without receiving my wrath. If we won, she couldn't talk to me for an hour. If we lost, I would stomp around for three hours. My anger continually wounded her until I repented and got healed. Jeanne's love has healed me of my emotional wounds so that now I can cry, express disappointment, or fear without getting angry. Anger is a destructive curse that is taught by example in many families. We need to be healed and repent of using anger to protect ourselves.

Speaking Judgments

When we judge, we walk in pride. We have our opinion about how things should be and how they should be done. We decide what is right. However, *"in whatever you judge another you condemn yourself; for you who judge practice the same things"* (Rom. 2:1 NKJV). I (Ken) used to argue with God, "I don't do those things I judge. I hate those things." Some time later God showed me how judgments work and why they connect me to the things and people I judge.

A judgment operates as a law. A law is a principle that works in every situation. Gravity operates under a specific law. We can ignore gravity, refuse to believe in gravity, or attempt to defy gravity, but we will function in that way to our own hurt. If I climb to the top of a high tower and presumptuously jump off, I will enact the law of gravity. Halfway down, I may decide that I have made a grave mistake and ask God to forgive me. He will forgive me, but that will not stop the law of gravity. I can repent all I want, but that will not stop the law of gravity from hurtling me to the ground. A judgment is like that; it operates all the time, and no matter how much we repent or ask forgiveness, it will still operate. But *"Jesus said, For judgment I am come into this world..."* (John 9:39). He alone is able to *"bear the sins..."* (Heb. 9:28). A judgment operates under two fixed laws: the law of sowing and reaping, and the law of increase. These are the same laws that every farmer depends upon to grow his crops. The law of sowing and reaping dictates that if a farmer plants wheat, he gets wheat; if he plants corn, he gets corn; if he plants acorns, he gets oaks. The law of increase dictates that if he plants 2-3 bushels of grain per acre, he will harvest 30, 60, or 100 bushels per acre. Time does not heal a judgment; it only guarantees that it will produce fruit.

The judgments we make against others are like seeds. They contain the ability to reproduce and over time to increase. We sow them against people or situations and will reap them in similar people and situations. If I sow a judgment against my mother, who was the primary woman in my life, I will likely reap it in my wife, who is the new primary woman in my life. Depending on the judgment and the circumstances, judgments may come to fruit in a year or two or a decade or two.

I (Ken) found myself being irritated over some of the small things my wife would do or say. The big things, like her smashing the car, didn't upset me. I went to God to find the seed that had spawned this root and discovered a judgment.

My mother is a brilliant woman who has always scored well on a Mensa test but centered her conversations on people and past events. These were trivial things in my mind since I was not a people person. I remember a judgment coming into my head that she "majors in the minors." Thirty years later, I started to reap that judgment in my wife.

Once that revelation became apparent, I repented and dealt with my accusation against my mother, as a judgment. In a very short time, my irritation with Jeanne's idiosyncrasies disappeared. My judgment had made life miserable for her, and nothing she or I did seemed to make any difference until it was properly dealt with. Once a law is operating, nothing we do can stop it. You cannot break one of God's laws, only confirm them. Jesus came not *"to destroy the law...but to fulfill"* it (Matt. 5:17). We can't stop the consequences, but the Cross can, so that we will not be destroyed under the judgment of it.

Paul encountered a law at work in him that he was helpless to stop; it was the law of sin. He said, *"I see another law in my members...bringing me into captivity to the law of sin...Who shall deliver me from the body of this death? I thank God through Jesus Christ"* (Rom. 7:23-25). Jesus is the answer to every law that is set in motion to destroy us. He said, *"Think not that I am come to destroy the law...I am not come to destroy, but to fulfill"* (Matt. 5:17). We cannot destroy a judgment once it has been instituted, only Jesus can, for *"whatever a man sows, that he will also reap"* (Gal. 6:7 NKJV). That is why we need to understand judgments in order to remove their destructive effects in our lives and those around us.

How to Deal With a Judgment

- Repent of believing the lie that fostered the judgment in the first place (this usually requires some revelation). The lie is the connotation that we assigned to the events; the truth is God's interpretation. Forgive anyone connected whom you have not forgiven.

- Disavow and break off the words (spoken or thought) connected with this judgment.

- Put the cross between what you have been sowing and the reaping of it. Ask Jesus to reap or bear the consequences of the judgment in His body, thus fulfilling the requirements of the law that we instituted.

- Ask God to put to death all the mindsets, neuron pathways, thought patterns, structures, and strongholds in our minds that facilitated this judgment.

- Ask God to give you a new heart to believe the truth about the situation and the best about the person against whom you made the judgment. The truth is the way God sees the people and situation. It will usually be the opposite of what we judged. We need to declare thing like, "I believe that no one meant to hurt me; I believe that You meant this for my good."

Judgments are often generalizations of specific events or extrapolations of an isolated incident. Words like *always* and *never* are usually involved in a judgment. Judgments destroy people and relationships, leaving no avenue for reconciliation. They allow us to justify murdering our friends, families, and neighbors without a cause or cure.

Judgments are in reality curses that release demonic force against our intended victims. Because they grow over time (law of increase), they distort every event out of proportion to the original situation and destroy our discernment. Jesus said,

> *Why worry about a speck in your friend's eye when you have a log in your own? How can you think of saying to your friend, "Let me help you get rid of that speck in your eye," when you can't see past the log in your own eye? Hypocrite! First get rid of the log in your own eye, then perhaps you will see well enough to deal with the speck in your friend's eye* (Matthew 7:3-5 NLT).

We think we see, but really we can't see past our judgments. Repent first; see clearly later—not to judge, but to help.

Racism

Racism is the prejudgment of a group based on assumptions or the limited observation of an individual. Racism is not based on facts but on prejudices that cannot be substantiated. We may even be OK with the individuals whom we know and still hate their race. Racism is illogical ethnic hatred usually based on hearsay and not experience. Even when we have had bad encounters, painting a whole people with the same brush is illogical. We know that no narrow band of behavior could be applied to our own nationality, yet it seems logical to apply it to another people group.

That everyone of a certain ethnic group looks the same to us only means that we do not know them well enough to see the individual differences. It is the same with personalities or actions. Our lack of familiarity makes all their actions look similar. People are not like the Borg (characters from the Star Trek series); they are individuals. Every nationality has its shame and its glory. To lump them all together lessens them as individuals and causes us to see them as less than human. At that point, we do not have to treat them as humans and can justify our suspicions and hatred.

Racism stems from our fear of anything different. God loves all His children: every race, color, tribe, and tongue. If we are in Him, we are all brothers and sisters—and persons to love, not fear.

Murder

Actual murders needs to be repented of to remove the blood off the family line, as many of our grandfathers, fathers, and uncles went to war. War often becomes an excuse to do horrific things that would never be considered in another setting. A mob reaction can motivate many atrocities. Mobs get their momentum from our yielding individual authority to the group rather than using one's conscience to make decisions. All that is necessary for the triumph of evil is for good men to do nothing.[2]

Gender Prejudice

Gender prejudice is a learned behavior usually derived from bad experiences or from the prejudices of an influential role model. If unchecked, it will attract a man-hating or a woman-hating spirit. A series of judgments may have initiated the fear or hatred.

Revenge and Retaliation

Revenge and retaliation derive from the spirit of unforgiveness. It is unforgiveness with a kicker. Two wrongs don't make a right no matter what it feels like. God gave me (Ken) a dream last year about retaliation. In the dream I was playing hockey. I had the puck on my stick and was skating down the boards when an opponent swung his stick and slashed me across the back of the legs. I went down in a heap, but the referee didn't see the infraction. I was furious and got up swinging my stick at the culprit. The referee saw my infraction and gave me a penalty.

I asked God what the dream meant, and He said, "Retaliation is worse than the original infraction and will be penalized this year." The original situation that hurt you may have been accidental or originated in an emotional moment. But revenge and retaliation are evil, intentional acts of vengeance. *"Vengeance is Mine; I will repay, saith the Lord"* (Rom. 12:19).

We once witnessed an altercation that erupted into retaliation. A woman driving a flatbed truck was in the front of a line of traffic, waiting for a light to change. All of a sudden, the man in the car behind her jumped out and ran up to her window. He was yelling and waving his hands as an argument erupted. She tried to roll up her window, to protect herself, but he grabbed it and tried to tear it off. She continued to crank up the window, squeezing his fingers. He jerked his hands out, but this only further enraged him. He started to kick the truck door and was swearing loudly.

This all happened in a few seconds, and we had no idea what set off the ruckus. I (Ken) was about to get out of our car to intervene when the woman swung into action. She revved up her motor and dropped the gearshift into reverse and rammed this guy's car. The truck deck caught the top of the radiator, destroyed the grill, and folded up the hood. She then smoked the tires as she sped away from the steaming car. The enraged guy stood there flapping his arms in unbelief. Road rage and retaliation don't make for peaceful solutions.

We don't overcome evil with evil. Our job is to *"overcome evil with good"* (Rom. 12:21). Jesus told us to *"love your enemies, bless them that curse you, do good to them that hate you, and pray for them which despitefully use you, and persecute you"* (Matt. 5:44). Revenge and retaliation come from an inability to forgive. They become a self-defense mechanism that God wants to dismantle. Isaiah said that *"the glory of the Lord will be your rear guard"* (Isa. 58:8 NASB). If we know that God has our back, we won't have to protect ourselves by hurting others. Some demonic spirits we may need to deal with include the following:

- Anger
- Fear
- Spirit of Haman (anti-Semitic spirit) (Esther 3:10)[3]
- Racism
- Gossip and Slander
- Man-Hating or Woman-Hating Spirit
- Lying Spirit
- Jezebel Spirit

Prayer:

Lord, I acknowledge the sin of "Slaying My Neighbor Secretly" in all its forms. I stand before You for myself and in proxy on behalf of the generations before me, on both my mother and father's side. We ask forgiveness for our sin of "Slaying My Neighbor," specifically for slaying through:

- Actual murder
- Thoughts of murder

- Hatred and anger

- Revenge and retaliation

- Slander, gossip, and maligning

- Racism

- Gender prejudice

Or for _____. I ask forgiveness back to the 4th generation, the 3rd, the 2nd, and for myself.

Forgive us for creating widows and orphans during wars.

*On the basis of the authority gained through receiving forgiveness, **I now break this curse** off of my children and me.*

Lord, I pray You cause me to quickly forgive and love those who have hurt me. I pray that I would not repay evil with evil, rather with good. Lord, give me the gift of love and Your love for others. I pray that I would not fear what I don't understand, but lean on You. Our words produce life or death; help us to always speak life.

Chapter 16

SLAYING AN INNOCENT

Cursed is he who accepts a bribe to strike down an innocent person
(Deuteronomy 27:25 NASB).

I saiah warned Israel that

...your hands are covered with the blood of your innocent victims. Wash yourselves and be clean! Let me no longer see your evil deeds. Give up your wicked ways. Learn to do good. Seek justice. Help the oppressed. Defend the orphan. Fight for the rights of widows. "Come now, let us argue this out," says the Lord. "No matter how deep the stain of your sins, I can remove it. I can make you as clean as freshly fallen snow. Even if you are stained as red as crimson, I can make you as white as wool. If you will only obey me and let me help you, then you will have plenty to eat. But if you keep turning away and refusing to listen, you will be destroyed by your enemies. I, the Lord, have spoken!" (Isaiah 1:15-20 NLT)

This curse comes into effect when some kind of reward or benefit is derived for injuring an innocent person. Jesus warned us against unjustly seeking profit, saying, *"Ye cannot serve God and mammon"* (Luke 16:13), which is gain.[1] This ungodly propensity manifests itself in the following ways.

Cliques

As social creatures, we tend to gather in narrow, exclusive groups, depending on our views or interests. Membership in these groups becomes a status symbol and thus highly prized. Very early our response to these cliques will reveal our value system.

Suppose we are playing with a friend at school when another group of kids invites us to play with them. The one stipulation is that our friend cannot join them. Decision time! Are we willing to abandon our friend and hurt his or her feelings so that we get to be a part of the "in crowd"? Are we willing to suffer rejection if we insist that our friend be included? Today, that "in crowd" has shifted from the playground to the school, the job, the church, and the club where we still get a benefit from excluding someone.

Jesus challenged us concerning our exclusive commitment to Him. He said,

> *Blessed are you when men hate you, and when they exclude you, and revile you, and cast out your name as evil, for the Son of Man's sake. Rejoice in that day and leap for joy! For indeed your reward is great in heaven, for in like manner their fathers did to the prophets* (Luke 6:22-23 NKJV).

We cannot let our desire to be accepted by the world's clubs cause us to exclude Jesus. For *"he who denies Me before men will be denied before the angels of God"* (Luke 12:9 NASB).

Peer Pressure

Peer pressure causes us to do things that would ordinarily violate our conscience. Mob mentality allows the group to be our guide rather than our own values.

Gangs

About 20,000 violent street gangs, motorcycle gangs, and prison gangs with approximately one million members are criminally active in the U.S. today. Many are sophisticated and well organized; all use violence to control neighborhoods and boost their illegal money-making activities, which include drug trafficking, robbery, theft, fraud, extortion, prostitution rings, and gun trafficking.[2] Some gangs even require you to murder before you can join them.

Bigotry

Bigotry can be a form of racism but is broader in its definition in that it can exclude or subdue any group. Status based on race, class, wealth, or social standing can erect barriers that devalue and subordinate the lower strata. The group with the most power will put up walls to keep the other groups out of the realms that would benefit them.

Apartheid in South Africa, segregation in the United States, the caste system in India, and the royalty/commoners system in Great Britain are all examples of bigotry. In Canada, the Chinese were not allowed to vote or work in any professional positions such as doctors, lawyers, and accountants until 1947, even though they had fought in WWII.[3] These same structures are layered throughout our societies to exclude the many from the privileges of the few. The exclusion of women from most of the realms of power in the world and the Church is a destructive barrier, active in society today.

Persecution

Persecution is the subversion of one segment of society to the benefit of another. In Germany, the Jews were persecuted and their property seized as they were conveniently blamed for all of Germany's woes following the First World War. More than 200 million people in over 60 nations are being denied their basic human rights for one reason only: they are Christians. The main reason Christians are being persecuted today is the simple fact that Christianity is growing fastest in countries where human rights are being violated or do not exist.[4]

Persecution is not just limited to religious groups; it is rampant in every structure of society where one group can gain an advantage by disenfranchising another. It has been going on since Cain slew Abel because God *"did not accept*

Cain and his gift. This made Cain very angry, and he looked dejected" (Gen. 4:5 NLT). The resulting persecution of his brother brought a curse on Cain (see Gen. 4:11) as it does on all persecutors.

Jeremiah had convinced King Zedekiah to proclaim liberty to all the bond-slaves in Jerusalem as Moses had directed. God was pleased that the leaders had responded, saying, "[You have] *done right in My sight...proclaiming liberty"* (Jer. 34:15). But they relented on their proclamation, and Jeremiah prophesied against them. God said, "[I proclaimed] *liberty...to the sword, to the pestilence, and to the famine....And I will give the men that have transgressed My covenant... into the hand of them that seek their life"* (Jer. 34:17-18;20). That persecution of the bond-slaves was the final drop that tipped the cup of retribution that God was storing up for the rebellion of Judah.

Scapegoats

God set up a system for a scapegoat to bear the sins of Israel (see Lev. 16:10). Aaron was to

> *...confess over it all the iniquities of the sons of Israel and all their transgressions in regard to all their sins; and he shall lay them on the head of the goat and send it away into the wilderness...The goat shall bear on itself all their iniquities to a solitary land* (Leviticus 16:21-22 NASB).

That practice is still used in many settings today. In families or groups there always seems to be someone who gets the blame for everything that happens whether he or she is involved or not.

We just had a prophecy where the prophet discerned that Jeanne and I had been ridiculously blamed by certain people for everything that had happened to them including WWII, the Indonesian tsunami, and Hurricane Katrina. That is an exaggerated case, but the truth is that many of us not only are blamed for, but also *take* the blame for, someone else's sin and mistakes.

Our friend Derrick just went through the "Curses to Blessings" seminar. He related this story:

As my worker was praying, breaking off this curse, I felt a sensation in my body and knew that God was showing me something in the spirit. As I zeroed my spirit in to hear, God started to speak about my role as a father. It became crystal clear that I had taken on guilt because, as a father, I had made many mistakes and had taken the blame for everything that went wrong in my family. I recognized that I had done the same thing to my father, and had, as a child, taken advantage of that weakness for my own advantage.

I was wearing guilt as covering: a form of self-flagellation for the mistakes I had made. After repenting and breaking the curse, Bernice (my wife) and I realized that we had gained more personal freedom and that we had a new release to operate in the church. When we are bound up under any false expectations, the removal of those chains will often bring a freedom in an unrelated area. Christ is willing and able to bear the sins. I knew this, but was stuck under this scapegoat curse and could not let the guilt go.

If you are one of those types of people, you are likely also a burden bearer. Burden bearers are sensitive individuals who feel others' emotional pain. The danger is that they will assign the feelings to themselves and take the blame for the cause of those feelings. All burden bearers are not scapegoats, but most scapegoats are burden bearers.

Jesus is the only one designated to be the scapegoat. He alone can bear our sins; He alone can cleanse our sins. If you are the designated scapegoat, break off that designation. You must reject that label and learn to give those feelings to the Lord to bear.

Abortion

Satan has always tried to kill prophesied deliverers. When it was time for Israel to come out of Egypt, Pharaoh commanded the midwives, *"If it be a son, then ye shall kill him"* (Exod. 1:16) in an attempt to destroy Moses. Herod *"slew all the children that were in Bethlehem"* (Matt. 2:16) in an attempt to destroy Jesus. Now, as Jesus prepares to return, there is a generation of overcomers rising up. For there is a *"generation yet unborn...a people yet to be created shall praise the Lord"* (Ps. 102:18 AMP). Satan is attempting to destroy this generation before they can inflict damage to his kingdom. Abortion is the tool he is using to defile the land with blood and pressure God to abandon us. Abortion may be legal, but it is still immoral: it gives a benefit for slaying an innocent one. It takes away the protection of the most helpless, and casts women, who were created to nurture babies, into the role of murderers. Yet none of us can accuse and say, "I don't know how they could do that." We all do the same things. You may argue and say, "I never had anything to do with an abortion." Abortion is just one fruit of a selfish root, which expresses itself differently in each of us.

Roots of Abortion

1. Most abortions are carried out on babies conceived in lust, not love.

2. Abortions are often carried out for reasons of convenience.

3. Abortions are carried out for reasons of finances.

4. Abortions are carried out from fear of rejection.

5. Abortions are carried out for reasons of timing.

6. Abortions are carried out for physical reasons, many of which are selfish.

7. Abortions are carried out for reasons of immaturity.

8. Abortions are carried out for other selfish reasons.

Each one of us has operated at one time or another in a lustful manner. We have all done what we should not have done for reasons of convenience, for various personal financial considerations, out of the fear of rejection, and when it was not a good time to do what was right. We have all said, "This is my body; I'll do what I want" (eat too much, laze around too much, stay up too late, go somewhere not appropriate, watch or listen to something not glorifying to God). We have all blown it because we were too immature to bear our own responsibilities. We have all been selfish and looked after our own self-interests ahead of another's.

We all know exactly why women had an abortion because we have all done the same thing; we have all sinned in those areas. We don't need to accuse those who have been part of an abortion; we need to heal and forgive them. We need to forgive the doctors and the nurses. We even need to forgive those who profit from selling baby parts as harvested human organs. We need to forgive the lawmakers and ourselves for fearing the wrath of some liberal if we speak out. We need to forgive the liberals who are lost and don't know the heart of God. We must forgive all who pressured a vulnerable, isolated young woman to cast off her baby. We need to pray for our society, which taught couples that career and personal achievement was more important than a baby's life. Most of all we need to forgive and heal the mothers and fathers who lost a child to this demoniacally inspired attack on the next generation of God's children.

We speak especially to the mothers who in their ignorance and weakness lost their babies. God loves you and does not condemn you. Ask and He will forgive you. Picture your child in your mind, wrapping your baby in a cuddly blanket. Hold your baby in your arms, say good-bye, and hand him or her to Jesus. He has received every little one and will keep them safe until you are reunited with them in Heaven. Jesus holds out His hand and places it on your head, softly saying, "Peace, be still. I care for this little one." We speak healing to your guilt and shame.

Hit Men

Someone in your family may have taken out a contract to kill someone. This will bring a curse upon you and your family. Someone may have paid you or a relative to lie in court or on a document so they could get a financial gain.

Being Mean-Spirited

I (Ken) used to be offensive and harsh in order to frighten people away from me so that I could have my own way. No one would confront me because they didn't want the conflict that would arise. This mean-spirited attitude destroyed relationships and hurt many tender people who got in my way. Some people attack others and put them down to feel better about themselves.

David was attacked by Shimei, a man of the family of the house of Saul, as he fled from Absalom.

> *He cursed, "Get out, get out, you man of blood, you base fellow! The Lord has avenged upon you all the blood of the house of Saul...Behold, the calamity is upon you because you are a bloody man!"* (2 Samuel 16:7-8 AMP)

David had never fought Saul and had nothing to do with his death. The attack was simply a release so that Shimei would feel better about his family's loss of the kingdom.

Hostile Takeovers

A hostile takeover is a business move that gains control of a company in order to sell the assets. There is no intention of running the company and keeping the employees working. Such a move is motivated by greed, not the good of the employees.

Stealing of Patents

This constitutes industrial espionage and intellectual theft. Rather than invest in their research and development, a company, or an individual, steals copyrighted material. Even unauthorized copying of movies and songs off the Internet would fall into this curse.

Plagiarism

This is the quoting of words or ideas and claiming them as your own. It is a sluggard's method of appearing more intellectual than he or she really is. Using the ideas with permission is not wrong; claiming that they are yours is.

Political Lies

Henry Kissinger once said, "Corrupt politicians make the other ten percent look bad." John Emerich Acton said, in the same vein, "Power tends to corrupt, absolute power corrupts absolutely."[5] Too many politicians have been willing to promise anything to get elected, misrepresenting themselves, their plans, and other politicians.

Identity Theft

This is the fastest rising form of deception and theft and is very destructive to our lives. It comes in the following forms:

Credit Card Fraud makes up 26% of all identity theft: Credit card fraud can occur when someone acquires your credit card number and uses it to make a purchase. [We just had $3,500 spent on our credit card, in Houston, by someone who got our number. We were never in Texas, and never lost the card or misplaced it. The credit card company was informed of when we were traveling, where we were going, and when we would return, but still failed to stop the fraud.]

Utilities fraud (18%): Utilities are opened using the name of a child or someone who does not live at the residence. Parents desperate for water, gas, and electricity will use their child's clean credit report to be approved for utilities.

Bank fraud (17%): There are many forms of bank fraud, including check theft, changing the amount on a check, and ATM pass code theft.

Employment fraud (12%): Employment fraud occurs when someone without a valid Social Security number borrows someone else's to obtain a job. [This does not include green card violations.]

Loan fraud (5%): Loan fraud occurs when someone applies for a loan in your name. This can occur even if the Social Security number does not match the name exactly.

Government fraud (9%): This type of fraud includes tax, Social Security, and driver license fraud.

Other (13%).[6]

There are over ten million victims in the U.S.A. alone, totaling over $50 billion.[7] This type of theft is not just a loss of property but is a violation of privacy, requiring an average of almost a week's time to clear up the mess. The mean resolution time is at a high of 40 hours per victim in 2006 compared to 28 hours in 2005 and 33 hours in 2003.[8]

Some demonic spirits that may need to be dealt with include the following:

- Jealousy
- Envy
- Greed
- Murder

- Pride
- Lust
- Guilt
- Shame

Prayer:

Lord, I acknowledge the sin of "Slaying an Innocent for a Reward" in all its forms. I stand before You for myself and in proxy on behalf of the generations before me, on both my mother and father's side. We ask forgiveness for our sin of "Slaying for Reward," specifically, for slaying through:

- Cliques
- Persecution
- Bigotry
- Scapegoats
- Abortion
- Hit Men
- Being Mean-Spirited
- Hostile Takeovers
- Stealing Patents
- Plagiarism
- Political Lies
- Identity Theft
- Gangs
- Peer Pressure

Or for _____. I ask forgiveness back to the 4th generation, the 3rd, the 2nd, and for myself.

*On the basis of the authority gained through receiving forgiveness, **I now break this curse** off of me and my children. Lord, I pray that it would be in my heart to rejoice with those who rejoice in their proper reward.*

Chapter 17

NOT AGREEING WITH THE LAW

*Cursed is he who does not confirm the words of this law
by doing them* (Deuteronomy 27:26 NASB).

"*The law is spiritual: but I am carnal*" (Rom. 7:14). That is why, in the flesh, we cannot keep the law: "*The life which I now live in the flesh, I live by the faith of the Son of God, who loved me, and gave Himself for me*" (Gal. 2:20). God said that

> ...*this shall be the covenant that I will make...I will put My law in their inward parts, and write it on their hearts...and they shall teach no more...saying, Know the Lord: for they shall all know Me* (Jeremiah 31:33-34).

The law, which was written in stone, was given on the original day of Pentecost. That day 3,000 people died (see Exod. 32:28). The New Covenant was written on hearts, through the release of the Holy Spirit, on the first Pentecost after Jesus was resurrected. That day 3,000 people were born into the Kingdom (see Acts 2:41).

The "*law was our schoolmaster to bring us unto Christ, that we might be justified by faith*" (Gal. 3:24). Imagine a car with a five speed, standard transmission. You cannot start that car in fifth gear; you will burn out the transmission. You must start it in first gear. Once you reach the maximum speed for first gear, you must shift, or you will burn out the engine. At that point, first gear becomes the biggest hindrance to obtaining highway speed. The law is like that; it is necessary to cause us to recognize sin. But once we see sin in our lives, the law becomes the biggest hindrance to freeing us from sin. We must shift our focus to Christ if we are to gain freedom.

> *For it is not merely hearing the Law [read] that makes one righteous before God, but it is the doers of the Law who will be held guiltless and acquitted and justified* (Romans 2:13 AMP).

We are to become an

> *...epistle of Christ...written not with ink but by the Spirit of the living God, not on tablets of stone but on tablets of flesh, that is, of the heart. God...made us...ministers of the new covenant, not of the letter but of the Spirit; for the letter kills, but the Spirit gives life* (2 Corinthians 3:3-6 NASB).

The following is a list of the many ways in which our actions do not agree with the spirit of the law, which was designed to lead us to Christ.

Those Who Don't Know Jesus

They didn't know Christ, but they were *"a law unto themselves: which shew [showed] the work of the law written in their hearts, their conscience also bearing witness"* (Rom. 2:14-15a). Their own consciences would alternately *"accuse or excuse one another"* (see Rom. 2:15b). We need to repent for those points at which our forefathers would not follow the light that God had given them (see John 1:9), where they called *"evil good, and good evil"* (Isa. 5:20) and tried to convert others to their camp. They may even have known the truth about God but didn't want to give up their lifestyle and didn't want others to go that way either. Jesus said of them, *"You neither enter yourselves, nor do you allow those who are about to go in to do so"* (Matt. 23:13 AMP). They did not want to come under the King, and each *"did that which was right in his own eyes"* (Judg. 21:25). Solomon called them fools (see Prov. 12:15).

Christians Who Are Disobedient to the Word

This includes Christians who are *"carnally minded* [which] *is death… because the carnal mind is enmity against God: for it is not subject to the law of God"* (Rom. 8:6-7).

Those who become legalistic in their approach to God are included as well: *"You who are trying to be justified by law have been alienated from Christ; you have fallen away from grace"* (Gal. 5:4 NIV).

It also constitutes all who are attempting to be justified by the law: *"For whoever keeps the whole law and yet stumbles at just one point is guilty of breaking all of it"* (James 2:10 NIV). The law is like a chain with ten links. You don't have to break all the links to break the chain.

Christians who are living in unforgiveness are likewise disobedient to the Word. Jesus said that *"if you do not forgive men their trespasses, neither will your Father forgive your trespasses"* (Matt. 6:15 NKJV).

Christians Who Don't Believe What God Says

This includes those who walk in doubt and unbelief. Jesus lumped together the

> *…fearful, and unbelieving, and the abominable, and murderers, and whoremongers, and sorcerers, and idolaters, and all liars, shall have their part in the lake which burneth with fire and brimstone: which is the second death* (Revelation 21:8).

Joyce Meyer says that miracles come in *cans*, not in *can'ts*. If you need a miracle, God *can*.

The double minded are part of this category as well. We are exhorted to

> *…ask in faith, nothing wavering. For he that wavereth is like a wave of the sea driven with the wind and tossed. For let not that man think that he shall receive any thing of the Lord. A double minded man is unstable in all his ways* (James 1:6-8).

Those who listen to what satan is saying rather than to what God is saying are also, essentially, unbelievers.

> ...*They did not welcome the Truth but refused to love it that they might be saved. Therefore God sends upon them a misleading influence, a working of error and a strong delusion to make them believe what is false* (2 Thessalonians 2:10-11 AMP).

Finally, there are those who listen to their feelings more than the Word of God. I (Jeanne) was a person whose feelings screamed to be obeyed. Through the training of the Lord, I learned to submit my feelings to the Word of the Lord.

Christians Who Demystify (Deny the Miracles of) the Bible

There are Christians who believe the truths are only stories, parables, and allegories. The denomination that I (Jeanne) grew up in didn't believe in miracles, yet even as a little child I knew that God is the most powerful force in the universe. I always hungered to know the God of the miracles in the Bible. When I met Jesus, I found not only the God of the Bible, but also the God of miracles in my life.

This category also includes those who believe that the Bible is not accurate and is written by human reason. The Bible says of itself that

> ...*no prophecy of the scripture is of any private interpretation. For the prophecy came not in old time by the will of man: but holy men of God spake as they were moved by the Holy Ghost* (2 Peter 1:20-21).

Paul adds that *"all scripture is given by inspiration of God, and is profitable for doctrine, for reproof, for correction, for instruction in righteousness"* (2 Tim. 3:16).

Some Christians won't believe unless they have experienced it themselves. The disciple Thomas refused to believe:

> *Except I shall see in His hands the print of the nails, and put my finger into the print of the nails, and thrust my hand into His side, I will not believe* (John 20:25).

Jesus chided him later when He appeared to all the disciples: *"Thomas, because you have seen Me, you have believed. Blessed are those who have not seen and yet have believed"* (John 20:29 NKJV).

There are also believers who use the Word as a weapon and bring condemnation instead of bringing forgiveness and healing. Jesus said to the woman taken in adultery, *"Neither do I condemn you; go and sin no more"* (John 8:11 NKJV). If we accuse, we are speaking as satan would, and bringing guilt, shame, and condemnation. It is the *"goodness of God that leads you to repentance"* (Rom. 2:4 NKJV). A pastor friend of ours told us that his family used the Word as a weapon of condemnation to control people. They operated in a religious and a self-righteous spirit. The Word given in love, with no condemnation, will draw people just as Jesus (The Word) did.

All of us have unredeemed areas in our minds where we can't agree with the Word. *"God is a Spirit: and they that worship Him must worship Him in spirit and in truth"* (John 4:24).

> *The...natural man does not receive the things of the Spirit of God, for they are foolishness to him; nor can he know them, because they are spiritually discerned* (1 Corinthians 2:14 NKJV).

There are generational strongholds in families, churches, and nations that resist the truths of God.

Some demonic spirits that may need to be dealt with include the following:

- Unbelief
- Rebellion
- Criticism
- Religiosity (doing it right)
- Anti-Christ
- Idolatry

Prayer:

Lord, I acknowledge the sin of "Not Agreeing With the Law" in all its forms. I stand before You for myself and in proxy on behalf of the generations before me, on both my mother and father's side. We ask forgiveness for our sin of "Not Agreeing With the Law," specifically, for not agreeing through:

- Not submitting my life to Jesus

- Being disobedient to the Word

- Not believing what God says

- Denying the miracles in the Word and in my life

Or for _____. I ask forgiveness back to the 4th generation, the 3rd, the 2nd, and for myself.

*On the basis of the authority gained through receiving forgiveness, **I now break this curse** off of my children and me. Lord, grant that I would have faith to walk in Your Word, know Your Word, and obey Your Word. Write Your laws in my heart and give me a willingness to obey in the Spirit. Put life back into the Word and give me a desire for it.*

"Give me understanding; that I may keep your law; yea, I will observe it with my whole heart" (Psalm 119:34 AMP).

Section C

PERSONAL CURSES

Chapter 18

CURSES ON HONORING SELF

Trusting in the Flesh

Whenever we trust in our own strength or that of another, we have entered into idolatry and placed ourselves under a curse. Depending on our own strength is presumptuous.

> Come now, you who say, "Today or tomorrow we will go to such and such a city, and spend a year there and engage in business and make a profit." Yet you do not know [the least thing] about what may happen tomorrow. What is the nature of your life? You are [really] but a wisp of a vapor (a puff of smoke, a mist) that is visible for a little while and then disappears [into thin air]. You ought instead to say, "If the Lord is willing, we shall live and we shall do this or that [thing]" (James 4:13-15 AMP).

I (Ken) was praying with a young man who came forward for ministry during a conference at our church. He was a hockey player and asked for prayer so that he could get along with his coach. He was very young looking, and I thought that he was likely a junior or college hockey player. He shared that every time he was put on the power play he was unable to produce any goals. That was the main problem with his coach.

This curse sprang to mind:

Cursed…is the strong man who trusts in and relies on frail man, making weak [human] flesh his arm…For he shall be like a shrub or a person naked and destitute in the desert; and he shall not see any good come, but shall dwell in the parched places in the wilderness (Jeremiah 17:5-6 AMP).

He was unable to produce when the coach put the heat on and now felt isolated and dry. Together we worked through the curse, first repenting on trusting in his own abilities; then forgiving the coach and repenting for his own rebellion; finally taking his own authority, that he had gained through repentance, and breaking off the curse.

After the service I discovered that this young man was a National Hockey League player. In fact, his team was on television that week. Jeanne and I were interested spectators, watching to see how the removal of the curse would affect his play. That night he scored two goals on the power play. We laughed as we joked, "This stuff really works." That year he had his best season, despite the team's poor showing. He even garnered a new million-dollar contract.

God is to be our only source of strength and hope. We declare with the psalmist,

Whom have I in heaven but You? And there is none upon earth that I desire besides You. My flesh and my heart fail; but God is the strength of my heart and my portion forever…It is good for me to draw near to God; I have put my trust in the Lord God (Psalm 73:25-28 NKJV).

Blessed is the man who believes in, trusts in, and relies on the Lord, and whose hope and confidence the Lord is. For he shall be like a tree planted by the waters that spreads out its roots by the river; and it shall not see and fear when heat comes; but its leaf shall be green. It shall not be anxious and full of care in the year of drought, nor shall it cease yielding fruit (Jeremiah 17:7-9 AMP).

Our own strength is like a cistern that dries up when the heat comes.

God wants us to root ourselves in Him so that our source of blessing will never dry up. Isaac sowed in a year of famine and *"received in the same year an hundredfold: and the Lord blessed him"* (Gen. 26:12). Our blessing does not depend on the economy or the weather but on our relationship with God. God will use circumstances to draw us to Him, but the circumstances won't dictate our results; our relationship will. *"Therefore I am well content with weaknesses, with insults, with distresses, with persecutions, with difficulties, for Christ's sake; for when I am weak, then I am strong"* (2 Cor. 12:10 NASB).

Prayer:

Lord, forgive me for trusting in others or myself rather than in You. Forgive me for taking matters into my own hands and trying to make situations work according to my wisdom. I now break this curse in Jesus' name.

Some demonic spirits that may need to be dealt with include the following:

- Man-pleasing Spirit
- Establishing Our Worth From Works
- Spirit of Mistrust
- Perfectionism
- Performance
- Independence
- Self-righteousness
- Unbelief
- Rebellion

Lord, help me to rely on You alone and not on myself or others. Help me to know You well enough to believe You love me and to trust You, that You have my highest good in Your heart.

Cursing Those Above Us

Do not curse a king, and...do not curse a rich man, for a bird of the heavens will carry the sound and the winged creature will make the matter known (Ecclesiastes 10:20 NASB).

Human nature wants to be on the top and resents anything or anyone that is above us. If we can't overcome them, we curse them. Paul said,

Let every soul be subject to the governing authorities. For there is no authority except from God, and the authorities that exist are appointed by God. Therefore whoever resists the authority resists the ordinance of God, and those who resist will bring judgment on themselves (Romans 13:1-2 NKJV).

If we hate being subject to authority, we are rebelling against God. Our opinion of the authority matters not; our submission does. Paul goes on to say that the authority *"is God's minister to you for good"* (Rom. 13:4). When we speak against what God has ordained, we empower winged creatures (demonic forces) (see Matt. 13:4,19) to bring to pass our words. Our cursing is an indication that we have hard hearts and can't hear what God is saying to us.

Even if those over us are evil, Jesus said, *"Do not resist an evil person. If someone strikes you on the right cheek, turn to him the other also"* (Matt. 5:39 NIV). Difficult authority structures are God's sculptors working to chip off our rough edges. We are urged

...that entreaties and prayers, petitions and thanksgivings, be made on behalf of all men, for kings and all who are in authority, so that we may lead a tranquil and quiet life in all godliness and dignity (1 Timothy 2:1-2 NASB).

When we curse our leadership, we will reap bad leadership. When we pray for them, it opens a door for God to use them to bless us.

Jeremiah told the captives in Babylon to *"seek the peace of the city where I have caused you to be carried away captive, and pray to the Lord for it; for in its peace you will have peace*" (Jer. 29:7 NKJV). Our natural tendency is to fight against anything that comes against us. When a swimmer is caught in a rip tide, the worst thing he can do is to swim against it. He must save his energy and not fight the current. If he can't escape it, ride it out; it will eventually turn and bring him back to the beach.

God puts us in similar circumstances that are designed to develop us, not destroy us. He is training us to trust Him even through the authority structures placed over us. They are designed to expose those unredeemed places within us. In the desert, the children of Israel *"murmured against Moses"* (Exod. 17:3) when there was no water. Moses was taken aback and *"said to them, 'Why do you quarrel with me? Why do you test the Lord?' "* (Exod. 17:2 NASB). Their complaint against Moses was actually against God. God said that they had *"put Me to the test these ten times and have not listened to My voice"* (Num. 14:22 NASB).

Moses called the place *Massah* and *Meribah*, meaning temptation and strife.[1] They had only been out of Egypt for less than six weeks and were still battling with the responsibilities of freedom. Their contention and strife resulted in an encounter with Amalek. *Amalek* means to exhaust[2] or lick up. Contention and strife exhaust everyone involved and open the door to all kinds of issues.

Jealousy and envy are connected with strife seven times in the New Testament.[3] That strife takes away our contentment. Paul could say,

> *...I have learned to be content whatever the circumstances. I know what it is to be in need, and I know what it is to have plenty. I have learned the secret of being content in any and every situation, whether well fed or hungry, whether living in plenty or in want. I can do everything through Him who gives me strength* (Philippians 4:11-13 NIV).

God wants us to *"prosper in all things and be in health, just as your soul prospers"* (3 John 2 NKJV). However, focusing on a doctrine of prosperity will bring in greed and pride.

That will result in

...envy, strife, railings, evil surmisings, perverse disputings of men of corrupt minds, and destitute of the truth, supposing that gain is godliness: from such withdraw thyself. But godliness with contentment is great gain. For we brought nothing into this world, and it is certain we can carry nothing out. And having food and raiment let us be therewith content. But they that will be rich fall into temptation and a snare, and into many foolish and hurtful lusts, which drown men in destruction and perdition. For the love of money is the root of all evil: which while some coveted after, they have erred from the faith, and pierced themselves through with many sorrows (1 Timothy 6:4-10).

Great wealth comes with a great burden; we should not envy those who have to carry that burden.

Prayer:

Lord, I ask You to forgive me for the sin of cursing those in authority and those with wealth and power, by speaking against them out of my opinions and judgments. I now break this curse, in Jesus' name.

Some demonic spirits that may need to be dealt with include the following:

- Spirit of Murder
- Gossip
- Rebellion
- Spirit of Criticism
- Jealousy and Envy
- Greed

Lord, give me a heart to pray for (even when I don't understand) and bless those in authority. Change my heart and mouth to bless and not to curse.

Not Tithing

"Return to Me, and I will return to you," says the Lord of hosts. "But you say, 'How shall we return?' Will a man rob God? Yet you are robbing Me! But you say, 'How have we robbed You?' In tithes and offerings. You are cursed with a curse, for you are robbing Me, the whole nation of you!" (Malachi 3:7-9 NASB)

Tithing is not something you have to do; it is something you get to do. It originated not with the law, but 450 years before, as a covenant response between Abraham and Melchizedek (see Gen. 14:18-24) and was continued with Jesus. The Bible says,

Here mortal men receive tithes, but there he receives them, of whom it is witnessed that he lives. Even Levi, who receives tithes, paid tithes through Abraham, so to speak, for he was still in the loins of his father when Melchizedek met him (Hebrews 7:8-10 NKJV).

Tithing connects us to Abraham and God's covenant to bless him and his descendants. His righteousness is imputed to us *"if we believe on Him that raised up Jesus...from the dead"* (Rom. 4:24). The tithe is a seed that will produce a harvest, if we believe. Not tithing produces a curse and destroys our harvest.

Years ago, we taught on tithing in a small group of six couples. Everybody agreed to tithe except one couple, who stated that they could not afford to do it. We tried to explain that tithing was not a cost but the guarantee of a benefit, but they didn't have the faith to do it. That was 25 years ago, and every one of us has prospered except that one couple. They still live in the same house they had then and are still struggling with financial problems. They couldn't trust God for small amounts of money, and God couldn't trust them with large amounts.

Haggai explains how the curse operates (see Hag. 1:3-6). God told them to consider their ways.

They were sowing much, but harvesting little. This is working hard and putting out a great deal of effort but getting no benefit back. This is investing—only to have your investments robbed or the bottom drop out of the market (stock, housing, commodities).

They were eating, but were still hungry. This is not being satisfied with what you get. Everything you start leaves you with a bad taste in your mouth. You purchase something but get no value for your money.

They were drinking without quenching their thirst. Thirst speaks of spiritual desire. Jesus said,

> *Whoever drinks of the water that I shall give him will never thirst. But the water that I shall give him will become in him a fountain of water springing up into everlasting life* (John 4:14 NKJV).

He confused His disciples when He challenged them, *"Unless you eat the flesh of the Son of Man and drink His blood, you have no life in you. Whoever eats My flesh and drinks My blood has eternal life"* (John 6:53-54 NKJV). They were looking at His blood as a literal requirement, like the law. Jesus wanted them to exercise faith and eat and drink in the spirit.

Tithing is the same; it is a spiritual exercise. If we do it as law, it will have no benefit. We must do it in faith. Jesus continued and said, *"It is the Spirit who gives life; the flesh profits nothing. The words that I speak to you are spirit, and they are life"* (John 6:63 NKJV). Our thirst will allow us to tithe in faith, and the life in the faith will produce our harvest.

They were clothed, but were not warm. God clothed Adam and Eve with skins. They became "dead" in those animals so that when God looked at them He didn't see their nakedness. We also are to be *"dead in Christ"* (1 Thess. 4:16 NKJV) and to *"put on Christ"* (Gal. 3:27 NKJV). When we don't tithe, His covering does not extend into those realms of unbelief and affects our finances.

They were earning wages, but it was as if their money bags had holes. If we don't tithe, that 100 percent of the money we kept will seem to slip through our fingers. Part of the covenant is that God *"will rebuke the devourer for your sakes, so that he will not destroy the fruit of your ground"* (Mal. 3:11 NKJV). That means things won't go wrong at the wrong time; things won't continually break down.

The government or the banks won't change the rules after you invested. The market may go down, but your stocks will go up. Our efforts are easily thwarted.

> *Except the Lord builds the house, they labor in vain that build it: except the Lord keeps the city, the watchman waketh in vain* (Psalm 127:1).

Their hopes came to nothing. Hope that doesn't have faith as its substance is just wishful thinking and will always disappoint. Without tithing, the enemy has a right to oppose and block our prayers. If we can't put our money where our mouth is, we are displaying our lack of faith. God's promises will *"not profit them, not being mixed with faith"* (Heb. 4:2). Why did their hopes come to nothing? Because *"I [the Lord] blew on it"* (Hag. 1:5-6;9-10). They considered their own homes while neglecting the Lord's house (see Hag. 1:9).

Only Christians and Jews can tithe. Everyone else can bring offerings, but the tithe is reserved for those in covenant relationship. Suppose I were to offer to go into business with you. I have all the money that you will need to start up and operate the business. I understand the business and have all the expertise to make it prosper. I have all the contacts and connections necessary for the success of the business. I have all the pull to make it run smoothly like a clock.

I want you to be the front person; I will be the silent partner. I will give you advice whenever you want it. Best of all, we will split the profits: 90 percent for you; 10 percent for me. Want to go into business? Most would say, "What is the catch? That's too good to be true." That is what tithing is all about: not giving 10 percent, but keeping 90 percent. When you look at it that way, it is an offer too good to pass up. Faced with the alternative, who would? Only one who doesn't believe in the *"goodness of God* [which] *endures continually"* (Ps. 52:1 NKJV).

When we were first married, we felt God wanted us to tithe. I (Ken) had just finished university and didn't have a job. Jeanne was working, but the tithe would put a stress on our finances. We felt a strong urge to obey and began tithing one Sunday. On Tuesday I got a job, and on Wednesday we received a small inheritance from my grandfather who had passed away two years before. Since then, God has abundantly supplied all we have needed and more.

Prayer:

Lord, I ask You to forgive me for not giving the tithe, which is Your due. I now break this curse in Jesus' name.

Some demonic spirits that may need to be dealt with include the following:

- Stinginess
- Unbelief
- Operating in Duty Rather Than With Joy
- Withholding
- Rebellion
- Spirit of Poverty

Lord, I call back justice for all that has illegally been taken by the enemy. I ask that You provide for me and my household. I call my harvest in for all I have sown in tithes and offerings.

Negligence Doing the Work of the Lord

Cursed be the one who does the Lord's work negligently (Jeremiah 48:10a NASB).

Everything we do, we are to do *"not with eyeservice, as menpleasers; but as the servants of Christ, doing the will of God from the heart"* (Eph. 6:6). Saul only partially destroyed Amalek when God had commanded utter destruction (see 1 Sam. 15:3). God expressed His disappointment, saying, *"I am grieved that I have made Saul king, because he has turned away from Me and has not carried out My instructions"* (1 Sam. 15:11 NIV). The last thing I want is for God to repent for His decision to commit some Kingdom business into my hands.

We all have *"gifts differing according to the grace that is given to us"* (Rom. 12:6). *"As each one has received a special gift, employ it in serving one another as good stewards of the manifold grace of God"* (1 Pet. 4:10 NASB). God wants us to give, *"not grudgingly, or of necessity; for God loves a cheerful giver"* (2 Cor. 9:7 NKJV). God told me that not every gift is an abiding gift, but every gift is an available gift. We can have them if we will use them freely for the Body. These are some of the ways we can be negligent in ministry.

1. Not Listening to the Promptings of the Holy Spirit

We are often impatient with God for not responding to our requests or to our disasters. But *"the Lord is not slack concerning His promise, as some count slackness, but is longsuffering toward us, not willing that any should perish but that all should come to repentance"* (2 Pet. 3:9 NKJV). Our disasters are usually of our own making, due to following our own agendas and not responding to God's.

We had a van that was leaking oil, but I (Ken) was negligent in getting it repaired and kept adding oil instead. We were heading back from a conference in Washington when Jeanne asked me if I had checked the oil. I didn't want to stop, though I too felt that the oil should be checked. I said, "It's OK. I'll check it when we gas up." I chose to ignore the voice inside, and the lack of peace, and continued driving.

About half an hour later, there was a big bang, and the van started to shudder. I thought we had broken the drive shaft, but as I looked out the rearview mirror, I saw the truth. There was a long black line of oil following us as we slowed down. The motor had blown, pushing a rod through the oil pan. My not responding to the voice of my wife confirming the voice of the Spirit cost us dearly. We had to catch a ride, get a tow, and borrow a car to get home (ten hours away). Then we had the expense of renting a trailer to bring the van back, and buying a new motor. All this occurred because I didn't want to stop for five minutes to put in some oil. We ignore the voice of the Spirit to our own hurt.

God disciplined Israel for not believing Him and possessing the land by sending them back into the desert. Israel compounded their original sin by ignoring the second command and presumptuously attacking the inhabitants of the land: *"The Amalekites and Canaanites who lived in that hill country came down and struck them and beat them down as far as Hormah"* (Num. 14:45

NASB). God's response to the disaster was to shrug His shoulders at what was happening to the army, turn to Moses, and explain to him the proper way to present offerings when they finally got into the land (see Num. 15:1-5). The army was in desperate need of help, but they were reaping their disobedience. The long-term goal of entering the land was more important than the short-term loss of a battle. When God is not responding to our cries, it is because He is talking about something more important: His agenda for us.

We are to be disciples (disciplined ones), like the angels *"that excel in strength, that do His commandments, hearkening unto the voice of His Word"* (Ps. 103:20). We must be ready to *"preach the word; be instant in season, out of season; reprove, rebuke, exhort with all longsuffering and doctrine. For the time will come when they will not endure sound doctrine"* (2 Tim. 4:2-3).

> *And that, knowing the time, that now it is high time to awake out of sleep: for now is our salvation nearer than when we believed. The night is far spent; the day is at hand* (Romans 13:11-12).

> *But sanctify the Lord God in your hearts: and be ready always to give an answer to every man that asketh you a reason of the hope that is in you* (1 Peter 3:15).

I (Ken) met a couple while ministering prophetic evangelism at a trade fair. This couple listened while I spoke into their lives about the love and destiny that God had for them. They had been raised in Christian homes but had never personally encountered Jesus. After a few minutes, they got up to leave, deciding not to make any commitment to God at that time. I felt urgency in my spirit that the conversation was not over but I was at a loss as to how to arrest their departure.

They were picking up their bags as the husband casually mentioned that though he had read some of the Bible, he never really understood all that he was reading. I said, "I can introduce you to the author of the book." Immediately, he sat back down. He had not been interested in knowing the answers from the Bible, but he desperately wanted to know the author of the Bible. In less than a minute both he and his wife asked Jesus to be Lord of their lives. We don't have to be wise to do God's will; we just have to listen to the Spirit and respond.

2. Not Doing Our Part of the Covenant

When God made His covenant with Abraham, He performed both sides of the pact by passing between the pieces (see Gen. 15). Abraham simply *"believed in the Lord; and He counted it to him as righteousness"* (Gen. 15:6). We believe God and enter into His finished work. He said it, we believe it, and that settles it.

> *And whatsoever ye do, do it heartily, as to the Lord, and not unto men; knowing that of the Lord ye shall receive the reward of the inheritance: for ye serve the Lord Christ* (Colossians 3:23-24).

To walk in this New Covenant we also must believe what God is saying to us.

> *This is the covenant that I will make with the house of Israel after those days, says the Lord: I will put My laws in their mind and write them on their hearts; and I will be their God, and they shall be My people. None of them shall teach his neighbor, and none his brother, saying, "Know the Lord," for all shall know Me, from the least of them to the greatest of them. For I will be merciful to their unrighteousness, and their sins and their lawless deeds I will remember no more* (Hebrews 8:10-12 NKJV).

We must believe that we are not the poor cousins who snuck in through the back door but are *"heirs of God and joint heirs with Christ"* (Rom. 8:17 NKJV). We have the Holy Spirit resident in us, and *"He shall teach you all things, and bring all things to remembrance, whatsoever I have said unto you"* (John 14:26). Stop thinking that you need to go to others to hear the Word of the Lord. He puts His "laws in your mind and writes them on your heart" (see Heb. 8:10 NKJV). Jesus said, *"He who believes in Me, the works that I do he will do also; and greater works than these he will do, because I go to My Father"* (John 14:12 NKJV). Our part of the covenant is to believe and obey.

3. Not Serving

God is merciful, but *"justice and judgment are the habitation of Thy throne"* (Ps. 89:14). *"Be not deceived; God is not mocked: for whatsoever a man sows, that shall he also reap"* (Gal. 6:7). There is a disturbing trend in the Body of Christ for us to act like kings. Jesus was a king, yet He *"came not to be ministered unto, but to minister, and to give His life"* (Mark 10:45).

We can serve in many ways. God taught me (Jeanne) to put my shopping cart in the designated corral when I am finished with it and not just shove it into the closest vacant parking stall. If I accidentally knock a dress off the rack, I don't just kick it out of the way; I hang it back up. I don't act like serving is beneath me or that my time is too precious to be considerate of others. There is one King, and His name is Jesus, and even He doesn't act like that. Jesus said, *"A disciple is not above his teacher, nor a servant above his master. It is enough for a disciple that he be like his teacher, and a servant like his master"* (Matt. 10:24-25 NKJV).

> *You call Me Teacher and Lord, and you say well, for so I am. If I then, your Lord and Teacher, have washed your feet, you also ought to wash one another's feet. For I have given you an example, that you should do as I have done to you* (John 13:13-15 NKJV).

4. Not Laying Down Our Lives

> *Therefore I urge you, brethren, by the mercies of God, to present your bodies a living and holy sacrifice, acceptable to God, which is your spiritual service of worship. And do not be conformed to this world, but be transformed by the renewing of your mind, so that you may prove what the will of God is, that which is good and acceptable and perfect* (Romans 12:1-2 NASB).

5. Not Loving Each Other

Jesus said, *"Don't misunderstand why I have come. I did not come to abolish the Law of Moses or the writings of the prophets. No, I came to accomplish their purpose"* (Matt. 5:17 NLT). Because He fulfilled the law, *"It is finished"* (John 19:30). But *"a new commandment* [is given]…*that you love one another; as I have loved you, that you also love one another"* (John 13:34 NKJV). That commandment we, through the power of the Holy Spirit, must fulfill. And *"greater love has no one than this, than to lay down one's life for his friends"* (John 15:13 NKJV). *"Love is the fulfillment of the law"* (Rom. 13:10 NKJV). *"By this shall all men know that ye are My disciples, if ye have love one to another"* (John 13:35).

God taught me (Jeanne) to love by putting a lady in my life who was very hard to love. If I said I would babysit for her children while she went to the doctor at 10:30, a lot more was expected. She would show up at 8:00 A.M. for breakfast; stay afterward for lunch; phone her husband to pick her up at suppertime; and let me feed the whole family supper. She was so lonely. I learned to love her and truly bless her. I also learned to be blunt and to set boundaries because she wouldn't respond to hints.

6. **Not Walking in the Spirit**

We are filled with the Spirit

...so that the righteous and just requirement of the Law might be fully met in us who live and move not in the ways of the flesh but in the ways of the Spirit [our lives governed not by the standards and according to the dictates of the flesh, but controlled by the Holy Spirit]. For those who are according to the flesh and are controlled by its unholy desires set their minds on and pursue those things which gratify the flesh, but those who are according to the Spirit and are controlled by the desires of the Spirit set their minds on and seek those things which gratify the [Holy] Spirit (Romans 8:4-5 AMP).

This is my (Jeanne's) secret power. I love to pray in the Spirit for hours at a time. Then I hear so much clearer and my emotions come in line with God's will.

For if you

...walk by the Spirit, and you will not carry out the desire of the flesh. For the flesh sets its desire against the Spirit, and the Spirit against the flesh; for these are in opposition to one another, so that you may not

do the things that you please. But if you are led by the Spirit, you are not under the Law (Galatians 5:16-18 NASB).

No Spirit; no profit.

Prayer:

Lord, forgive me for doing the work of the Kingdom negligently and not with my whole heart. I now break this curse and open myself up to Your direction. Lord, my life is not my own. Help me to give over my life to You to serve You.

Lord, I ask You to forgive me for being negligent in doing Your work. I now break this curse in Jesus' name.

Some demonic spirits that may need to be dealt with include the following:

- Selfishness
- King Attitude
- Fear
- Fear of Man
- Captive Spirit

Lord, my life is not my own. Help me to give over my life to You to serve You.

Chapter 19

CURSES ON IMPROPER RESPONSES

Operating in Unsanctified Mercy

Cursed be the one who restrains his sword from blood (Jeremiah 48:10b NASB).

At times we are called upon to hold others accountable in love. If we choose to withhold the exhortation that the Lord is asking us to give, we literally withhold the sword of the Lord.

> *The Lord disciplines those He loves, and He punishes everyone He accepts as a son. Endure hardship as discipline; God is treating you as sons. For what son is not disciplined by his father? If you are not disciplined (and everyone undergoes discipline), then you are illegitimate children and not true sons. Moreover, we have all had human fathers who disciplined us and we respected them for it. How much more should we submit to the Father of our spirits and live! Our fathers disciplined us for a little while as they thought best; but God disciplines us for our good, that we may share in His holiness. No discipline seems pleasant at the time, but painful. Later on, however, it produces a harvest of righteousness and peace for those who have been trained by it* (Hebrews 12:6-11 NIV).

We operate in unsanctified mercy when we do any of the following:

1. Operate in Human Compassion

Sympathy is not a fruit of the Spirit; it is a fruit of the flesh. We feel bad for people and let them off the hook. There is nothing wrong with empathizing with people, but it is not a basis for action. Saul empathized with the king of the Amalekites *"and...spared Agag"* (1 Sam. 15:9). Samuel was furious that Saul had shown compassion to Agag. Saul had won the battle and showed deference to another king. Samuel called, and

> *Agag came to him delicately and...said, Surely the bitterness of death is past. And Samuel said, As thy sword has made women childless, so shall thy mother be childless among women. And Samuel hewed Agag in pieces before the Lord* (1 Samuel 15:32-33).

Human compassion comes from the soul realm and expects that people will respond to the compassion shown. When people don't respond correctly, we get mad or disappointed. God-ordained mercy does not respond to a poor reaction, for it was not motivated by feelings but by obedience. If God is happy with what we did, nothing else matters. If it does matter how people react, then we did it for the wrong reasons. Because God never disappoints, our disappointment is a sure sign that God did not tell us to show mercy.

We have been fooled into giving people money when they were not in a real need and just wanted a "free lunch." We must learn the difference between a con and Holy Spirit conviction. God always has a plan even if we don't know it. He may want lack to prompt someone to cry out to Him or learn to trust Him. If we come rushing in whenever the baby cries, he or she will learn to cry to us instead of to God. When we give prematurely, and get in between the person and God's dealings, the lesson will only need to be repeated. Be the intercessor, not the mediator; that position belongs to Jesus alone (see 1 Tim. 2:5).

God ordered the destruction of all the inhabitants of Canaan so they would not infect Israel with their demonic practices. He said,

> *You shall make no covenant with them and show no mercy to them... shall not intermarry with them...For they will turn your sons away from following Me to serve other gods* (Deuteronomy 7:2-4 NASB).

> *But if you do not drive out the inhabitants of the land from before you,*
> *then those you let remain of them shall be as pricks in your eyes and*
> *as thorns in your sides, and they shall vex you in the land in which*
> *you live. And as I plan to do to them, so I will do to you* (Numbers
> 33:55-56 NASB).

God is more loving than we are, but He is also wiser. Submitting to His wisdom is always our best protection.

The Corinthian church tolerated a degrading sexual sin and had mercy on the man engaged in it. Paul lambasted their "spiritual approach" of not judging this sin. He said,

> *Shouldn't this person and his conduct be confronted and dealt*
> *with?...You must not simply look the other way and hope it goes*
> *away on its own. Bring it out in the open and deal with it in the*
> *authority of Jesus our Master...Hold this man's conduct up to public*
> *scrutiny* (1 Corinthians 5:1-4 MSG).

Pussyfooting around, trying not to embarrass someone, is not mercy; it's the fear of man. *"Do you not know that a little leaven leavens the whole lump?"* (1 Cor. 5:6 NASB). If I have gangrene in my hand, it is stupidity, not mercy, to not cut it off. Sin is contagious; righteousness is not (see Hag. 2:12-13). We are not to elevate our opinions but must hate what God hates, and love what God loves.

We are in charge of the ministry teams at our church. One Sunday, at the end of the service, we were releasing the teams to pray with the people who came to the front. By the Spirit, God directed my (Jeanne's) focus toward one young man on the ministry team. I approached him and asked him to not minister at this time. I felt that he had unrepentant sin, and I didn't want him laying hands on people. Later he shared his unrepentant sin with me and went for some counseling. The Holy Spirit loved him enough not to allow him to enter a battle for someone else when his sin had left him open to attack. In this situation, covering, not compassion, was required.

Eli, the priest, had two sons who were defiling the tabernacle. They took by force the meat offered to the Lord for themselves and threatened the people. They also seduced the women who came to worship.

> *Eli was very old, and heard all that his sons did unto all Israel; and how they lay with the women that assembled at the door of the tabernacle of the congregation. And he said unto them, Why do ye such things? For I hear of your evil dealings by all this people. Nay, my sons; for it is no good report that I hear: ye make the Lord's people to transgress* (1 Samuel 2:22-24).

This mild rebuke confirmed that Eli was not willing to confront the sins of his sons, but actually preferred them above God.

God holds those in charge responsible for the actions of those under them. God sent a prophet to confront Eli and linked him directly to his sons' actions. He prophesied,

> *Why do you kick at My sacrifice and at My offering which I have commanded in My dwelling, and honor your sons above Me, by making yourselves fat with the choicest of every offering of My people Israel?* (1 Samuel 2:29 NASB)

Eli's unsanctified mercy toward his sons resulted in his whole family being removed from the priesthood (see 1 Kings 2:27).

That same principle applies to discipline in our families. God says that "*He who spares his rod hates his son, but he who loves him disciplines him promptly*" (Prov. 13:24 NKJV). Modern wisdom disagrees with corporal punishment and has elevated reason as the proper method of instruction. Admittedly, many children have been abused and punished more harshly than necessary, but that does not detract from God's wisdom.

Solomon noted that "*foolishness is bound in the heart of a child; but the rod of correction shall drive it far from him*" (Prov. 22:15). "*Blows that wound cleanse away evil, and strokes [for correction] reach to the innermost parts*" (Prov. 20:30 AMP).

God is preparing us to rule and reign with Him. Remember, discipline is an expression of love (see Heb. 12:6-11). I don't discipline the neighbors' children because I don't have a love relationship with them: they are not my children. We are telling our children that they are not loved, not worth loving, if we won't discipline them. Subconsciously, they will feel that they aren't worth our effort, and they will be right, if we continually manipulate by showing compassion and not justice.

2. Operate in Human Wisdom

Joshua began the invasion of Canaan by following God's instructions. They got specific strategies for each battle and won every time they obeyed. Then they started to rely on their own wisdom. They went up against Ai with just a few men, unaware that they had transgressed at Jericho. They depended on their own wisdom and were defeated (see Josh. 7:1-10). The defeat was a shock and a wake-up call that something was wrong. Once they got instructions from God, the battle was easily won, but the lesson was not learned.

The Gibeonites knew that they were in trouble and devised a plan to align with Israel through deceit. The Gibeonites claimed they were from far off and showed some stale bread as proof.

> *So the men of Israel took some of their provisions, and did not ask for the counsel of the Lord. Joshua made peace with them and made a covenant with them, to let them live* (Joshua 9:14-15 NASB).

Israel relied on their own wisdom, and the Gibeonites created problems for Israel for the next 500 years (see 2 Sam. 21:1).

We once rented a house to a "Christian" family. Originally, we were trying to sell the house but were not having much success. They came in and looked casually around, not seeming too interested until they found out we were Christians. Immediately they started talking about spiritual things and forgot about the house. After a few minutes, they shifted back to the house but this time with the idea of renting. They were looking for a good church and thought that if they were in the community, they would attend ours.

I (Ken) listened to their story and really liked this couple and was determined to help them achieve their goals. We decided to rent it to them; the deal was sealed with a handshake and not a check or a contract. They told us a tale of hardship, and we decided to let them come in early with their furniture. When the day to sign the contract came, there was only enough money to put down a damage deposit.

Because I (Ken) used the Jezebel spirit to control people, I was also subject to being controlled by that spirit. So I caved and agreed to collect the rest of the money in two weeks: *"The wisdom of this world is foolishness with God"* (1 Cor. 3:19 NKJV). The rest of the story you can imagine; it took a month for us to detach these leeches from our house and our lives. Jeanne had a check in the spirit about them right after the first meeting, but I ignored her because I wanted to "help." I finally contacted their former church, which they had given as a reference, and found that this was not the first time they had pulled this scam.

Sin does not evaporate, and time will not heal the wounds sin creates; only repentance does. I had to repent of listening to my wisdom and my emotions without checking with God. Human wisdom says, "Let sleeping dogs lie," but God calls us to deal with our sins. Jesus urges us to *"agree with your adversary quickly"* (Matt. 5:25 NKJV). Hebrews pleads, *"To day if ye will hear His voice, harden not your hearts"* (Heb. 3:7-8).

David took the *laissez faire* attitude when it came to his family. He did nothing when Ammon raped his half-sister; he did nothing when Absalom murdered Ammon; and he did nothing when Absalom left Israel or when he returned. David pleaded, *"Deal gently for my sake with the young man, even with Absalom"* (2 Sam. 18:5), even though he was in rebellion and had started a civil war. After Absalom was killed, David mourned, *"O my son Absalom—my son, my son Absalom—if only I had died in your place! O Absalom my son, my son!"* (2 Sam. 18:33 NKJV).

Had David died earlier to his own wisdom and lack of action, his son might have stayed under his authority and lived.

3. **Align With the Culture Rather Than With the Kingdom**

We are commanded not to

...be conformed to this world, but be transformed by the renewing of your mind, so that you may prove what the will of God is, that which is good and acceptable and perfect (Romans 12:2 NASB).

Sin is not just a lifestyle choice; it is sin and abhorrent to God. James minces no words, declaring,

You adulterous people, don't you know that friendship with the world is hatred toward God? Anyone who chooses to be a friend of the world becomes an enemy of God (James 4:4 NIV).

God intervened for Israel with the Syrians because they had belittled Him by asserting that He was only *"God of the hills, but He is not God of the valleys"* (1 Kings 20:28). He gave Ben-hadad, the Syrian king, into Ahab's hands and *"appointed* [him] *to utter destruction"* (1 Kings 20:42). Ahab followed the custom of the day and showed him mercy and let him live (see 1 Kings 20:31-34). God was furious and vowed to Ahab, *"Your life shall go for his life, and your people for his people"* (1 Kings 20:42 NKJV). When God moves on our behalf, we are responsible to follow His dictates.

The constant challenge is to remember that we *"are no longer foreigners and aliens, but fellow citizens with God's people and members of God's household"* (Eph. 2:19 NIV). Now, *"we are ambassadors for Christ"* (2 Cor. 5:20), and as such, are not subject to the laws of this realm.

If you have died with Christ to the elementary principles of the world, why, as if you were living in the world, do you submit yourself to decrees, such as, "Do not handle, do not taste, do not touch!"... in accordance with the commandments and teachings of men? (Colossians 2:20-22 NASB)

It is easy to adapt to the customs and reason of this realm, but that is not where we are called to live. Israel had to fight heathen customs of working on the Sabbath and resist the pressure to intermarry with the heathen. Today, sexual relations before marriage are encouraged. To close our eyes and accept this as a standard is unsanctified mercy. More often it is fear of offending that prompts our silence. God said,

> *...not to keep company with anyone named a brother, who is sexually immoral, or covetous, or an idolater, or a reviler, or a drunkard, or an extortioner—not even to eat with such a person* (1 Corinthians 5:11 NKJV).

Tact is required, but it cannot be an excuse for ignoring God's Word.

Prayer:

Lord I ask You to forgive me for operating in unsanctified mercy. I now break this curse off my life in Jesus' name.

Some demonic spirits that may need to be dealt with include the following:

- Man-pleasing Spirit
- Spirit of Apathy
- Self-protection
- Rebellion

Lord, give me the courage to speak Your truth in love in every situation.

Not Honoring and Thanking God

> *If you do not take it to heart to give honor to My name...then I will send the curse upon you and... your blessings* (Malachi 2:2-3 NASB).

I heard a story about a man working on a roof. It was a frosty morning, and he slipped and started to slowly slide off. He grasped at the shingles, but everything was so slippery that he kept creeping toward the edge. In his panic, he cried out, "God, help me!" Just then, he caught his pants on a protruding nail, which arrested his slide. Relieved, he called back to God, "Don't worry about me; I got caught on a nail. I'm OK." We often assign chance to God's providence in our lives and are not thankful.

We went fishing with our eldest son, Shannon, when he was about five or six. We had caught several fish when Shannon said we needed to pray and thank God, right now! We did, and those were the best tasting fish we ever had. *"Out of the mouth of babes...You have perfected praise"* (Matt. 21:16 NKJV).

We are not thankful because we don't believe that God really loves us. He is so concerned about us that He sets in motion events that are often cosmic in magnitude, for our benefit. When Deborah was celebrating Israel's victory over Sisera, she proclaimed, *"From the heavens the stars fought, from their courses they fought against Sisera"* (Judges 5:20 AMP). The Bible doesn't say how the stars fought, but Deborah was quick to acknowledge divine intervention in her victory. Joshua also had a dramatic, divine intervention when he fought the battle of the five kings.

The Lord cast down great stones from Heaven upon them, *"and they died: they were more, which died with hailstones than they whom the children of Israel slew with the sword"* (Josh. 10:11). Even *"the sun stood still, and the moon stayed, until the people had avenged themselves upon their enemies"* (Josh. 10:13). God loves us and will go to extraordinary measures to bring us to our destiny.

An unthankful heart cannot receive or remember the good done for it. We knew a lady who received a thousand dollars as an anonymous gift one Sunday. Later at a Bible study we were all asked if anyone had a testimony of what God had done for them that week; she could think of nothing special. The Bible study had been specifically praying for her family's financial difficulties, and some of them had even contributed to the gift. With no recall of blessings, faith has a hard time growing. We begin to think that all the good that happens to us is our doing.

> *Hezekiah was sick to the point of death; and he prayed to the Lord and He answered him and gave him a sign. But Hezekiah did not make return [to the Lord] according to the benefit done to him, for his heart became proud [at such a spectacular response to his prayer];*

therefore there was wrath upon him and upon Judah and Jerusalem (2 Chronicles 32:24-25 AMP).

If we don't acknowledge God's goodness, we will not get the next level of blessing.

Jesus commanded ten lepers to

...go shew yourselves unto the priests. And it came to pass, that, as they went, they were cleansed. And one of them, when he saw that he was healed, turned back, and with a loud voice glorified God, and fell down on his face at his feet, giving him thanks: and he was a Samaritan. And Jesus answering said, Were there not ten cleansed? But where are the nine? There are not found that returned to give glory to God, save this stranger. And He said unto him, Arise, go thy way: thy faith hath made thee whole (Luke 17:14-19).

Ten were cleansed, but only the thankful one was made whole.

This unthankfulness is one of the signs of the endtimes, as Paul says:

...in the last days perilous times shall come. For men shall be lovers of their own selves, covetous, boasters, proud, blasphemers, disobedient to parents, **unthankful,** *unholy, without natural affection, trucebreakers, false accusers, incontinent, fierce, despisers of those that are good, traitors, heady, high minded, lovers of pleasures more than lovers of God; having a form of godliness, but denying the power thereof* (2 Timothy 3:1-5).

"*The fool hath said in his heart, There is no God*" (Ps. 14:1). We become god in our own life when we deny that there is a God. That is the point at which wisdom departs from us. Refusing to honor and thank God likewise denies the existence or relevance of God.

For even though they knew God, they did not honor Him as God or give thanks, but they became futile in their speculations, and their foolish heart was darkened (Romans 1:21 NASB).

...Therefore God gave them over in the lusts of their hearts to impurity (Romans 1:24 NASB).

When we are thankful, we do not grumble and complain. Complaining is an attribute of pride: I deserve better; I could do better; I don't like____. We are commanded to

...do all things without grumbling or disputing; so that you will prove yourselves to be blameless and innocent, children of God above reproach in the midst of a crooked and perverse generation, among whom you appear as lights in the world (Philippians 2:14-15 NASB).

That is our calling—to be *"the light of the world"* (Matt. 5:14 NASB). But we don't shine, and we don't honor God when we grumble.

God wants us to prosper, especially in the middle of discipline, but we need the right attitude. Even before Israel went into captivity, God declared, *"I know the plans I have for you...plans to prosper you and not to harm you, plans to give you hope and a future"* (Jer. 29:11 NIV).

...Because you did not serve the Lord your God joyfully and gladly in the time of prosperity, therefore in hunger and thirst, in nakedness and dire poverty, you will serve the enemies the Lord sends against you (Deuteronomy 28:47-48 NIV).

A thankful heart is an honoring, worshipful heart.

Prayer:

Lord, I ask forgiveness for not thanking or being grateful for all You do. I now break the curse that results from these actions in Jesus' name.

Some demonic spirits that may need to be dealt with include the following:

- Ingratitude
- Negativity
- Complaining spirit

- Pride

- Dishonoring

- Hopelessness

- Self-exaltation

- Self-righteousness

Lord, give me a thankful heart that is ever praising You for all Your benefits.

Stealing and Lying

> *This is the curse that is going forth over the face of the whole land [on]...everyone who steals...and everyone who swears [falsely]* (Zechariah 5:3-4 NASB).

Lack of character and integrity is the main blight on the Church's testimony. David's adultery and subsequent murder gave *"occasion to the enemies of the Lord to blaspheme"* (2 Sam. 12:14 NASB). Paul urged us to give *"no offence in any thing, that the ministry be not blamed"* (2 Cor. 6:3). You are going to suffer for righteousness' sake, but *"let none of you suffer as a murderer, or as a thief, or as an evildoer, or as a busybody"* (1 Pet. 4:15). Jesus is sanctifying and cleansing us to *"present...to Himself a glorious church, not having spot, or wrinkle, or any such thing, but that it should be holy and without blemish"* (Eph. 5:27).

God is holy, so we need to be *"holy in all manner of conversation"* (1 Pet. 1:15). The psalmist asks,

> *Who may climb the mountain of the Lord? Who may stand in His holy place? Only those whose hands and hearts are pure, who do not worship idols and never tell lies* (Psalm 24:3-4 NLT).

It is *"the knowledge of the truth that leads to godliness"* (Titus 1:1 NIV). Lying is our self-effort, our fleshly strength, trying to gain an advantage or protect ourselves. We use lies to hide those selfish intentions that we have hidden in the dark.

Jesus bluntly stated that the prideful Jews, who were challenging Him, were just like their

> *... father the devil, and the desires of your father you want to do. He was a murderer from the beginning, and does not stand in the truth, because there is no truth in him. When he speaks a lie, he speaks from his own resources, for he is a liar and the father of it* (John 8:44 NKJV).

Lies reveal those parts of our souls that are still aligned with satan's agenda.

I (Ken) had to repent for not loving the truth (see 2 Thess. 2:10). I called it exaggeration, but it was just lying. I called it bluffing, but it was just lying. I did not like the truth about me, so I lied to myself and refused to see the truth. We lie because we don't believe that God could love us the way we are. Fear and self-hatred drive us into the habit of lying so often that we will lie even when there is no reason to lie.

Peter believed that because he felt brave, he would never be afraid. He single-handedly stood up to the mob that came to take Jesus (see John 18:10). But the truth was not what Peter felt, but what Jesus said. Peter said to Jesus,

> *"Lord, with You I am ready to go both to prison and to death!"* [Jesus replied]...*"I say to you, Peter, the rooster will not crow today until you have denied three times that you know Me"* (Luke 22:33-34).

Peter's self-confidence was boasting, but it was a lie. He had no comprehension that it was a lie because *"the heart is deceitful above all things, and desperately wicked: who can know it?"* (Jer. 17:9). The truth is found in a person, not a set of facts or assumptions. Jesus said, *"I am the way, the truth, and the life"* (John 14:6). The *"words* [He speaks]...*they are spirit, and they are life"* (John 6:63). If we do not love the truth, we do not love the Lord, for He is the truth. Liars *"have their part in the lake which burneth with fire...which is the second death"* (Rev. 21:8).

"God, who cannot lie" (Titus 1:2 NKJV), takes lying seriously. He cannot lie because everything He says happens. We were designed to speak with the same

authority. Our words are containers of power to be used to create the world in cooperation with the Father. Lying brings confusion, which kills faith, thus nullifying God's intentions. Satan has deluded the world that truth is relevant and not knowable, and that lying is OK in some circumstances. God hates lying and has excluded liars from the New Jerusalem. Outside its gates are

> *... the dogs and those who practice sorceries (magic arts) and impurity [the lewd, adulterers] and the murderers and idolaters and everyone who loves and deals in falsehood (untruth, error, deception, cheating)* (Revelation 22:15 AMP).

Stealing is a physical form of lying. God included it in the Ten Commandments and connected it with lying, cheating, murder, and adultery (see Lev. 19:11; Jer. 7:9; Hos. 4:2). Jesus used the example of a thief to contrast himself with satan, who was a *"thief [come]...to steal and kill and destroy. I came that they may have and enjoy life, and have it in abundance (to the full, till it overflows)"* (John 10:10 AMP). Abundant life comes as a gift, but if we try to grab, it becomes greed.

Greed is a fruit of the root of lust. God once asked me, "When is enough, enough?" The answer that popped into my mind was, "Never." The Bible says, *"The horseleach hath two daughters, crying, Give, give"* (Prov. 30:15). This verse introduces those *"things that are never satisfied"* (Prov. 30:15). A leech will suck so much blood that it will literally burst. Even human leeches are like that, never satisfied.

We have found that greed is associated with a spirit of poverty. That spirit convinces us that there is a limited supply, and that if you have more, I must have less. That is a worldly mindset. In the Kingdom there is abundance. When God supplied, *"he that gathered much had nothing over, and he that gathered little had no lack"* (Exod. 16:18). Greed is about accumulating more than your need and more than your due.

It encourages hoarding to the detriment of others.

> *There is one who scatters, yet increases more; and there is one who withholds more than is right, but it leads to poverty. The generous soul*

will be made rich, and he who waters will also be watered himself. The people will curse him who withholds (Proverbs 11:24-26 NKJV).

Greed shows a dependence on things and makes them our supply rather than God Himself.

He tried to teach that to Israel as they prepared to enter the land. He gave them fresh manna every morning; they could not store it, except prior to the Sabbath, when it would not rot (see Exod. 16:13-35). He taught the same thing concerning the Sabbath rest of the land once they entered the Promised Land. God said that when they asked,

> *"What shall we eat in the seventh year, since we shall not sow nor gather in our produce?" Then I will command My blessing on you in the sixth year, and it will bring forth produce enough for three years* (Leviticus 25:20-21 NKJV).

Israel never learned abundance and consistently operated in greed. Jesus said, *"Beware, and be on your guard against every form of greed; for not even when one has an abundance does his life consist of his possessions"* (Luke 12:15 NASB).

Israel's captivity lasted for a 70-year period, equivalent to the 490 years Israel did not keep the Sabbath. The 70 years of captivity was equivalent to the rest the land was denied during that time (see 2 Chron. 36:21). They were greedy and didn't trust God to supply the abundance in the sixth year to compensate for the loss of the seventh Sabbath year. God warned them that He would give the land its rest when they were taken into captivity (see Lev. 26:34-35).

> *Whoever can be trusted with very little can also be trusted with much, and whoever is dishonest with very little will also be dishonest with much. So if you have not been trustworthy in handling worldly wealth, who will trust you with true riches? And if you have not been trustworthy with someone else's property, who will give you property of your own? No servant can serve two masters. Either he will hate the one and love the other, or he will be devoted to the one and despise the other. You cannot serve both God and Money* (Luke 16:10-13 NIV).

Like a partridge that hatches eggs it did not lay is the man who gains riches by unjust means. When his life is half gone, they will desert him, and in the end he will prove to be a fool (Jeremiah 17:11 NIV).

God sees everything: *"The darkness shall not hide from You...the darkness and the light are both alike to You"* (Ps. 139:12 NKJV). And our stealing will not stop God's justice: *"There is one who scatters, and yet increases all the more, and there is one who withholds what is justly due, and yet it results only in want"* (Prov. 11:24 NASB). Ultimately, *"the wealth of the sinner is laid up for the just"* (Prov. 13:22).

Prayer:

Lord, I ask forgiveness for the sin of lying and stealing in all their forms. I ask You to forgive me for trusting in deception to get what I want. I now break this curse off of my life in Jesus' name.

Some demonic spirits that may need to be dealt with include the following:

- Dishonesty
- Lying
- Lack of Integrity
- Stealing
- Cheating
- Exaggerating
- Lack of trust in God

Lord, help me to trust You to supply all of my needs and to walk in honesty and integrity. Give me a new heart to love truth. Lord, cause me to trust You for all my needs and to be content with what I have.

Section D

ENACTING THE BLESSING

Chapter 20

BLESSINGS THAT SET US ON HIGH

God's intention in pronouncing the curses was not to punish but to bless. The curses are designed to alert us to the iniquity in our families and in us so that we can repent, ask forgiveness, and restore the family to its destiny. *"Christ hath redeemed us from the curse of the law, being made a curse for us"* (Gal. 3:13). We enact that redemption by believing He paid for our transgression, by asking for and receiving forgiveness for our families and ourselves, canceling the curses in Jesus' name, and declaring the blessings upon our family.

If you have stood in proxy and asked forgiveness for all your family's iniquities, it is time to enact the blessings that Moses spoke over Abraham's children. We will deal with each one individually, but this is the list:

> *If you diligently obey the Lord your God, being careful to do all His commandments which I command you today, the Lord your God will set you high above all the nations of the earth. All these blessings will come upon you and overtake you if you obey the Lord your God: Blessed shall you be in the city, and blessed shall you be in the country. Blessed shall be the offspring of your body and the produce of your ground and the offspring of your beasts, the increase of your herd and the young of your flock. Blessed shall be your basket and your kneading bowl. Blessed shall you be when you come in, and blessed shall you be when you go out. The Lord shall cause your enemies who rise up against you to be defeated before*

you; they will come out against you one way and will flee before you seven ways (Deuteronomy 28:1-7 NASB).

As we did with the curses, we are going to explore all the aspects of the blessings, that we might, in faith, claim them for our lives. The first seven blessings are considered in this chapter, and the remaining seven in the next.

God Wants to Elevate Us

"The Lord your God will set you high above all the nations of the earth" (Deut. 28:1 NASB). God wants to put us into a place of authority. He has *"made us kings and priests to our God; and we shall reign on the earth"* (Rev. 5:10 NKJV). Don't worry about what you go through. Jesus said,

> *Blessed are you when men hate you, and when they exclude you, and revile you, and cast out your name as evil, for the Son of Man's sake. Rejoice in that day and leap for joy! For indeed your reward is great in heaven, for in like manner their fathers did to the prophets* (Luke 6:22-23 NKJV).

For we know that *"if we suffer, we shall also reign with Him"* (2 Tim. 2:12).

God has already begun to set up His Kingdom. Jesus said that if He *"cast out devils by the Spirit of God, then the kingdom of God is come unto you"* (Matt. 12:28). He told His disciples to *"heal the sick...and say to them, 'The kingdom of God has come near to you' "* (Luke 10:9 NKJV). Part of the blessing is to enter the Kingdom and perform healings and miracles, and to cast out demons. *"For the kingdom of God does not consist in words but in power"* (1 Cor. 4:20 NASB). Jesus encouraged His disciples by saying, *"The works that I do shall he do also; and greater works than these shall he do; because I go unto My Father"* (John 14:12).

We need to get excited, not fearful, because in the last days

> *...shall the God of heaven set up a kingdom, which shall never be destroyed: and the kingdom shall not be left to other people, but it shall break in pieces and consume all these kingdoms, and it shall stand for ever* (Daniel 2:44).

Your kingdom is an everlasting kingdom, and Your dominion endures throughout all generations (Psalm 145:13 NASB).

We are a part of that Kingdom, which is on the earth now. Our prayers, intercessions, praise, and proclamations can change governments and events. God said,

Let the high praises of God be in their mouth, and a two-edged sword in their hand, to execute vengeance on the nations and punishment on the peoples, to bind their kings with chains and their nobles with fetters of iron, to execute on them the judgment written; this is an honor for all His godly ones (Psalm 149:6-9 NASB).

Do you not know that the saints (the believers) will [one day] judge and govern the world?...Also that...we [Christians] are to judge the [very] angels and pronounce opinion between right and wrong [for them]? (1 Corinthians 6:2-3 AMP)

God is preparing us to walk in His power and authority, to set us high over nations and demonic structures. He has *"raised us up together, and made us sit together in the heavenly places in Christ Jesus"* (Eph. 2:6 NKJV).

Get ready for *"the people that do know their God shall be strong, and do exploits"* (Dan. 11:32). Believe it and receive it; this is for you.

Lord, I declare that You *"will set* [me] *high above all the nations of the earth"* (Deut. 28:1 NASB).

God Wants His Blessings to Overtake Us

Blessings Are an Empowerment

"The blessing of the Lord makes one rich, and He adds no sorrow with it" (Prov. 10:22 NKJV). The blessings are not the riches; they are an empowerment to get "the stuff." The Hebrew root for *blessing* is *bârak*, which means to kneel.[1] When applied to God, it indicates worship or adoration; when used with men, it

implies speaking a benefit. When Isaac blessed Jacob, he empowered him: "*May peoples serve you, and nations bow down to you; be master of your brothers*" (Gen. 27:29 NASB).

When Esau complained about Jacob stealing his blessing, Isaac replied, "*Behold, I have made him your master, and all his relatives I have given to him as servants*" (Gen. 27:37 NASB). Isaac didn't make Esau Jacob's servant; he empowered Jacob to be the master. God's blessing has empowered us with a seed that will produce fruit. "*For whatever is born of God overcomes the world*" (1 John 5:4a NKJV). That is the power of the spoken blessing. If we believe it and receive it, it will come to pass. For "*this is the victory that overcometh the world, even our faith*" (1 John 5:4b).

Blessings Will Be Experienced Here

Our doctrines limit what we can believe for. If we don't believe in divine healing, we will not have faith to pray for it. If we don't believe in prophecy, we will not have faith to function in it. If we don't believe that God wants us to be blessed in this life, we won't know how to receive it. Jesus declared that

> *There is no man that hath left house, or brethren, or sisters, or father, or mother, or wife, or children, or lands, for My sake, and the gospel's, but he shall receive an hundredfold now in this time, houses, and brethren, and sisters, and mothers, and children, and lands, with persecutions; and in the world to come eternal life* (Mark 10:29-30).

Our faith cannot be based solely on earthly benefit or just on a heavenly reward. We live in two realms and should be able to walk in both realms as Jesus did. He prayed that God's "*will be done in earth, as it is in heaven*" (Matt. 6:10). He gave the Church the

> *…keys of the kingdom of heaven; and whatever you bind (declare to be improper and unlawful) on earth must be what is already bound in heaven; and whatever you loose (declare lawful) on earth must be what is already loosed in heaven* (Matthew 16:19 AMP).

The children of Israel experienced a physical blessing by inheriting the promises given to them that had spiritual implications. We experience a spiritual blessing by inheriting our promises, which have physical implications.

Poverty Is Not a Sign of Holiness

Poverty is actually a sign of the curse being active in our lives. The Bible says that

> *...all these curses shall come on you and...they shall be upon you for a sign...upon you and your descendants forever...You shall serve your enemies...in hunger and thirst, in nakedness and in want of all things; and He will put a yoke of iron upon your neck until He has destroyed you* (Deuteronomy 28:45-48 AMP).

David praised God for His blessings, saying, *"I have not seen the righteous forsaken, nor his seed begging bread"* (Ps. 37:25). When we walk in God's provision we are walking in *"a land flowing with milk and honey"* (Exod. 13:5). Many are so paranoid about being linked to prosperity preaching that they forget that Jesus came that we *"might have life, and that* [we]*...might have it more abundantly"* (John 10:10).

Lack is not a sign of sin being present in one's life; rather it is an indication of a curse operating. We are either under a curse or under a blessing. God hates mixture (see Deut. 22:11), and these two manifestations don't mix. *"No fountain* [can] *yield* [both] *salt water and fresh"* (James 3:12). Poverty and abundance come from two separate sources; one needs to be resisted, and one needs to be embraced. Satan uses our poverty mindsets to block the blessings that God wants to release. We must change our thinking to receive our inheritance.

Jesus was not poor. That is a mistaken conclusion that is deduced from twisting the Scriptures to fit this false doctrine. When Jesus was rejected at a Samaritan village, He responded to one who wished to follow Him with the statement: *"Foxes have holes and birds of the air have nests, but the Son of Man has nowhere to lay His head"* (Luke 9:58 NKJV). This was not saying that He had no home, for He had earlier taken some of His disciples to His dwelling place (see John 1:39). He was stating that in that city there was no place for Him to dwell, for they had rejected Him (see Luke 9:52-53).

Though Jesus *"was rich, yet for your sakes He became poor, that you through His poverty might become rich"* (2 Cor. 8:9 NKJV). He was also *"made...to be sin for us...that we might become the righteousness of God in Him"* (2 Cor. 5:21 NKJV). He didn't *live* in poverty any more than He *lived* in sin; He was *made* both, that there might be a divine exchange. He became sin, on the cross; He also became poor, on the cross.

Poor people don't have treasurers, but Jesus did. Judas was both the treasurer and *"a thief...having the bag (the money box, the purse of the Twelve), he took for himself what was put into it [pilfering the collections]"* (John 12:6 AMP). If there were only pennies in the bag, what he took would have been noticed. He was able to steal from the abundance that was in the bag, undetected. Jesus knew, but none of the other disciples did. Jesus never rebuked him for his thefts because the money in the bag was not Jesus' supply; God was.

Even on the Passover night, when Judas went out to betray Jesus, some of the disciples

> *...thought that, since Judas had the money box (the purse), Jesus was telling him, Buy what we need for the Festival, or that he should give something to the poor* (John 13:29 AMP).

Jesus was the one giving, not the poor one receiving.

His real wealth was not stored in a bag but in the storehouse He owned in Heaven.

Jesus manifested His access to that wealth by feeding 5,000 men plus women and children out of those resources. His disciples asked if they should spend 200 denarii to feed the crowds, warning that it would not be enough (see John 6:7).

Two hundred denarii is the equivalent of two-thirds of a year's wages, which in the U.S.A. in 2008 was over $52,000.[2] On this occasion, Jesus chose to ignore the money in the bag (the 200+ denarii) and tap into the larger resource that He had available. He gave thanks for the five loaves and two fishes that a lad had supplied and *"then took the loaves, and...He distributed to those who were seated; likewise...the fish as much as they wanted"* (John 6:11 NASB). The fact that the disciple considered feeding them at all showed that they had considerable funds.

Jesus fed two such groups in a couple of weeks. If 200 denarii would barely give everyone just a little, it is easy to calculate that two filling lunches would have cost over 600 denarii. That is well over $100,000 worth of food. Because Jesus operated in abundance, not from a position of wealth, He was no poorer by feeding them than He would have been richer by not.

Abundance is the answer to poverty, not wealth. Abundance is sufficiency and more for whatever the situation requires. Abundance is like cash flow; it continues to come and does not require us to *"store up treasures here on earth, where moths eat them and rust destroys them, and where thieves break in and steal"* (Matt. 6:19 NLT). Rather, abundance comes because we have

> *...treasures in heaven, where moths and rust cannot destroy, and thieves do not break in and steal. Wherever your treasure is, there the desires of your heart will also be* (Matthew 6:20-21 NLT).

God has been training us to live in abundance and trust Him, not money, jobs, or the stock market, for our supply. If I (Ken) made a small wage one year and triple the next, it didn't seem to matter. There was always enough for our needs. We are preparing to go to Korea and Hong Kong as we write this. An emergency one-day job came up two days ago that paid for all the expenses. We had already booked the trip, and now it is covered. Abundance is always tied to faith and obedience.

Heaven is a place of great wealth. It is described as having *"foundations of... all manner of precious stones...gates...[of] pearls...[and streets of] pure gold"* (Rev. 21:19,21). There is no lack, or sickness, or want in Heaven. Jesus has access to everything in Heaven and *"as He is, so are we in this world"* (1 John 4:17 NKJV). Like the children of Israel coming out of Egypt, through the wilderness into the Promised Land, so we have moved out of the land of lack, through the land of just enough, to the land of plenty.

Lord, I declare that *"all these blessings will come upon* [me] *and overtake* [me as I] *obey the Lord* [my] *God"* (Deut. 28:2 NASB).

We Are Blessed in the City and in the Country

"All these blessings shall come upon you and overtake you" (Deut. 28:2 AMP). They will catch up to you and run you down. You will not be able to avoid them wherever you are. David prophesied that *"surely goodness and mercy shall follow me all the days of my life"* (Ps. 23:6). This psalm is full of the blessing of the Lord. David also said that God would *"prepare a table before me in the presence of my enemies; You anoint my head with oil; my cup runs over"* (Ps. 23:5 NKJV).

What do blessings running us down in the street look like? We book a hotel room, and they upgrade us free of charge; we get bumped off our airplane, and they rebook us on a later flight. Now they are forced to put us in first class because there is no more room in economy. The flights work out such that we catch up to the plane we just got bumped from. Only now, for the inconvenience, we receive complimentary tickets to anywhere the airline flies. We use those tickets for a holiday, and again they bump us coming home. They pay for the hotel and the meals, extending the holidays by one day. This time they give us three free tickets to anywhere they fly because our son is with us. That is called favor.

There is no striving to get blessed, just an abiding in God's goodness. The vine does not struggle to produce fruit; it just stays connected to the vine. *"As the branch cannot bear fruit of itself, unless it abides in the vine, neither can you, unless you abide in Me"* (John 15:4 NKJV). There is no striving to produce.

The High Priest was not allowed to sweat in his service at the temple (see Ezek. 44:18), and neither are we as *"priests unto God"* (Rev. 1:6). Jesus *"ordained you, that ye should…bring forth fruit, and that your fruit should remain"* (John 15:16).

Lord, I declare that I shall be *"blessed…in the city, and blessed…in the country"* (Deut. 28:3 NASB).

Our Children Will Be Blessed

Our Children's Destiny

The psalmist prayed, *"May the Lord give you increase, you and your children. May you be blessed of the Lord"* (Ps. 115:14-15 NASB).

> *Behold, children are a heritage from the Lord, the fruit of the womb is a reward. Like arrows in the hand of a warrior, so are the children of one's youth. Happy is the man who has his quiver full of them; they shall not be ashamed, but shall speak with their enemies in the gate* (Psalm 127:3-5 NKJV).

There is great spiritual power against all intruders when a family is united.

Ten times in the Old Testament, we read that God blessed them, saying, *"Be fruitful and multiply"* (Gen. 1:28). God said, *"As truly as I live, all the earth shall be filled with the glory of the Lord"* (Num. 14:21). He is going to use us to accomplish that. His blessings will ensure that *"one generation shall praise Your works to another, and shall declare Your mighty acts"* (Ps. 145:4 NASB). As you walk in God's blessings, *"all your children shall be taught by the Lord, and great shall be the peace of your children"* (Isa. 54:13 NKJV).

This is the Scripture that God gave me (Jeanne) when our sons were teenagers. They were a wild bunch, always doing crazy things and getting into trouble. We felt like we were in a canoe, paddling only feet away from the top of Niagara Falls. It was a scary, stressful time until God gave me this word. I used to be afraid of death, but now that I survived teenagers nothing scares me. And God was true to His Word and brought the peace to pass.

Family Destiny

Jesus' sacrifice on the cross fulfilled the prophetic words that filled the Scriptures. He said, *"Search the Scriptures…it is these that testify about Me"* (John 5:39 NASB). He was also fulfilling Abraham's family destiny. It was said that in Abraham's *"seed shall all of the nations of the earth be blessed"* (Gen. 22:18). It is through the generations walking together that God is able to bless the world.

There is a pressure from the devil for each generation to accuse the other. The older generation accuses the younger of being rebellious. The younger accuses the older of being indifferent and of making mistakes that will cost them.

The Pharisees, who were a cross-generational religious sect, accused their forefathers before Jesus, saying, *"If we had lived in the days of our father, we would not have been partakers with them in the blood of the prophets"* (Matt. 23:30 NKJV). Jesus turned their accusations back on them, saying, *"You are testifying against yourselves that you are the descendants of those who murdered the prophets"* (Matt. 23:30-31 AMP). Their accusation linked them to the atrocities that their fathers had done, ensuring that the sin would be repeated. *"Therefore, indeed, I send you prophets, wise men, and scribes: some of them you will kill and crucify"* (Matt. 23:34 NKJV).

God is sending

> *...Elijah the prophet before the coming of the great and dreadful day of the Lord. And he shall turn the heart of the fathers to the children, and the heart of the children to their fathers, lest I come and strike the earth with a curse* (Malachi 4:5-6 NKJV).

The prophetic blessing allows each generation to see past their wounds to the truth that the family is one. The forerunner Elijah is preparing the way for the King and the Kingdom to come. God will set families in proper order before the fullness of the Kingdom is manifest.

Yet Jesus said,

> *Don't imagine that I came to bring peace to the earth! No, I came to bring a sword. I have come to set a man against his father, and a daughter against her mother, and a daughter-in-law against her mother-in-law. Your enemies will be right in your own household! If you love your father or mother more than Me, you are not worthy of being Mine* (Matthew 10:34-37 NLT).

Jesus doesn't want divided loyalties.

God has to be first in our affections. Unhealthy soul ties hold most family connections together; these ties are the cause of most of the hurt and anger in families. Jesus is severing these soul ties so that He can build families again in the spirit. The spirit of Elijah will reconnect the hearts of the generations in their proper order. Let that prophetic mantle guide you in moving your family into its blessing.

It feels great for us when we host a seminar, and one of our sons and his wife are a part of the ministry team, another son is looking after the book table, and our third son and his wife are praying for us as they live hundreds of miles away.

World Destiny

The promise to Abraham went beyond the bounds of the Promised Land. Paul said, "*The promise to Abraham or to his descendants* [is] *that he would be heir of the world...through the righteousness of faith*" (Rom. 4:13 NASB). God is creating a new generation of spiritual children who will inherit the blessings of Abraham.

> *Beloved, now are we the sons of God, and it doth not yet appear what we shall be: but we know that, when He shall appear, we shall be like Him; for we shall see Him as He is. And every man that hath this hope in Him purifies himself, even as He is pure* (1 John 3:2-3).

God wants to use our families to bring His blessings to the whole world.

Lord, I declare that You shall bless "*the offspring of* [my] *body*" (Deut. 28:4a NASB).

Our Work and Labor Will Be Blessed

The original curse God spoke to Adam was

> *Cursed is the ground because of you; in toil you will eat of it all the days of your life. Both thorns and thistles it shall grow for you; and*

*you will eat the plants of the field; by the sweat of your face you will
eat bread* (Genesis 3:17-19 NASB).

Toil, sweat, and poor results are products of the curse. A good return from
sweatless work is the promise of the blessings. God cursed Adam's self-effort to
achieve success. God warned me (Ken) that I would not be able to achieve success through self-effort or will power. I would have to act in faith.

Faith is always birthed in God. He speaks a word; we hear it, believe it, and
declare it into our realms of authority. *"Faith is the substance of things hoped for,
the evidence of things not seen"* (Heb. 11:1). Faith is not belief. We try to work up
our faith by believing harder or proclaiming, *"Lord, I believe; help my unbelief!"*
(Mark 9:24 NKJV).

Faith is an actual substance. The word *substance* means to set under or
undergird, essence, or person.[3] The same word is used earlier in Hebrews referring to Jesus as *"being the brightness of His glory and the express image of His
person"* (Heb. 1:3 NKJV).[4]

So the substance of faith is the person of God. We receive God as a seed of
what we are hoping for. If it is planted in our heart, and we water it, and don't
choke it out with weeds, it will produce (see Matt. 13:3-8). The seed is the Word
(see Matt. 13:19), a piece of Jesus that has life in it, which will produce a harvest.
Faith is a substance that will grow by itself; an idea is a thought that has no life
and requires toil to make it manifest. Faith is a God idea; schemes are just good
ideas.

I (Ken) counseled a young couple who were stepping into business to learn
to operate in faith. This is their testimony.

Our construction company was less than a year old when we won a six-
figure contract. We were a little intimidated. Ken and I were discussing
the project when he challenged me to include faith in business. Quoting
Romans 10:17, he said, "Faith needs a word [*rhema*] in order to operate
in faith—no word, no faith. Without those, you're doing business like
everyone else in the world, relying on your own cleverness, charm, and
hard work. Is that *really* what you want to trust in?"

My wife and I took that challenge to heart. We each asked God for a word upon which to anchor our faith for this big project, and we both got one. Cam got, "Be confident in the blessing," and Teresa got, "Don't fear prosperity." We recited those words, especially when significant moments of decision arose throughout the project. Even though some "bad" things happened on-site—including an injured worker and accidental property damage caused by our crew—we had favor with the building inspector, the general contractor, and the trades.

The original contract ballooned to three times its initial value, as each decision on-site went in our favor. Incidentally, the injured worker had no lost time and didn't require ongoing compensation, though he "should" have, and the damage caused by our crew was easily and cheaply repaired. I believe God tipped the scales in our favor because we sought Him for a word and believed Him to perform it.

The Book of James encourages us not to say,

> *"Today or tomorrow we will go to such and such a city, spend a year there, buy and sell, and make a profit"; whereas you do not know what will happen tomorrow. Instead you ought to say, "If the Lord wills, we shall live and do this or that"* (James 4:13-15 NKJV).

Get a word so that you can operate in faith, *"for whatever is not of faith is sin"* (Rom. 14:23 NKJV). *"So faith comes from hearing, and hearing by the word of Christ"* (Rom. 10:17 NASB). We get a word for each job so that we can do those jobs in faith and not fear. It is always amazing how those particular Scriptures meet the needs of the problems that arise. Hidden in the Word are the keys to the unforeseen circumstances.

> *Without faith it is impossible to please God, because anyone who comes to Him must believe that He exists and that He rewards those who earnestly seek Him* (Hebrews 11:6 NIV).

We must believe that He is a rewarder to get a reward. The two blind men who cried after Jesus arrested His attention.

> *...Jesus said to them, "Do you believe that I am able to do this?" They said to Him, "Yes, Lord." Then He touched their eyes, saying, "It shall be done to you according to your faith"* (Matthew 9:28-29 NASB).

Blessings in business depend on your faith, not your savvy.

Jacob used many underhanded tactics to grasp what he wanted. But what you sow, you will reap, and Jacob had his wages *"changed...ten times...*[by Laban]; *but God did not allow him to hurt me"* (Gen. 31:7 NKJV). In the natural, Jacob would have walked out of that abusive situation with nothing, but God gave him revelatory strategies. God used genetic principles of animal husbandry to prosper Jacob. He showed him in a dream how to breed the animals for his benefit (see Gen. 31:11-12). I (Ken) have had many dreams of how to do things at work that had stumped me. This is part of God blessing whatever work we do.

The Kingdom principles work even when the economy isn't. *"There was a famine in the land....then Isaac sowed in that land, and received in the same year an hundredfold"* (Gen. 26:1,12 NKJV). Prices go up, and you get rich when you harvest a bumper crop and everyone else has nothing.

God told Jeremiah to *"buy...the field for money...for the city is given into the hand of the Chaldeans"* (Jer. 32:25). God is the best counter-cyclical trader ever because He knows where the bottom is. The land was going for next to nothing because Israel was being invaded. But God asked Jeremiah, *"Is there any thing too hard for Me?"* (Jer. 32:27). He knew that *"houses and fields and vineyards"* (Jer. 32:15) would be sold again and that this was a good time for Jeremiah to buy for his family's sake. God even told him how to store the deed so it would last until the captivity was over (see Jer. 32:14).

Our family has experienced similar blessing under duress. My (Ken's) grandfather farmed in the Palliser Triangle, an area in southern Alberta and Saskatchewan originally deemed too dry to farm. He farmed there during the drought years of the depression. Even though it was too dry to harvest a seeded crop, he managed to prosper and expand the farm as others were packing it in.

Peter had *"toiled all the night, and...taken nothing"* (Luke 5:5), but when he responded to Jesus' revelation on where to fish, *"they caught a great number of fish, and their net was breaking"* (Luke 5:6 NKJV). God has all the toil-less strategies on how to prosper. When Peter needed to pay some taxes, Jesus told him to go fishing, and the taxes came to him (see Matt. 17:27). Job says, *"If they obey and serve Him, they shall spend their days in prosperity, and their years in pleasure"* (Job 36:11 NKJV).

There are more verses in the Bible about money than there are about love because God is interested in your heart: *"Where your treasure is, there will your heart be also"* (Matt. 6:21). *"You cannot serve God and mammon (deceitful riches, money, possessions, or whatever is trusted in)"* (Matt. 6:24 AMP). If your heart is right about money, then your actions will be right. If your heart is right, God will anoint you to do the jobs He has appointed you to do.

> *He has filled* [Bezalel] *with the Spirit of God, with ability and wisdom, with intelligence and understanding, and with knowledge and all craftsmanship, to devise artistic designs, to work in gold, silver, and bronze, in cutting of stones for setting, and in carving of wood, for work in every skilled craft. And God has put in Bezalel's heart that he may teach, both he and Aholiab...He has filled them with wisdom of heart and ability to do all manner of craftsmanship, of the engraver, of the skillful workman, of the embroiderer in blue, purple, and scarlet [stuff] and in fine linen, and of the weaver, even of those who do or design any skilled work. Bezalel and Aholiab and every wise hearted man in whom the Lord has put wisdom and understanding to know how to do all the work for the service of the sanctuary* (Exodus 35:31–36:1 AMP).

Israel had constantly complained in the wilderness about the leadership, and the lack of water and food. There was little danger that when they entered the land that they would be poor, lacking the necessities and continuing to gripe and resent God. The real danger going into the land, for the children of Israel, was that they would not know how to handle the prosperity. Moses warned them that if they

...did not serve the Lord...with joy and gladness of heart, for the abundance of everything [then]*...you shall serve your enemies, whom the Lord will send against you, in hunger, in thirst, in nakedness, and in need of everything* (Deuteronomy 28:47-48 NKJV).

God will bless our work, if we let Him; but we will only keep it if we thank Him.

Lord, I declare that You shall "[bless]*...the produce of* [my] *ground and the offspring of* [my] *beasts*" (Deut. 28:4b NASB).

Our Investments and Holdings Will Be Blessed

There is much talk these days about green investments, but God wants us to go further and make righteous investments. Jesus said,

Sell your possessions and give to those in need. This will store up treasure for you in heaven! And the purses of heaven never get old or develop holes. Your treasure will be safe; no thief can steal it and no moth can destroy it (Luke 12:33 NLT).

This clashes with all our logic because we don't trust what Jesus is saying.

The rich young ruler encountered a similar roadblock in his attempt to justify himself. Jesus put His finger on the one idol he had: money. He said, "*Sell all that you have and distribute to the poor, and you will have treasure in heaven*" (Luke 18:22 NKJV). God cannot lie; if Jesus said it, it is true. But that doesn't make it any easier to follow. Logic says, amass a large fortune, and the money will make more money. Jesus said, give it away, and you will have a fortune.

The Jews were not even allowed to charge interest to each other (see Deut. 23:20), and they were required to lend whenever someone asked and give him as much as he needed (see Deut. 15:8). All debts were to be cancelled every seven years (see Deut. 15:2). "*He who has pity on the poor lends to the Lord, and that which he has given He will repay to him*" (Prov. 19:17 AMP).

All Hebrew slaves were to be released every seven years and supplied with enough to restart their lives (see Deut. 15:12-15). All land sales reverted to the original owner every 50 years as did all the rural houses (see Lev. 25:10-34). They were told to let the land go fallow every seven years (see Lev. 25:2-8). All these impacted the normal transaction of business and made the people dependent on God and responsible to each other. *"How hard it will be for those who are wealthy to enter the kingdom of God!"* (Mark 10:23 NASB).

God is not opposed to us making money or even to us getting rich, but He knows the temptations that money brings.

> *For the love of money is the root of all evil: which while some coveted after, they have erred from the faith, and pierced themselves through with many sorrows* (1 Timothy 6:10).

God did allow the Jews to charge interest to strangers and to keep foreign slaves. In the parable of the talents, Jesus commended those who traded and made profit—and rebuked the one who didn't even make any interest (see Matt. 25:15-29).

> *He who is faithful in what is least is faithful also in much; and he who is unjust in what is least is unjust also in much. Therefore if you have not been faithful in the unrighteous mammon, who will commit to your trust the true riches? And if you have not been faithful in what is another man's, who will give you what is your own? No servant can serve two masters; for either he will hate the one and love the other, or else he will be loyal to the one and despise the other. You cannot serve God and mammon* (Luke 16:10-13 NKJV).

Jesus laid out three criteria for God to increase us:

- Faithful in little; faithful in much

If you are not able to keep a small house clean, why would God burden you with a larger one? Because we managed a small business for years, we were ready when the million-dollar contracts came along.

- Faithful with money; faithful with true riches (spiritual authority)

If you can't tithe when money is tight, there will always be a reason not to when times are good. We used to tithe on what we needed as if we already had the money that we had faith for. We consistently got excited when God's blessings exceeded our faith. Now we have a ministry that touches God's real treasure: His people.

- Faithful with what belongs to others; faithful with your own

When you borrow something and it breaks, do you repair it and return it in better condition than you got it? Do you even return it? We mistakenly borrowed the wrong trailer from a friend and took the neighbor's instead. It got a flat, and we bought a new tire instead of just fixing the old one. Imagine the neighbor's surprise when he got home, and the trailer in his backyard had sprouted a new tire. When the error was explained, we all had a good laugh, and God was glorified with our faithfulness.

If we can pass these three measuring posts, we won't fall under the lure of gain.

To enter into the covenant promises and reap the full benefit of God's favor, we must be willing to tithe. Tithing is the seal on the covenant that keeps the devourer away and ensures our blessing (see Mal. 3:11). If you know you are under God's protection and provision, giving is not hard; it is fun. God *"loves a cheerful giver"* (2 Cor. 9:7 NKJV). Being hilarious in our giving pleases the heart of God.

Jesus' approach to owning possessions was that everything belonged to God and He was the steward of what was the Father's. He knew that *"the earth is the Lord's, and the fullness thereof, the world, and they that dwell therein"* (Ps. 24:1), for God had said, *"The silver is Mine, and the gold is Mine"* (Hag. 2:8).

Even though Jesus never chided extravagance, He was frugal. He never let anything go to waste. After He fed almost 10,000 people, He told His disciples to *"gather up the fragments that remain, that nothing be lost"* (John 6:12). He and the disciples either ate the leftovers for a few days or gave them to the poor. He silenced those who criticized the use of a year's wages in costly oil[5] (see John 12:5-7) to anoint Him, while praising the widow for putting in her two mites[6] (see Luke 21:2-4). The heart of the giver was what impressed Him. We may not all be kings, but as the King's servants, we live in the palace and eat the King's food.

Lord, I declare that You shall "[bless]...*the increase of* [my] *herd and the young of* [my] *flock*" (Deut. 28:4c NASB).

Our Provisions and Groceries Will Be Blessed

The picture of the cornucopia, the overflowing basket or the horn of plenty, has always been a symbol of abundance. The blessings of the Lord are like that: overflowing. When Jesus fed the thousands of people, there was always an overflow. Later, the disciples were worried because they had brought no bread with them.

> But Jesus, aware of this, asked, "Why are you discussing among yourselves the fact that you have no bread?...Do you not yet discern (perceive and understand)? Do you not remember the five loaves of the five thousand, and how many [small hand] baskets you gathered? Nor the seven loaves for the four thousand, and how many [large provision] baskets you took up?" (Matthew 16:8-10 AMP)

Lack was not an issue with Jesus because He did not have a poverty mindset like the disciples did. For even though *"the kingdom of God is not* [about] *meat and drink; but righteousness, and peace, and joy"* (Rom. 14:17), it makes provision for the meat and drink. The Kingdom operates on the laws of thermodynamics. The first law of thermodynamics, commonly known as the law of conservation of matter, states that matter/energy cannot be created, nor can it be destroyed.[7] Because Jesus understood that, even though they could not see the bread, it was available to them just as it had been to feed the thousands.

Friends of ours, Bill and Bernice, were in Holland, with their six kids, on a long-term mission. They had little support and were trusting the Lord to look after them. Bernice decided to cook a Cornish game hen for their New Year's day feast, as that was all they could afford. They had lots of vegetables and potatoes from the garden, but they needed more meat. That little bird was going to supply only a mouthful of meat for the eight of them. They prayed, and God told Bernice that He would supply what they needed.

They went to church that morning expecting that someone might give them a turkey or some chickens. All they got from the church was six more guests for dinner. Six Bible school students had nowhere to go, and Bill invited them to share the meal with their family. Now that game hen needed to feed 14.

The guests went first to fill up their plates. Bill saw each one take two pieces of meat along with the vegetables. He was more shocked when next the kids dished up, taking two pieces also. When Bill and Bernice served themselves, the pot was still full of game hen pieces. It got even better when everyone went back for seconds. God stretched that bird to fill 14 plates twice, *"as much as they wanted"* (John 6:11 NKJV). God said to Bill, "Trust Me; love men."

God has a multitude of delivery systems for our provision. Elijah hid from King Ahab during the drought, which he had spoken into being. God gave him instructions, and he

> *...went and dwelt by the brook Cherith...and the ravens brought him bread and flesh in the morning, and bread and flesh in the evening; and he drank of the brook* (1 Kings 17:5-6).

It wasn't long until the brook dried up, and God gave him new instructions. God is not static, and neither is His provision. What works for a while may not work later.

George Mueller had over 2,000 orphans in his care in the late 1800s.[8] He depended upon a supernatural supply to feed his children. One Christmas, the orphans asked for a special dessert that they normally could not afford. Mr. Mueller agreed, and bananas were the choice of the majority. They ate their Christmas meal and reset the table in anticipation of their dessert. They prayed and thanked God for His special provision and then waited.

In a few minutes, there was a knock on the door. Dozens of stevedores were outside with lorries full of bananas. God is extravagant with His love. There was a dock strike going on, and the shipment of bananas was sitting in the hold of a ship docked at the quay. The bananas were going to rot there if they weren't unloaded. The stevedore offered a solution. If the bananas were given to George Mueller's orphanage, they would unload them on Christmas morning. God knows how to bless and honor the faith of His children.

When satan tempted Jesus about His provision in the wilderness, Jesus replied, *"It is written, Man shall not live by bread alone, but by every word that proceedeth out the mouth of God"* (Matt. 4:4). Though Jesus had the capacity to change the stones to bread, He chose to rely on God's methods of providing. He was walking out a pattern that we would be able to follow.

So when the brook dried up, God moved Elijah in with a widow and gave her supernatural provision. She only had *"a handful of meal in a barrel, and a little oil in a cruse"* (1 Kings 17:12). Elijah prophesied over the ingredients, and *"the bin of flour was not used up, nor did the jar of oil run dry, according to the word of the Lord, which He spoke by Elijah"* (1 Kings 17:16 NKJV). God can bless your provisions whether you have little or much, but we need to be fluid in our responses to God. The Holy Spirit is depicted as a river, not a lake, because He is always moving. We will need a second word from the Lord If our circumstances change, as they did with Elijah. Stubbornness is not faith and is not a fruit of the Spirit.

In the wilderness, Israel experienced miraculous provision in the form of the manna. But

> *...the manna ceased on the day after they had eaten some of the produce of the land, so that the sons of Israel no longer had manna, but they ate some of the yield of the land of Canaan during that year* (Joshua 5:12 NASB).

God can supply miraculously or abundantly.

God used Israel to demonstrate to us how much He loves us and will supply for us if we can trust Him. He said to Israel,

> *If you want to live securely in the land, follow My decrees and obey My regulations. Then the land will yield large crops, and you will eat your fill and live securely in it. But you might ask, "What will we eat*

during the seventh year, since we are not allowed to plant or harvest crops that year?" The answer is, "I will order My blessing for you in the sixth year, so the land will produce a crop large enough for three years" (Leviticus 25:18-21 NLT).

God wants to overflow your baskets so that you have more than enough groceries to eat and to give away as a blessing to others. If we never step out in faith, we will never see the provision He promised.

Lord, I declare that You shall "[bless]…[my] *basket"* (Deut. 28:5a NASB).

Our Kneading Bowls Will Be Full and Blessed

There is no smell on earth like the smell of fresh-baked bread. Bread has long been called the "staff of life." Jesus drew on that analogy, saying,

> *For the Bread of God is He who comes down out of heaven and gives life to the world…I am the bread of life. He who comes to Me shall never hunger* (John 6:33,35 NKJV).

Entering into covenant with God and anticipating the blessing gives us access to this bread and fills us to overflowing.

That bread is in us, if *"Christ…dwell*[s] *in* [our]…*hearts by faith"* (Eph. 3:17). If we have Him in us, we can give Him away.

> *Sanctify the Lord God in your hearts: and be ready always to give an answer to every man that asketh you a reason of the hope that is in you with meekness and fear* (1 Peter 3:15).

God wants to bless us with not just food, but life.

Jesus wants to be fresh bread for us every day. The bread of His Presence, the showbread, was baked daily. We too are to partake daily of that bread from Heaven. That is part of the blessing, to receive fresh revelation each day. God told me (Ken) that Heaven was going to be special for me. Because I am a teacher, new revelation gets me very excited. God said that Heaven was going to be like that. Every day He would reveal something about Him that I had not seen before. There was enough revelation that throughout eternity I would not get to the end of understanding all His facets.

Be hospitable and

> *...cheerfully share your home with those who need a meal or a place to stay. God has given each of you a gift from His great variety of spiritual gifts. Use them well to serve one another* (1 Peter 4:9-10 NLT).

> *Do not forget to entertain strangers, for by so doing some have unwittingly entertained angels* (Hebrews 13:2 NKJV).

We minister to God by ministering *"to the least of these My brethren"* (Matt. 25:40).

Lord, I declare that You shall bless my *"kneading bowl"* (Deut. 28:5b NASB).

Going In and Out We Shall Be Blessed

We went to a gathering in Quebec City and felt impressed to extend our stay past the conference dates. The day after the conference, an Air France jet skidded off the runway and burnt at Pearson International in Toronto, shutting down the airport for over a day. Anyone traveling east to west in Canada was affected. We watched on television as the thousands of passengers across the country were stranded or diverted because of this crash (no one was seriously injured). We watched but were not affected as we enjoyed two more days of relaxation. By the time we were ready to travel, the backlog had cleared up, and we had no problems. We were blessed going in and coming out. However, this blessing is not just about traveling and going from one place to another.

There are two aspects to blessings: giving and receiving. God prophesied to Abram, *"I will bless you [with abundant increase of favors]...and you will be* a blessing [dispensing good to others]" (Gen. 12:2 AMP). Though we all like to receive, Jesus said, *"It is more blessed to give than to receive"* (Acts 20:35).

We must love to both give and receive. Many have a wrong concept about cheerfully receiving and are unable to be a beneficiary. We must thankfully receive before we have something to give. *Yâdâh* is the Hebrew word translated "thankful." Its root is *yâd*, which means an open hand.[9] We need to have an open hand to properly receive. If our hand is closed, we are taking, not receiving.

I saw a short film about a man traversing the Kalahari Desert. He needed to find water and came to a place where there was a troop of monkeys. As the monkeys watched him, he drilled a narrow hole in a termite mound and deposited some nuts inside one of its small compartments. He then pretended to sleep under the monkey's tree.

Curiosity overcame one of the monkeys, and he ran over to the termite mound and wriggled his front paw inside. When he discovered the nuts, he grasped as many as he could in his fist and attempted to withdraw. With his fist full of nuts, it was too big to navigate the hole, and he screamed as he struggled to extract his treasure.

The explorer jumped up and placed a small rope around the monkey's neck. Caught, he released his trove of nuts. He was fed some salt and later released to lead the man to the watering hole. The monkey could have easily escaped if he would have released what was in his hand. Open your hand in thanksgiving so that you receive the bounty of the Lord and don't get caught by greed.

We may give things to You, God, but *"all this store that we have...cometh of Thine hand, and is all Thine own"* (1 Chron. 29:16).

Lord, I declare that that I shall be *"blessed...when* [I] *come in, and blessed...when* [I] *go out"* (Deut. 28:6 NASB).

Bless and Empower Us to Drive Our Enemies Back

The enemy has been working to keep us out of our promises. God told Joshua to *"be strong and of good courage; do not be afraid, nor be dismayed, for the Lord your God is with you wherever you go"* (Josh. 1:9 NKJV). If we know that *"God is for us,* [then] *who can be against us?"* (Rom. 8:31 NKJV). If we know we are loved, then we will have no fear (see 1 John 4:18).

Fear is a spirit (see 2 Tim. 1:7), and it is not particular about whom it attacks. The blessing Moses spoke was that the enemy would be afraid and flee. Rahab, the harlot, told the spies

> *...that the terror of you has fallen on us, and that all the inhabitants of the land have melted away before you. For we have heard how the Lord dried up the water of the Red Sea...and what you did to the two kings of the Amorites...whom you utterly destroyed...Our hearts melted and no courage remained...because of you* (Joshua 2:9-11 NASB).

A friend of ours, who is very evangelistic, decided to pass out tracts in a seedy area of Edmonton. People cautioned her about being a young lady working those streets, but she felt secure in God's protection. She went out and started to give tracts to anyone who would take them. Suddenly a man with crazed eyes grabbed her. She responded with what was in her—praise and tongues. Just as quickly as he had grabbed her, the man took off in fear. The enemy has no power when faith attacks fear.

God is in the process of establishing His Kingdom in the earth. *"His Kingdom is an everlasting kingdom and His dominion is from generation to generation"* (Dan. 4:3 NASB). Jesus said, *"If I with the finger of God cast out devils, no doubt the kingdom of God is come upon you"* (Luke 11:20). The power of God accompanies the blessings of God, which brings deliverance. The Gospel of the Kingdom includes *"healing every sickness and every disease among the people"* (Matt. 9:35). If we are citizens of the Kingdom, we can function in the power of the Kingdom. The disciples did. They were given *"power to tread on serpents and scorpions, and over all the power of the enemy"* (Luke 10:19).

In the movie *Apocalypto,* the main character, Jaguar Paw, is fleeing for his life from a band of furious Mayans. He flees, in survivor mode, until he crosses into his own territory. At that point, a shift occurs in his response to the pursuit. He stops and declares to himself, "I am Jaguar Paw; this is my jungle, and I am not afraid." Sensing the power of that declaration, he no longer runs to escape. Now it is only to buy time, till he gains an advantage and is able to attack. When the fear left, he could see his provision, his weapons, all around him.[10]

The blessing of God allows us to see His strategy for defeating any foe. Joshua was given a strategy to defeat Jericho (see Josh. 6); David was given a strategy to defeat the Philistines (see 2 Sam. 5:19-25); Jehoshaphat was given a strategy to defeat Ammon and Moab (see 2 Chron. 20:10-24). Every strategy was radically different, as the Spirit dictated, but each defeated the enemy and put them to flight.

When Goliath was taunting the army of Israel, a spirit of fear overcame them, and *"they were dismayed and greatly afraid"* (1 Sam. 17:11). But the giant did not intimidate David, even though he was only 17. His brothers were upset at his cocky attitude and accused him of wanting to see a battle. But David did not want to see a battle; he had no fear and wanted to participate in one. When David killed Goliath, the fear that had rested on the camp of Israel crossed the valley and attacked the Philistines. And *"when the Philistines saw that their mighty champion was dead, they fled"* (1 Sam. 17:51 AMP), even though they greatly outnumbered the Israelis.

Paul said, *"The God of peace will bruise Satan under your feet shortly"* (Rom. 16:20 NKJV). That is the fulfillment of the original prophetic word to Eve designed to drive our enemy away. And *"the last enemy that will be destroyed is death. For 'He has put all things under His feet' "* (1 Cor. 15:26-27 NKJV).

I declare that *"the Lord shall cause* [my] *enemies who rise up against* [me] *to be defeated before* [me]; *they will come out against* [me] *one way and will flee before* [me] *seven ways"* (Deut. 28:7 NASB).

Chapter 21

HEIRS OF THE PROMISES

M oses continued with Israel's blessings. As children of Abraham (see Rom. 4:16), we also are heirs to these promises.

The Lord will command the blessing upon you in your barns and in all that you put your hand to, and He will bless you in the land which the Lord your God gives you. The Lord will establish you as a holy people to Himself, as He swore to you, if you keep the commandments of the Lord your God and walk in His ways. So all the peoples of the earth will see that you are called by the name of the Lord, and they will be afraid of you. The Lord will make you abound in prosperity, in the offspring of your body and in the offspring of your beast and in the produce of your ground, in the land which the Lord swore to your fathers to give you. The Lord will open for you His good storehouse, the heavens, to give rain to your land in its season and to bless all the work of your hand; and you shall lend to many nations, but you shall not borrow. The Lord will make you the head and not the tail, and you only will be above, and you will not be underneath, if you listen to the commandments of the Lord your God (Deuteronomy 28:8-13 NASB).

Bless and Fill Your Storehouses

"The Lord will command the blessing on you in your storehouses" (Deut. 28:8 NKJV), which today would represent our bank accounts. There is a great division in the Body of Christ around wealth. The Scripture is often quoted that *"it will be difficult for a rich man to get into the kingdom of heaven"* (Matt. 19:23 AMP)—difficult, but not impossible. The disciples were amazed and asked, *"Who then can be saved?"* (Matt. 19:25 AMP). Their wonder was due to the popular doctrine that money was a mark of approval from God. This in turn indicated that God showed favoritism because everyone knew that not all those with money were righteous. We need to take our doctrines to their conclusions to see if they really make sense and are in line with the Word.

Solomon said, *"The wealth of the sinner is stored up for the righteous"* (Prov. 13:22 NASB). This is not some fantasy reserved for Heaven or the millennium; what is good for Heaven and the millennium is good for now.

> *All Scripture is given by inspiration of God, and is profitable for doctrine, for reproof, for correction, for instruction in righteousness, that the man of God may be complete, thoroughly equipped for every good work* (2 Timothy 3:16-17 NKJV).

We need righteous doctrine to function righteously. John prayed, *"In all respects* [may] *you...prosper and be in good health, just as your soul prospers"* (3 John 2 NASB).

Prosperity is a good thing to pray for. If it wasn't, then we should pray that we don't prosper, that we don't have good jobs, and that our children do without. That may seem ridiculous, but it is the logical outcome of the non-prosperity doctrine. Any attempt to help the poor and needy would also be counterproductive if we don't want people to prosper. In fact, we couldn't save money or invest because it might make us rich. The prosperity doctrine has suffered abuse, not because the doctrine is wrong, but because our hearts are wrong.

Lack is a sign of the curse; prosperity is a sign of blessing. As stated earlier, there is great wealth in Heaven: streets of gold, gates of pearls, and foundations of precious stones. Jesus prayed, *"Thy kingdom come, Thy will be done in earth, as it is in heaven"* (Matt. 6:10). God's will in Heaven is prosperity; we need to pray that down to earth.

Power and money are amplifiers.

> *He who is faithful in a very little thing is faithful also in much; and he who is unrighteous in a very little thing is unrighteous also in much* (Luke 16:10 NASB).

If we are evil without much money, we will be worse with it. We are not told to have riches; we are advised that *"if riches increase, set not your heart upon them"* (Ps. 62:10). Riches don't make the man: the man makes the riches. One such man was R.G. LeTourneau.

R.G. LeTourneau, as the father of the modern earthmoving industry, was responsible for 299 inventions. These inventions included the bulldozer, scrapers of all sorts, dredgers, portable cranes, rollers, dump wagons, bridge spans, logging equipment, mobile sea platforms for oil exploration, and many others. He introduced into the earthmoving and material handling industry the rubber tire, which today is almost universally accepted. He also invented and developed the electric wheel.

His life's verse was Matthew 6:33: *"Seek ye first the kingdom of God and His righteousness; and all these things shall be added unto you."*

LeTourneau said that the money came in faster than he could give it away, and he gave away 90 percent of everything he made. He was convinced that he could not out-give God. "I shovel it out," he would say, "and God shovels it back, but God has a bigger shovel."[1]

God allowed Jeanne and me to give away well over $150,000 in 2008. We had been praying since 1994, when we gave away our first $10,000 gift, that we would be able to give away $100,000. We plan to give away $1,000,000, when we get that much. We don't know how, just as we didn't know how we gave away the $150,000 and the $10,000. But God knows how; we just need to believe that our storehouse will be overflowing when He says to give into the Kingdom. Faith is like a muscle: the more you use it, the stronger it becomes.

Money is not evil or good; it is neutral. The heart's intent with money is the deciding factor. Jesus warned us to *"beware of covetousness, for one's life does not consist in the abundance of the things he possesses"* (Luke 12:15 NKJV). To the rich man Jesus described in the following verses, money became a curse and contributed to his demise. *"So is he who lays up treasure for himself, and is not rich toward God"* (Luke 12:21 NKJV). Gain is not godliness, *"but godliness with contentment is great gain. For we brought nothing into this world, and it is certain we can carry nothing out"* (1 Tim. 6:6-7 NKJV).

You can't recognize the righteous by their bank accounts; *"ye shall know them by their fruits"* (Matt. 7:16).

Prosperity is like every other gift from God; everyone who has faith can have it. Jesus said, *"All things are possible to him that believeth"* (Mark 9:23). We must cry out, *"Lord, I believe; help Thou mine unbelief"* (Mark 9:24). God wants to give you the faith and the character to handle great wealth.

David could handle wealth. He laid up an estimated $750,000 out of his own resources to build the temple (see 1 Chron. 29:3-4). Solomon could not. He spent his money on vanities and women. Solomon started the work on the house of Lord and *"was seven years in building it...But Solomon took thirteen years to build his own house"* (1 Kings 6:38; 7:1 NKJV). He also built the house of the Forest of Lebanon, the Hall of Pillars, the Hall of Judgment for the throne, and a house for Pharaoh's daughter who was one of his wives. These were all of costly stones and hewn timbers (see 1 Kings 7:2-12).

Solomon *"had seven hundred wives, princesses, and three hundred concubines, and his wives turned his heart away...after other gods"* (1 Kings 11:3-4 NASB). Wealth amplified his self-centeredness because he put no constraints on his own desires. He said,

> All that my eyes desired I did not refuse them. I did not withhold my heart from any pleasure...Thus I considered all my activities...and behold all was vanity and striving after wind and there was no profit (Ecclesiastes 2:10-11 NASB).

His wealth destroyed him, and he lost most of the kingdom for his heirs. Godly men often fall because increased money and power amplifies the cracks in their character.

> *A good man out of the good treasure of his heart brings forth good; and an evil man out of the evil treasure of his heart brings forth evil. For out of the abundance of the heart his mouth speaks* (Luke 6:45 NKJV).

It is not wealth but abundance that counts. Even if you have little, God has chosen *"the poor of this world rich in faith, and heirs of the kingdom which He promised to those who love Him"* (James 2:5).

Lord, I declare that You *"will command the blessing upon...[my] barns"* and my bank accounts (Deut. 28:8a NASB).

Bless (Empower) Everything That We Do

My (Jeanne's) brother said to us, "If you win; you win. If you lose; you win." That is the spiritual equivalent of the Midas touch: everything you touch turns to gold. Paul said, *"All things work together for good to those who love God, to those who are the called according to His purpose"* (Rom. 8:28 NKJV).

> *...What then shall we say to these things? If God is for us, who is against us? He who did not spare His own Son...will He not also with Him freely give us all things? Christ...also intercedes for us. Who will separate us from the love of Christ? Will tribulation, or distress, or persecution, or famine, or nakedness, or peril, or sword?...But in all these things we overwhelmingly conquer through Him who loved us* (Romans 8:31-37 NASB).

God wants us so in tune with His will that He can do our will. David was *"a man after His own heart"* (1 Sam. 13:14). God liked David and treated him like His son, correcting him but also allowing him freedom of expression. Moses built the tabernacle and was told to *"be sure that you make everything according to the pattern I have shown you here on the mountain"* (Exod. 25:40 NLT). Every detail was exactly as God showed him.

David wanted the ark of God close to him, so he too built a tabernacle. He erected it in the wrong place, used the wrong materials, used the wrong pattern, staffed it with the wrong people, had the wrong order of service, and went in where kings were not allowed. He did it all wrong but with the right heart. God was so enamored with his heart's desires that He must have exclaimed, "I like this boy! He had a better idea than I did. When We set the tabernacle up again in the last days, We will use his idea instead of Mine" (see Amos 9:11).

God wants to bless everything we do as we are in fellowship with Him. *"God waited patiently while Noah was building his boat"* (1 Pet. 3:20 NLT). He gave Joshua total success against impossible odds. Even when Joshua ventured out on his own and made a mistake with the Gibeonites, God didn't abandon him (see Josh. 9).

Joshua was so sure of God's favor that he could command,

> *"O sun, stand still at Gibeon, and O moon, in the Valley of Aijalon."…*
> *the sun stopped in the middle of the sky and did not hasten to go down*
> *for about a whole day. There was no day like that before it or after it,*
> *when the Lord listened to the voice of a man; for the Lord fought for*
> *Israel* (Joshua 10:12-14 NASB).

God listened to Joshua and stopped the rotation of the earth. Since the moon never set either, He must have stopped it as well. These are not isolated events; Deborah rejoiced that *"the stars fought from heaven, from their courses they fought against Sisera"* (Judg. 5:20 NASB). God arranged the cosmic forces necessary to answer the requests, eons before the day that faith arose in Joshua and Deborah. He is willing to bless us the same way.

We got our car helplessly stuck on a muddy back road when we were young. We had no money for a tow truck and needed the car the next day. We went back to where we were camping and asked the Lord for help. I had just read in the Bible about Moses commanding the Red Sea to part and God sending an east wind that opened the sea. In Alberta an east wind brings rain, but that night after we prayed for a drying wind, the east wind began blowing hard. But it didn't rain, and we were able to drive the car out with no difficulties. *"The Lord is gracious and full of compassion, slow to anger and great in mercy. The Lord is good to all: and His tender mercies are over all His works"* (Ps. 145:8-9).

We often lose faith because we cannot see the hand of God in a situation. We need to trust even if we cannot see. When Jesus was crucified the disciples all lost heart, and even after He showed Himself to them, they went back to fishing (see John 21:3). Satan and all his cohorts were excited at defeating God's Messiah until He rose from the dead, plundered Sheol, and *"led captivity captive"* (Eph. 4:8 NASB). Jesus' death on the cross was not the defeat satan had hoped for, but the victory God had planned. Had hell *"known, they would not have crucified the Lord of glory"* (1 Cor. 2:8).

Balaam learned that when God *"has blessed...I cannot reverse it"* (Num. 23:20 NKJV). Receive the blessings,

> *...for God's gifts and His call are irrevocable. [He never withdraws them when once they are given, and He does not change His mind about those to whom He gives His grace or to whom He sends His call]* (Romans 11:29 AMP).

Lord, I declare that You *"will command the blessing upon...all that* [I] *put* [my] *hand to"* (Deut. 28:8b NASB).

Bless in the Land (Our Relationships)

God appeared to Solomon at night after he had dedicated the temple and said,

> *If My people, who are called by My name, shall humble themselves, pray, seek, crave, and require of necessity My face and turn from their wicked ways, then will I hear from heaven, forgive their sin, and heal their land* (2 Chronicles 7:14 AMP).

God was not just talking about the dirt, but the relationships in the land. God wants to bring peace and harmony to the land; therefore, He must heal its wounds.

Some of those wounds have been done directly to the land through pollution and exploitation. Most have resulted from the conflicts and unrighteousness that occur on the land between individuals and peoples. When Cain killed Abel and shed the first blood on the ground, there was a response from the earth. God said,

> *The voice of your brother's blood is crying to Me from the ground. And now you are cursed by reason of the earth, which has opened its mouth to receive your brother's [shed] blood from your hand. When you till the ground, it shall no longer yield to you its strength* (Genesis 4:10-12 AMP).

"Watchmen for the Nation" has been bringing the Church in Canada to a place of intercession and repentance for the sins of the fathers in the land. They first dealt with the sins Canada inflicted on the Jews, then worked through French, English, First Nations, Inuit and Metis issues. Their success has prompted other nations to look at the strife and bloodshed that they have inflicted on their citizens and native peoples. It is the Church's job to repent and heal the land.

There is an aspect of the creation that we tend to ignore in modern society. God speaks of creation as being animated or alive. When Jesus came to Jerusalem, He told the Pharisees that if the people did not praise Him, *"the stones would immediately cry out"* (Luke 19:40). Joshua made a covenant with Israel and set up a great stone saying,

> *…this stone shall be a witness unto us; for it has heard all the words of the Lord which He spake unto us: it shall be therefore a witness unto you, lest ye deny your God* (Joshua 24:27).

The creation responds to us. It is not dead and passive but has a will of its own. Paul said,

> *For all creation is waiting eagerly for that future day when God will reveal who His children really are. Against its will, all creation was subjected to God's curse. But with eager hope, the creation looks forward to the day when it will join God's children in glorious freedom from death and decay. For we know that all creation has been groaning as in the pains of childbirth right up to the present time* (Romans 8:19-22 NLT).

The creation is waiting eagerly, has a will, anticipates, and is groaning. These are not just literary expressions; they indicate an animated entity that is actively participating in God's plan.

The Lord told Moses that the sins practiced in the land of Canaan defiled the people. He added that *"the land is defiled; therefore I visit the iniquity of it upon it, and the land itself vomits out her inhabitants"* (Lev. 18:25 AMP). The land is connected to the people and their destiny. Conflict affects the land not just the people on it. When Amos prophesied against Jeroboam, he was accused of treason. The priest of Bethel warned the king that *"the land is not able to bear all his words"* (Amos 7:10 AMP). Strife between people causes *"confusion and every evil work"* (James 3:16), which eventually tears a people apart and causes a land to be barren.

God is sending Elijah to prepare the way for the establishment of His Kingdom. He is doing that by *"turning the heart of the fathers to the children, and the heart of the children to the fathers* [anything less would force God to]...*come and smite the earth with a curse"* (Mal. 4:6). This unity is the blessing that Jesus foresaw. He prayed that *"they...may be one in Us: that the world may believe that Thou hast sent Me"* (John 17:21). Jesus told the Father that He was giving us *"the glory and honor which You have given Me, that they may be one [even] as We are one"* (John 17:22 AMP). God is blessing (empowering) us to be one with Jesus, the Father, the Holy Spirit, the creation, and each other. Then the work of the cross reaches its climax.

> Lord, I declare that You will *"bless* [me] *in the land* [and the relationships] *which...*[You give me]" (Deut. 28:8c NASB).

Establish Us as His Holy People

The Word says that *"He who called you is holy, you also be holy in all your conduct, because it is written, 'Be holy, for I am holy' "* (1 Pet. 1:15-16 NKJV). God never asks us to try to do anything; He commands us, then blesses or empowers us to do it. Both the Hebrew[2] and Greek[3] roots of *holy* mean to be clean. He will *"sanctify and cleanse* [us]*...with the washing of water by the word"* (Eph. 5:26 NKJV).

We have a special friend, Chang Su Yoo, in Korea who took his extended family through generational repentance using the "Curses to Blessings" workbook on February 13, 2010. We include a portion of the resulting testimony using his words. The entire testimony is quoted later.

> On the 20th of February, I was on my business trip to Tokyo and had a chance to meet my father who is resting [taking a break] there. My father officially proclaimed that he was a Christian about four months ago, and he did not know that my sister and my family had just repented of our generational sins. While we were having lunch together, he said he wanted to tell me about a wonderful dream that he had in the morning of the 14th of February, which is right after we had repented. He had a dream, and he felt that he was cleansed from sins. I asked him what the dream was about. He said that he was in a deep mountain where a waterfall was. The waterfall to him was very fresh, and he dipped himself into the very clean water pond. He had a very special feeling, as if all of his sins were cleansed. I had to shout, praising Jesus, since the Lord was telling me through my natural father that our repentance had been received as the Holy Spirit had asked me to proclaim. I told my father that our God is a good and nice God. *Hallelujah!*

God is the one who makes us holy. Jesus is *"the author and finisher of our faith"* (Heb. 12:2 NKJV). *"His divine power has given to us all things that pertain to life and godliness, through the knowledge of Him"* (2 Pet. 1:3 NKJV).

You are a chosen generation, a royal priesthood, a holy nation, His own special people, that you may proclaim the praises of Him who called you out of darkness into His marvelous light (1 Peter 2:9 NKJV).

God has made us *"kings and priests...and we shall reign on the earth"* (Rev. 5:10 NKJV).

God is calling us holy and righteous; that is His assessment. We may not feel it, but feelings lie; God does not. *"By His doing you are in Christ Jesus, who became to us wisdom from God, and righteousness and sanctification, and redemption"* (1 Cor. 1:30 NASB). Holiness is not about right and wrong. Christians often define their holiness as "not sinning." What you are not does not say who you are. Saying a house is not a car does not help define what a car is. Saying a Christian is one who does not sin puts the emphasis on us and what we do. We become the center, the focal point, instead of Jesus.

That is what the law does; it emphasizes our weaknesses. The Jews tried to establish their righteousness by doing things right.

For not knowing about God's righteousness and seeking to establish their own, they did not subject themselves to the righteousness of God. For Christ is the end of the law for righteousness to everyone who believes (Romans 10:3-4 NASB).

We cannot attain righteousness by following the law. Legalism will not create purity; it only creates pride. *"For by grace are ye saved through faith; and that not of yourselves: it is the gift of God: not of works, lest any man should boast"* (Eph. 2:8-9).

The Pharisees followed the law as best they could, tithing even from their herb gardens all the *"mint and anise and cumin...omitt*[ing] *the weightier matters of the law, judgment, mercy, and faith"* (Matt. 23:23). Their self-efforts only made them hypocrites, and they, in turn, made their converts *"twice as much a son of hell"* as they were (see Matt. 23:15 NIV). When we were young parents, we put our children under the law, thinking it would control them. It only made them rebel. As we grew in knowledge of God's grace, we repented, and our children were able to come through their rebellion.

Holiness can only be obtained by faith. *"The one who does not work, but believes in Him who justifies the ungodly, his faith is credited as righteousness"* (Rom. 4:5 NASB). *"For the promise to Abraham or to his descendants that he would be heir of the world was not through the Law, but through the righteousness of faith"* (Rom. 4:13 NASB).

The blessing is the gift of righteousness and holiness imparted to us through Jesus. To receive it, we need to believe.

Let the Holy Spirit *"convict the world of sin, and of righteousness, and of judgment"* (John 16:8 NKJV). The Holy Spirit convicts three separate groups of three separate things: unbelievers of sin, believers of righteousness, the devil of judgment (see John 16:9-11).

We need to be convicted of our righteousness in Jesus, *"for in Him we live and move and have our being"* (Acts 17:28 NKJV). Only then we can walk in our blessing and be holy as God commanded us.

I declare that the Lord *"will establish* [us] *as a holy people to Himself, as He swore to* [us], *if* [we] *keep the commandments of the Lord* [our] *God and walk in His ways"* (Deut. 28:9 NASB).

People Will See and Call Us Blessed

We are an *"epistle, written in...hearts, known and read of all men"* (2 Cor. 3:2). The world may not come and look inside the church building, but they do look inside of us. Because we are blessed we become *"the light of the world. A city set on a hill cannot be hid...*[therefore] *let your light so shine before men that they may see your good works and glorify your Father...in heaven"* (Matt. 5:14,16).

Your blessings make you a beacon to the world. Because Jesus is alive and active on the earth, we have a relationship that all other religious people wish they had: we have a Father who loves us and empowers us. He takes impossible situations and not only allows us to survive, but to conquer. When the Ark of the Covenant was brought into Israel's encampment, their enemies cried, *"God is come into the camp"* (1 Sam. 4:7). We are even more blessed because the Kingdom of God is within us (see Luke 17:21). That blessing is designed *"to arouse Israel [to see and feel what they forfeited] and so to make them jealous"* (Rom. 11:11 AMP).

Jesus elicited a response from everyone—supporters and critics alike. They either loved Him or hated Him, but no one could ignore Him. The critics of the early church complained that *"these who have turned the world upside down have come here too"* (Act 17:16 NKJV). In most of the world, the modern church is considered irrelevant and dismissed as a crutch for the weak. What happened to cause the shift?

We stopped considering ourselves as blessed and powerful. When the children of Israel said we were *"in our own sight as grasshoppers...so were we in their sight"* (Num. 13:33), they had no faith to go into battle. We must recognize that the blessings that are on us make the world look at Jesus, who is alive in us. Will power, intellect, and emotion are no substitute for faith and the Kingdom. Paul asked the Galatians, *"He who supplies the Spirit to you and works miracles among you, does He do it by the works of the law, or by the hearing of faith?"* (Gal. 3:5 NKJV).

In a vision, I (Jeanne) saw Jesus standing by a door in a schoolroom. He opened the door and revealed a set of stairs. He said to me, "School is over. Step out into the unknown that I have prepared for you." Ever since that vision, doors have opened for us to go to other nations. God has more for you also. Seek Him; He will open doors into His blessing especially prepared for you.

Without power, the Gospel just becomes words or philosophy. Christianity then just becomes one of many religions, making it no better than any other. But the blessing of the Gospel comes *"not with enticing words of man's wisdom, but in the demonstration of Spirit and power"* (1 Cor. 2:4). That power sets us apart from mere philosophies. People admire the Church when it does the good works that man can do, such as feeding the poor and looking after the homeless. They react to the Church when we do the impossible, such as miracles and healings. Power demonstrations will always draw a crowd and elicit a reaction—sometimes hateful.

Paul wrote, *"A great and effective door has opened to me, and there are many adversaries"* (1 Cor. 16:9 NKJV). We think opposition is a closed door. Opposition is not a closed door, but it requires God to intervene and say, *"I have set before you an open door, and no one can shut it"* (Rev. 3:8 NKJV). When you joyfully and confidently stand *"without being frightened in any way by those who oppose you. This is a sign to them that they will be destroyed, but that you will be saved—and that by God"* (Phil. 1:28 NIV). People see the blessing on you even when they don't want to. They hate us because we remind them of their doom. We need to express love to remind them of God's hope.

Lord, I declare that *"all the peoples of the earth will see that* [we] *are called by the name of the Lord, and they will be afraid of* [us]" (Deut. 28:10 NASB).

We Shall Have Abundance of All Good Things

Abundance is more than enough to do everything that God has called you to do and beyond. When Jesus fed the thousands, there was a lot left over (see Matt. 16:9-10). When Peter caught the fish to pay his taxes, there was enough money in its mouth to pay for Jesus also (see Matt. 17:27). The desert was a place of just enough; the Promised Land flows with milk and honey.

Abundance does not require wealth to create more wealth; it requires faith to create more wealth. The effort to acquire wealth often brings the clutter of things that we don't need, including distracting opportunities. To walk in abundance requires us to stop striving and rest in God's provision. Abundance requires stewardship, not necessarily ownership. If we are *"faithful in the unrighteous mammon…* [God] *will commit to your trust true riches"* (antithesis of Luke 16:11).

God wants us to be abundant in every realm of life; He wants us to live big or be fat in the Holy Spirit. Our spirits may be poor, but connected to His Spirit we are rich. He wants us to prosper in health, long life, and in our relationships. He wants to give us a full cup of

- Honor and respect (see Deut. 26:19; 1 Sam. 2:30; John 12:26)

- Acceptance (see 1 Sam. 18:5; Eph. 1:6)

- Love (see Deut. 7:13; Song of Sol. 2:4; John 3:16; 14:23)

- Adventure or exploits (see Dan. 11:32; John 14:12)

We are ordinary, middle-class people, with no wealth, or fame, or special education. Yet God has allowed us to meet some real royalty, and eat with them in God's Kingdom. Many of God's generals have come to our house and sat down to a meal with us. Why? Because God loves to bless and prosper His children. He will bless you if you seek Him.

Jesus said,

> no one who has left home or brothers or sisters or mother or father or children or fields for Me and the gospel will fail to receive a hundred times as much in this present age (homes, brothers, sisters, mothers, children and fields—and with them, persecutions) and in the age to come, eternal life (Mark 10:29-30 NIV).

The abundant life, *"full of days, riches, and honor"* (1 Chron. 29:28), is what God wants to bless us with as we live for His glory.

Lord, I declare that You *"will make [us] abound in prosperity"* (Deut. 28:11a NASB).

We Will Be Blessed With Favor

It's not what you know, but who you know that counts. That holds true in the spiritual as well as the natural realm. God believes in nepotism and will always favor His children. Even in prison, Joseph was favored by God:

> But the Lord was with Joseph, and showed him mercy, and gave him favor in the sight of the keeper of the prison. And the keeper of the

prison committed to Joseph's hand all the prisoners...The keeper of the prison looked not to any thing that was under his hand; because the Lord was with [Joseph]*...and that which he did, the Lord made it to prosper* (Genesis 39:20-23).

Daniel was taken captive to Babylon, but *"God...brought Daniel into favor... of the chief of the eunuchs"* (Dan. 1:9 NKJV). And Daniel continued even unto the first year of King Cyrus (see Dan. 1:21). We need to put Daniel's rule into perspective:

He was *"chief of the magicians"* (Dan. 4:9 NKJV), or the head advisor to Nebuchadnezzar, the Babylonian king.

Belshazzar inherited the kingdom from Nebuchadnezzar, and at *"Belshaz-zar's command, Daniel was...proclaimed the third highest ruler in the kingdom"* (Dan. 5:29 NIV). Daniel's promotion came even though he had just pronounced the king's demise.

When Darius conquered Babylon, Daniel's favor continued. He should have died with the rest of the conquered leadership (see Dan. 5:30). Instead, *"...it pleased Darius to set over the kingdom an hundred and twenty princes, which should be over the whole kingdom; and over these three presidents; of whom Dan-iel was first"* (Daniel 6:1-2).

He was promoted to prime minister because he pleased the king and had favor. Later when Daniel was condemned to the lion's den, the king was *"deeply distressed and set his mind on delivering Daniel"* (Dan. 6:14 NASB). Daniel's light had shone so brightly that the king saw it and responded: *"Your God whom you constantly serve will Himself deliver you"* (Dan. 6:16 NASB).

So *"Daniel enjoyed success in the reign of Darius and in the reign of Cyrus the Persian"* (Dan. 6:28). Daniel affected Cyrus as he walked in integrity before him and prepared him to receive God's orders. God called him by name (see Isa. 44:28) and stirred

...the heart of Cyrus to put this proclamation into writing..."This is what King Cyrus of Persia says: 'The Lord, the God of heaven, has

given me all the kingdoms of the earth. He has appointed me to build him a Temple at Jerusalem in the land of Judah' " (Ezra 1:1-2 NLT).

Favor for Daniel and a prophetic word from God, reversed the fortunes of a whole nation and brought them out of captivity. *"Do you see a man who excels in his work? He will stand before kings"* (Prov. 22:29 NKJV). Hard times are coming, just as they did for Daniel.

> *For behold, darkness will cover the earth, and deep darkness the peoples; but the Lord will rise upon you and His glory will appear upon you. Nations will come to your light, and kings to the brightness of your rising* (Isaiah 60:2-3 NASB).

God's favor will cause us not just to survive, but to be *"more than conquerors through Him that loved us"* (Rom. 8:37).

Even in a bad place, when we fall out of favor with men, trust the favor of the Lord.

> *They will lay their hands on you and persecute you...and you will be led away before kings and governors for My name's sake. This will be a time (an opportunity) for you to bear testimony. Resolve and settle it in your minds not to meditate and prepare beforehand how you are to make your defense and how you will answer. For I [Myself] will give you a mouth and such utterance and wisdom that all of your foes combined will be unable to stand against or refute* (Luke 21:12-15 AMP).

Learn to see yourself as a child of the King: King Jesus. Close your eyes and see Him looking at you. See the love He has for you. He is giving you a blank check from Heaven. He has already signed His name in blood on the check. He is telling you He wants to bless you. Cash it in at the bank in Heaven. Your God loves you because you are His child, the child of a King.

God's favor is over us just as it was over Israel.

He allowed no man to do them wrong; in fact, He reproved kings for their sakes...saying, "Touch not My anointed, and do My prophets no harm" (Psalm 105:14-15 AMP).

As children of Abraham, God will *"bless those who bless you, and I will curse him who curses you; and in you all the families of the earth shall be blessed"* (Gen. 12:3 NKJV). We are highly favored, *"for it is your Father's pleasure to give you the kingdom"* (Luke 12:32 NKJV).

I declare that the Lord will make "[us] *abound in prosperity* [and in favor]...*in the land which the Lord swore to* [our] *fathers to give* [us]" (Deut. 28:11b NASB).

We Will Be Blessed With Rain From Heaven

The Lord *"will open to you His good storehouse, the heavens, to give rain to your land in its season"* (Deut. 28:12 NASB). Rain is a blessing straight out of the treasury of Heaven, which God uses to discipline us with. The Promised Land

...is not like the land of Egypt...where you sowed your seed and watered it with your foot laboriously as in a garden of vegetables. But the land which you enter to possess is a land of hills and valleys which drinks water of the rain of the heavens (Deuteronomy 11:10-11 AMP).

Self-effort does not produce in the Kingdom of Heaven. In the world (Egypt), self-effort, irrigation with water wheels, worked, but in the Kingdom we need God to pour out His blessings just as Israel needed rain. In the world, we need stability and uniformity, like the flat irrigation land in Egypt, to make things work. The Promised Land is hills and valleys, ups and downs that force us to rely on God. God used the rain, or lack of it, for correction but also for communication.

When a drought wracked the land during David's reign, he turned to God and asked Him why. God answered, *"It is for Saul, and for his bloody house, because he slew the Gibeonites*" (2 Sam. 21:1). God wanted to remove the blood off the land, and He communicated that by removing the blessing. If the blessing is not present, we are under a curse that God wants to remove. It is not a punishment; it is a course correction.

God wants to connect the blessing to His righteousness so that He can reveal and remove those unhealed, unsanctified, and unredeemed areas in our lives. He ties the timing of blessings to His covenant with us. God said, "*I will give you rain in due season, and the land shall yield her increase*" (Lev. 26:4). If His covenant is not kept, He promises to

> ...*break the pride of your power; and...make your heaven as iron, and your earth as brass: and your strength shall be spent in vain: for your land shall not yield her increase* (Leviticus 26:19-20).

The withholding of rain blocked the production of fruit in the land, which always brought Israel to their knees and produced repentance. God wants fruit in us, not just repentance. Seedtime and harvest (see Gen. 8:22) were guarantees of the covenant to which God connected seasons. Rain is good if it does not fall in harvest time. We need to recognize the seasons in our lives, and "*through faith and patience inherit the promises*" (Heb. 6:12). If we don't, we will try to harvest when it is seedtime and wonder what happened.

We were not ready earlier in our lives for some of the things that we are doing now in the Kingdom. God had to develop our character so we wouldn't fall when the blessings came. The blessings came, not always in our time frame, but always in His. Our weakness does not block God's strength, for His "*strength is made perfect in weakness*" (2 Cor. 12:10).

God removed Gideon's strength for battle so that Israel could not "*boast to Me that they saved themselves by their own strength*" (Judg. 7:2 NLT). The blessing is waiting to be released in its proper season. God wants us to trust Him, commune with Him, and rest in Him so that the blessings will bless us and not harm us.

I declare that *"the Lord will open for* [us] *His good storehouse, the heavens, to give rain to* [our] *land in its season"* (Deut. 28:12a NASB).

God Will Bless Us With Righteousness From Heaven

Rejoice in the Lord your God: for He hath given you the former rain moderately and He will cause to come down for you the rain, the former rain, and the latter rain (Joel 2:23).

Sometimes the translations only hint at the root meanings of the words. This is such a case. Joel is predicting the rain that will come and bring a harvest. The language he used veils the means of receiving that harvest.

The Hebrew word for "former rain" is *môreh*,[4] from the root *yârá*.[5]

- *Yârá* means to flow (as water, rain) or to shoot an arrow, to point out (as with a finger), or to instruct, or teach

- *Môreh* means archer or teacher, or early rain (from *yârá*)

The Hebrew word for "moderately" is *tsedâqâh*.[6]

- *Tsedâqâh* means rightly or moderately or righteousness

Put that all together, and we see that God was instructing Israel in righteousness, using the rain or the blessings as a teacher. Once we have been trained in righteousness, then God says,

The threshing floors will be filled with grain; the vats will overflow with new wine and oil. I will repay you for the years the locusts have eaten (Joel 2:24-25 NIV).

Our ability to respond rightly to the blessing and the correction determines our relationship with the Father.

As you endure this divine discipline, remember that God is treating you as His own children...If God doesn't discipline you as He does all of His children, it means that you are illegitimate and are not really His children after all (Hebrews 12:7-8 NLT).

Paul learned this ability to righteously live in dependence was his access to power. He said,

> *I know how to get along with humble means, and I also know how to live in prosperity; in any and every circumstance I have learned the secret of being filled and going hungry, both of having abundance and suffering need. I can do all things through Him who strengthens me* (Philippians 4:12-13 NASB).

We are righteous because He is righteous, for *"by the righteousness of One the free gift came upon all men"* (Rom. 5:18). This is our true blessing. By faith, we with *"Abraham believed God and it was counted unto him for righteousness"* (Rom. 4:3). Jesus said that we *"are clean through the word, which I have spoken unto you"* (John 15:3).

We are a blessed people. Every other religion tries to appease their gods. We have believed and appropriated what He did so that we have *"through faith subdued kingdoms, wrought righteousness,* [and] *obtained promises"* (Heb. 11:33).

Lord, I declare that You will *"rain righteousness upon* [us]" (Hos. 10:12).

We Are Blessed to Lend and Not Borrow

We are not going to experience any more lack. We will have enough to lend to any in need; that is the promise. To walk in that fullness we must walk in the Spirit and be able to hear what God is saying. Our salvation is free, but is to be *"work*[ed] *out...with fear and trembling"* (Phil. 2:12-13 NKJV).

In ministry, we see that it is truly God who should bear the responsibility and receive the glory for the increase: Paul *"planted, Apollos watered, but God gave the increase. So then neither he who plants is anything, nor he who waters, but God who gives the increase"* (1 Cor. 3:6 NKJV). Our work does not bring the increase, but the increase does not come without our work. *"This is the work of God, that ye believe on Him* [Jesus] *whom He hath sent"* (John 6:29).

If we work, in faith, the principles God laid out, He will bring the blessing. *"He who has pity on the poor lends to the Lord, and that which he has given He will repay to him"* (Prov. 19:17 AMP). God is more than willing to pay for what we give away. Jeanne and I have for years given our time ministering in the Kingdom.

When we were young, God told us that He would pay us for our labor. The inheritance and the benefits that the Lord pays would bankrupt any church that tried to match them. We get to travel, write books, and minister all over the world and not have to charge anything. I believe in paying those who labor in the Kingdom, but we are able to function without compensation because we had a specific word concerning our finances.

We need to shift our thinking from slaves to that of sons and daughters. A slave or a hireling works for wages; a son has an inheritance. Working for wages keeps you going from paycheck to paycheck. An inheritance gives you a share of the Kingdom and access to all its resources.

Lord, I pray that You heal all the wounds that prevent us from believing that we are sons and daughters of the most High. Increase our faith to believe that we have enough to *"do exceeding abundantly above all that we ask or think, according to the power that worketh in us"* (Eph. 3:20).

God wants us out of debt, for *"the borrower is servant to the lender"* (Prov. 22:7). He wants us free to serve Him, not bound to serve others. Pray that God will get you out of debt, remembering that He will meet all your needs, not all your "greeds." Many who have money are still stuck in a poverty mindset, believing that there is a limited supply.

Some are the opposite and spend like drunken sailors only to wake up wondering where all the money went. We need a proper attitude, not a stupid attitude. There is more than enough to do whatever God tells you to do, not what you feel like doing. The Kingdom operates on faith, a word from God, and not on feelings.

Wrong thoughts will stir up wrong emotions, which will push us to perform wrong actions. Those actions will coalesce into habits that will take us in the wrong direction. Those habits, done long enough, become the basis for our character. Our character will determine our destiny. The only way to change the direction we are going is to repent, which means to turn around. We must stop thinking lack so we can stop hoarding and being greedy.

Israel's laws were designed to prevent poverty by ensuring each family retained their ancestral property. The Jews never stepped into an abundance mentality and continued to grab rather than receive from God. God brought a curse on Israel because of those who

> *...join house to house [and by violently expelling the poorer occupants enclose large acreage] and join field to field until there is no place for others and you are made to dwell alone in the midst of the land* (Isaiah 5:8 AMP).

We are told, *"Don't look out only for your own interests, but take an interest in others, too"* (Phil. 2:4 NLT). We can only do that if we know God will look after us as we look after others.

We are one Body, and

> *...there should be no division or discord or lack of adaptation [of the parts of the body to each other], but the members all alike should have a mutual interest in and care for one another. And if one member suffers, all the parts [share] the suffering; if one member is honored, all the members [share in] the enjoyment of it* (1 Corinthians 12:25-26 AMP).

We are all *"stewards of the mysteries of God"* (1 Cor. 4:1) and responsible to have the whole Body share in them.

> *Who then is the faithful and sensible steward, whom his master will put in charge of his servants, to give them their rations at the proper time? Blessed is that slave whom his master finds so doing when he comes. Truly I say to you that he will put him in charge of all his possessions* (Luke 12:42-44 NASB).

When God first started to give me (Ken) revelation, I was afraid to share what I got with just anybody. I had a poverty mindset and was afraid I might never get another revelation. I wanted to share this revelation where it would have the most impact, and I would get the most recognition. When God showed me a miniscule amount of the vastness of His wisdom, I was overwhelmed. I have been flooded with God's revelation and realize there is more than enough to go around. I pray that you may

> ...*have the power to understand, as all God's people should, how wide, how long, how high, and how deep His love is. May you experience the love of Christ; though it is too great to understand fully. Then you will be made complete with all the fullness of life and power that comes from God* (Ephesians 3:18-19 NLT).

I (Jeanne) sing a little song from Sunday school that expresses how God wants to bless:

> *You have to give it away*
> *Pass it around*
> *Turn your basket upside down*
> *I can tell by your smile*
> *And the twinkle in your eye*
> *The Master has taught you how to multiply*
> *Yes, the Master has taught you how to multiply.*[7]

> *He that spared not His own Son, but delivered Him up for us all, how shall He not with Him also freely give us all things?* (Romans 8:32)

Our little is much in the Master's hand.

I declare that *"the Lord will open for* [me] *His good storehouse, the heavens...and* [I] *shall lend to many nations, but* [I] *shall not borrow"* (Deut. 28:12c NASB).

We Will Be the Head and Not the Tail

You know that the rulers of the Gentiles lord it over them, and their great men exercise authority over them. It is not this way among you, but whoever wishes to become great among you shall be your servant, and whoever wishes to be first among you shall be your slave; just as the Son of Man did not come to be served, but to serve, and to give His life a ransom for many (Matthew 20:25-28 NASB).

Our first priority if we want to be the head is to act like the tail. Jesus said,

You call Me Teacher and Lord, and you say well, for so I am. If I then, your Lord and Teacher, have washed your feet, you also ought to wash one another's feet. For I have given you an example, that you should do as I have done to you. Most assuredly, I say to you, a servant is not greater than his master; nor is he who is sent greater than he who sent him. If you know these things, blessed are you if you do them (John 13:13-17 NKJV).

Clothe yourselves with humility toward one another, because, "God opposes the proud but gives grace to the humble." Humble yourselves, therefore, under God's mighty hand, that He may lift you up in due time (1 Peter 5:5-6 NIV).

The biggest challenge that everyone must overcome is to not *"think of himself more highly than he ought to think"* (Rom. 12:3). The disciples asked Jesus, *"Increase our faith"* (Luke 17:5). Jesus gave a strange answer. He told the story of the servant who worked in the field and then came in to give his master supper. Jesus emphasized an attitude that they should have.

This attitude was the answer to greater faith. He said that the master would not give the servant any thanks for doing what he was commanded to do. *"So likewise you, when you have done all those things which you are commanded, say, 'We are unprofitable servants. We have done what was our duty to do' "* (Luke 17:10 NKJV). Our faith is increased because we are not expecting a reward from men but rather from God alone. If we can do that, we are free from the tyranny of pleasing men and can *"be the servant of Christ"* (Gal. 1:10).

With our hearts right, God can exalt us and then the *"Gentiles shall come to thy light, and kings to the brightness of thy rising"* (Isa. 60:3). You will draw people to God because they will be attracted to Jesus in you. God's blessings will change the way people deal with you. Just as David was shocked at the favor God brought him, so shall the Holy Spirit cause us to exclaim, *"You gave me victory over my accusers. You appointed me the ruler over nations; people I don't even know now serve me. As soon as they hear of me, they submit"* (Ps. 18:43-44 NLT).

God's Spirit on a land changes attitudes toward His people. Israel was weak and under constant pressure from the surrounding nations. Before David was made king, the surrounding nations continually plundered and harassed Israel. That changed when God entered the fray on Israel's side. God told David, when you hear

> *...the sound of marching in the tops of the balsam trees, then you shall go out to battle, for God will have gone out before you to strike the army of the Philistines...Then the fame of David went out into all the lands; and the Lord brought the fear of him on all the nations* (1 Chronicles 14:15,17 NASB).

The fear of the Lord subdued Israel's enemies as they recognized the hand of God covering David with power.

After Jehoshaphat sent out Levites to teach the law to the people,

> *the fear of the Lord fell on all the kingdoms of the lands surrounding Judah, so that they did not make war with Jehoshaphat...The Philistines brought Jehoshaphat gifts and silver as tribute, and the Arabs brought him flocks* (2 Chronicles 17:10-11 NIV).

The nations round about saw the light of revelation emanating from Judah as they responded to the Word. God shone a light on them that brought the awe of the fear of the Lord to the surrounding nations. *"When a man's ways please the Lord, He maketh even his enemies to be at peace with him"* (Prov. 16:7).

Rahab told Joshua's spies that fear had overcome all the warriors in Jericho. They heard the tales of God's power, which parted the Red Sea and destroyed the Egyptians.

> *When we heard of it, our hearts melted and everyone's courage failed because of you, for the Lord your God is God in heaven above and on the earth below* (Joshua 2:11 NIV).

God is placing us over all the nations. We will see it if we look through the eyes of faith. He did the same thing for Israel. God told Moses,

> *This day I will begin to put the dread and fear of you upon the nations under the whole heaven, who shall hear the report of you, and shall tremble and be in anguish because of you* (Deuteronomy 2:25 NKJV).

We are the head and not the tail. Persecution and hatred that rise against us do not change that fact. Jesus encouraged us to *"fear not, little flock; for it is your Father's good pleasure to give you the kingdom"* (Luke 12:32). It is hard to be humble if you are nothing. But God has made us the head and not the tail; therefore,

> *...let this mind be in you, which was also in Christ Jesus: who, being in the form of God, thought it not robbery to be equal with God. But made Himself of no reputation, and took upon Him the form of a servant...He humbled Himself, and became obedient unto death, even the death of the cross. Wherefore God also hath highly exalted Him, and given Him a name, which is above every name* (Philippians 2:6-9).

Humility is not a sign of weakness; it is a declaration that my Father is in control, and I do not have to fight for myself. I can rest in the fact that the God of the universe likes me. Jesus declared, *"I have given them the glory that You gave Me, that they may be one as We are one"* (John 17:22 NIV). His glory and love makes us the head and not the tail.

Lord, Your goodness has *"blessed us with all spiritual blessings in heavenly places in Christ"* (Eph. 1:3).

I pray that the eyes of your heart may be enlightened, so that you will know what is the hope of His calling, what are the riches of the glory of His inheritance in the saints, and what is the surpassing greatness of His power toward us who believe (Ephesians 1:18-19 NASB).

That you might trust Jesus whom God

...raised...from the dead and seated...at His right hand in the heavenly places, far above all rule and authority and power and dominion, and every name that is named, not only in this age but also in the one to come. And He put all things in subjection under His feet, and gave Him as head over all things to the church, which is His body, the fullness of Him who fills all in all (Ephesians 1:20-23 NASB).

I declare that *"the Lord will make* [me] *the head and not the tail, and* [I] *only will be above, and* [I] *will not be underneath, if* [I] *listen to the commandments of the Lord* [my] *God"* (Deuteronomy 28:13 NASB).

CALL DOWN YOUR BLESSINGS

We once took a river trip from our hotel in Mexico to a quaint village set on the most beautiful beach, in an unspoiled bay. The river was small but clear and cool compared to the ocean. We had only gone about a mile, when the river slowed, and we entered a mangrove forest. There was a channel cut through the overhanging trees that was just big enough for two boats to pass through. The branches of the mangroves formed a canopy that at times became more like a tunnel than a forest. For the next 20 minutes, we meandered through this dark mass of branches and leaves that were reaching out to close the alleyway through which we were passing.

Eventually we emerged from the mangrove swamp as the river sped up and the mangroves receded. The river returned to its full width as it swung to within a few hundred yards of the ocean, and we docked on the backside of the little fishing village. Our guide told us that it had taken nearly two months to originally clear a path through the swamp from the hotel to the village. Now they must go in once a week with machetes and cut off all the branches they can reach. If they don't, the grove would fill in the passage within a month.

Our lives are like that; we can have free access to the beauty of our destiny if someone is willing to clear the passage. Once the way is open, we need to continually cut off anything that would try to block the access. The big job is the original asking of forgiveness and repentance to clear through the family's morass of iniquity, traditions, and sins. Once those have been cleared away, we must repent on a daily or weekly basis for our own sins to keep the river flowing freely. There is freedom and destiny waiting for all who will take sword in hand and wade into their family's past and lovingly cut off the blockages.

The Bible lays open the lives of the ordinary people of God and follows their journeys, some into destiny, some into destruction. They were just like us: they lusted, were idolaters, fornicated, tempted, and murmured (see 1 Cor. 10:5-10).

> *Now these things happened to them as an example, and they were written for our instruction, upon whom the ends of the ages have come* (1 Corinthians 10:11 NASB).

The generation that escaped Egypt never learned their lessons and all died in the wilderness, short of their Promised Land. Like them, we are on our journey to our Land of Promises. They could not enter with any of the sinners of the past generations still among them (see Num. 26:64-65). We cannot enter our Land of Promises with any of the iniquity of the past generations still clinging on to us. That is why we must deal with generational curses.

The story of Aaron's family presents the perfect picture of how a curse can cause the loss of a family's destiny and how a blessing can open the door to them for a higher realm of authority. Aaron, the High Priest, had four sons, two of which died because of a presumptuous act and left no children. The remaining two, Eleazar and Ithamar, each had families that simultaneously functioned in the priesthood.

Eleazar's son Phinehas ran a spear through a couple who were flaunting their fornication right in front of Israel's leaders. The leaders were interceding for the plague that was a result of the people joining themselves to Moab in idolatrous, sexual worship. God responded to Phinehas' zeal and pronounced a *"covenant of peace...for him and his descendants after him,* [and] *a covenant of a perpetual priesthood"* (Num. 25:12-13 NASB).

Ithamar's family functioned in the priesthood, alongside Eleazar's, for four hundred years until his descendant Eli, who was the last of the judges. Eli's sons, Phinehas and Hophni, were evil, seducing the women at the tabernacle and bullying the worshipers for their meat offerings. God responded to their sins:

I will judge and punish [Eli's] house forever for the iniquity of which he knew, for his sons were bringing a curse upon themselves [blaspheming God], and he did not restrain them (1 Samuel 3:13 AMP).

That curse resulted in

- The loss of the priesthood (see 1 Sam. 2:30)
- A shortening of the family's life spans (see 1 Sam. 2:30-33)
- Family emotional problems (see 1 Sam. 2:33)
- Family financial problems (see 1 Sam. 2:36)
- Family employment problems (see 1 Sam. 2:36)

This curse had an immediate effect, with Eli, Hophni, Phinehas, and Phinehas' wife all dying on the same day. The curse reached its climax when *"Solomon expelled Abiathar [descendant of Eli] from being priest to the Lord, fulfilling the word of the Lord which He spoke concerning the house of Eli in Shiloh"* (1 Kings 2:27 AMP). It is interesting that *Abiathar* means, "Father of superfluity,"[1] or "redundancy." *Redundant* means "unnecessary,"[2] which is what Eli's line had become.

One branch of the family was cursed and cut off because of the actions of their forefathers. The other branch was blessed and remained priests to the Lord because of the actions of one ancestor. Jesus came both to bear the consequences of the family's sin and to release the family's blessing. Just as we had to ask forgiveness for our sins to access our personal destiny, so we have to ask forgiveness for the family's sins to enter the family destiny.

Many people have come to us after breaking off the generational curses and admitted that they had not expected much. They all said that they thought they had done this stuff before but now realized this was different. They came out feeling lighter, as if a burden had been removed. We started by dealing with our own family "stuff" and got immediate results with our son and ourselves. We then migrated to our friends and saw immediate results in their lives. There were healings, financial turnarounds, relationships restored, spiritual growth, and the removal of depression, etc. We had so many requests for help that we developed a seminar and now have expanded it to this book. It is exciting to see what God does in our lives as we stand in the gap for our families. We ministered to a couple at a "Curses to Blessings" seminar, whose son was in a psych ward with schizophrenia. After they went through the curses, they called down the blessings for their family. Their son called that night and said, "I wish I could feel this good every day." They were so excited that their prayers were already making a difference. Another lady, Corrine, wrote us a note saying that her brother had an amazing healing of his hip on the Monday after the weekend seminar. She added that her son had also received a healing during the seminar.

At another seminar, I (Jeanne) noticed that a man was in the back during the blessing time, stomping his feet. I thought he was upset with the ministry, so I went back to check on him. Robert laughed and said that he was checking to see if his healing was real. He told us that he had broken his back in a car accident years before and had been off work, sometimes for a year at a time, the pain was so bad.

Robert said,

I went to get prayed over and was the first person up. I could barely walk and could hardly bend down. After the people prayed over me, I returned to my seat. When I sat down, I knew something had happened. I told my wife I was going out back for something but never told her what for. As I was out back, I proceeded to bend over and twist from side to side. At that point, I knew God had healed me, so I went back to my seat, but I again left to do the same thing—never telling my wife about the healing because I wanted to make sure it was true. The third time I went back, Jeanne saw me and asked what was going on. I told her I couldn't believe it, but God had healed me. She told me to believe it. We both went up to the front, running all the way. She told the audience what had happened. We danced and shared the joy. Before the prayer, I could barely walk, and from that instance to today (eight years later), I have never had any pain in my back or suffered with it at all.

Robert has a second healing that was even more dramatic. He had trouble with polyps in his intestines and had several operations to remove these cysts. The doctors recently found a large polyp the size of his thumb at the beginning of his duodenum. He shared,

The doctor had a meeting with me and showed me a picture of it, explaining that he must remove it as it could cause severe problems in the future. If it ruptured, I would bleed to death in minutes.

He explained to me that removing this polyp could, and most likely would, cause a hemorrhage. At that point, they would have to surgically open me to stop the massive bleeding. The doctor explained he would do the gastroscopy, and while doing it, he would have to have an O.R. room booked, on standby, and have doctors, anesthesiologists, etc., ready in case I proceeded to hemorrhage. The day came, and I was scared as I went in for the procedure.

After the procedure was done, the doctor came into the recovery room in the day ward and talked to my wife, Lynette, who asked him what happened. He told her that he didn't remove the polyp, and Lynette asked him if I would have to come back again. The doctor said that when he got to the spot where the polyp was, to remove it, it wasn't there. He said he looked at the spot where the polyp had been, but it was gone, and the area was just like it should be, smooth with no sign that a polyp had ever been there.

My wife asked him what happened to the polyp, and he said that he had no idea where it went. My wife said, "I do." He seemed upset, adding that he wasted his time, money on a new piece of equipment, the O.R. room booking, and the doctors standing by for the expected emergency.

The polyp didn't just slough off, or else I would have bled to death. The doctor had the pictures, but no explanation. Those "before-and-after" photographs are the proof that God did a miracle healing.

Healings don't always manifest immediately as miracles. One lady phoned me (Jeanne) and asked if she would be healed of cancer if she came to the seminar. I said we couldn't guarantee that, but that it couldn't hurt to come. She came and went through all the repenting and asking for forgiveness, broke off the curses, and received the blessing during a prophetic time at the end. She phoned a week later, angry and complaining that she wasn't healed. I challenged her to continue believing and to give God time. Two weeks later, this excited lady called Tangie, who had been her seminar worker, rejoicing that she no longer had cancer. God is faithful.

Our seminar doesn't get people healed; the healing power of Jesus does. The seminar, and this book, only give an outline of removing generational curses that block the blessings. Our good friend Chang Su Yoo in Korea had an exciting testimony with the removal of generational curses. Over the years, he had several tumors in his neck that had been removed but kept coming back.

He shared,

On February 9, 2010, seven tumors were found when I took an ultrasonic scan. The 0.8 cm tumor grew to 1.3 cm, and other tumors spread out over the whole neck.

I asked the Lord to give me the names of people who I should ask to intercede in prayer for me. Ken and Jeanne wrote to me concerning what the Lord said to them, regarding my tumors, dated February 10th. They said that the three tumors that the Lord cured earlier were linked to David killing Goliath. Nevertheless, there were still four more giants (see 2 Sam. 21:16-22) that were left to be killed, meaning that I need to get rid of the cancer root. The root would be found in family and ancestral sins, and I need to repent on their behalf. On the 10th of February, my son, who is at Bethel School of Supernatural Ministry, received a word from the Lord that He would pull out all the roots of the cancer this time.

When I sat in front of the Lord, I asked Him to show me the sins of my family. The Lord told me to first repent of my sin (see Ezek. 18). As a result, I started to repent of my sins and asked for the best timing to ask forgiveness for my ancestors' sins. On the 12th of February, my son's group received a word from the Lord that this tumor is there to show the glory of God.

Ken and Jeanne sent us a "Curses to Blessings" manual on February 13th, which is a day before Korea Lunar New Year Day. My sister and her family visited us that day; we started to worship in the evening and asked Holy Spirit to show us what we needed to repent of on behalf of our ancestors. The major areas were idolatry (Buddhism and shamanism), adultery, killing, fighting, being harsh toward neighbors, and greed. At the last moment of prayer, Holy Spirit told me to proclaim that the repentance had been received and that the Lord had thrown it behind His back. He said He doesn't remember anything. *Hallelujah!*

On the 14th of February, Ken and Jeanne received a word from the Lord. They said that the Lord had cured the three tumors the first time, but this was a new attack. As the Lord hardened Pharaoh's heart and mind and defeated the Egyptians by overthrowing them in the Red Sea, the Lord will handle this cancer for good and free me from its bondage. The Lord will show His glory in this final victory.

On the 17th of February, while I was meditating on Acts 16:3, the Lord said that I had to go through with the operation. I had been asking the Lord to heal me as He had done previously but told Him that I would submit to His will. If I needed to have an operation, I said that I was ready to go through with it. On February 20th, I was on a business trip to Tokyo and had a chance to meet with my father who was on a short retreat there. My father officially proclaimed that he is a Christian about four months ago. He did not know that my sister and my family repented of our family's generational sins days earlier.

While we were having lunch together, he said he wanted to tell me about a wonderful dream that he had in the morning of the 14th of February, which is right after we had repented for the generational sins. In this dream he felt that he was cleansed from sins. I asked him what the dream was about. He said that he was in a deep mountain where a waterfall was. The falls to him were very fresh, and he dipped himself into the very clean water pond. He had a very special feeling as though all of his sins were cleansed. I had to shout praises to Jesus since the Lord was telling me, through my natural father, that our repentance had been received just as the Holy Spirit had told me to proclaim. I told my father that our God is a good and nice God. *Hallelujah!*

On the 21st of February, my partner and friend, Pastor Hwan Sik Kim's wife received a word from the Lord that I was standing at Gilgal. The Lord was going to give me a monument to be remembered forever, and this would be a sanctification point.

On February 25th, I went to the hospital to check with the doctor. I had a blood test, and they did an ultrasonic scan. The doctor said that there was one tumor; the size was 0.84 cm, and he wanted to inject ethanol into the tumor. I was so surprised since there was no mention of the seven tumors. Also, the size of the tumor shrank from 1.3 cm to 0.84 cm. I told him that I would have the injection since I had peace of mind.

Later, while I was in the ultrasonic scan room again, I asked the doctor who was responsible for the injection about the numbers of tumors I had. She said I had three and that the other two are less than 0.3 cm and not worth looking at. *Hallelujah!* The Lord took care of all the tumors, and He shrank the remaining ones. I took the injection, and while I was lying down in the recovery room for an hour, I noticed that I had just had my operation. God is faithful, and He gives us the best of the best. Amen!

That is the result of breaking off generational curses. Only recently did we recognize that calling down the blessings would release what had been bottled up by the curses. Apprehending those blessings is done by faith, as is everything in the Kingdom. We reviewed our family histories to see what blessings had been birthed and the ones that had been aborted. We began to call the blessings down over our own lives for a period of six months when we started to see things shift.

I (Jeanne) loved my grandmothers. My maternal Grandma Cummings was very domestic, helping with mending, babysitting, sewing, or whatever was needed for the household as she lived with us. She was widowed early with five children to raise, but her pioneering spirit allowed her to help her children even after they had families of their own.

My Grandma McCullough also had to raise five children on her own. She came from a wealthy British family and immigrated to Canada as a missionary, though she did not receive the Lord until she was in her 60s. Her father was an architect and an artist, and her mother was an advocate for women's rights. Her culture and refinement carried her with grace through the financial struggles of the depression. Though she had little, she was generous to the poor and disadvantaged. She was full of energy, putting on plays for the community, helping the needy, working as the first policewoman in Edmonton, and later as a department store detective. There were always candy and presents for us kids when she came to visit us. We were excited with everything that grandma did. I even remember once running home from school to watch her on television.

She always advocated for and was involved with social issues, such as the school for the deaf. She organized to help the homeless get beds and shelter so they wouldn't freeze to death in Edmonton's cold winters, and worked with the girls in the home for unwed mothers. I lived with her for a short time after graduating high school, and there were always hampers to pack, gifts to wrap, and donations to collect for whatever project was on the top of her help list. She knew everybody and got Christmas cards from various dignitaries, the police chief, mayors (past and present), the premier of the province and even several prime ministers of Canada (I counted four of their cards one Christmas).

Grandma McCullough celebrated life and did everything with exuberance and dignity. Her funeral packed the biggest downtown cathedral, and the procession to the cemetery was accompanied with a full police escort. The Phoebe McCullough Park in Edmonton is named in her honor. Grandma Cummings was quieter and concentrated on her family circle but was no less impactful on our family. Both of them operated in the destiny that belonged to their families but neither achieved the fullness of what God had for them.

My (Ken's) great-grandfather, Gustavus Adolphus Eoll, was born in Sweden of British and German descent. He was converted to Jesus at an early age and immediately began his evangelistic lifestyle of distributing Christian literature, tracks, and Bibles. He was unpredictable in his enthusiasm and tossed a set of tracts into the Queen of Sweden's carriage. He would have been arrested if the Queen had not intervened, after seeing the intent of the package. Years later, two of the royal princes visited him in Egypt and told how that rash act had led to both their conversions and that of their mother.

Gustavus' father had fallen out with his grandfather, Baron Drake, and as a result, changed the family name. After his father suddenly died, Gustavus reconciled with his grandfather and was designated to inherit the fortune and the title. His grandfather's untimely death and a fire that destroyed some vital papers shifted the inheritance to his aunt. He never challenged the ruling, and charted his own course, becoming a physician in France. Later, moving to England, he was influenced by George Mueller, who started the first orphanages in Britain and became his personal physician.

That contact prompted him to start ministering to seamen in Bristol, and he eventually opened seamen's homes in London and Cardiff. God led him to take this ministry to Port Said, Egypt, shortly after the Suez Canal opened. He estimated that he gave away 1,500,000 Scriptures in 37 languages over his 29 years of ministry; nursing sick sailors, clambering aboard their ships with bags of Bibles, and rescuing sailors lost in the evil world of Port Said. His prayer was that "young men would ask God how they could circulate the Word, that the Word would remain when heaven and earth passes away."[3]

My granddad, Ormy Harrington, was an entrepreneurial farmer. He came up to Canada from Oregon in the early 1900s, losing a brother, and crossing the Red Deer River in covered wagons. He helped settle southern Alberta, farming 15 sections of land at the peak of the drought years. He was a county Reeve, head of the rural electrification for his area, and was instrumental in bringing in the first telephones to that part of the country. My dad, Robert, had the same progressive and innovative spirit. He helped found the first anhydrous-ammonia fertilizer co-op in western Canada and was one of the pioneers of large feedlots in Alberta, with a 1,200 head lot of his own. My dad and my granddad had the ability to make whatever they couldn't buy. They also did not reach the destiny that God had intended, but they prepared me to apprehend all that God has for our family.

After contemplating our spiritual heritage, we felt we needed to call down the 1,000 generations blessings (see Deut. 7:9). We walked in a wooded trail behind our house and daily began to call down the things we knew were in the family and the things we didn't know. I (Jeanne) prayed for that practical pioneering spirit and all the other giftings associated with my Grandma Cummings' side. I claimed the favor and the influence that belonged to my Grandma McCullough's line. I (Ken) prayed for spiritual riches, the governmental authority, the financial inheritance, and the ability to get the Word of God out from my mother's side. I called in the pioneering spirit to overcome adversity, the governmental authority, the entrepreneurial giftings, the inventiveness, and the leadership skill from my father's side.

We claimed all the gifts and callings that had been aborted, the dreams and inheritances that had been lost, and the destinies and purposes that had never been apprehended or called in. Since we started to call in all that belonged to our family lines, our lives have shifted. We have published three books, including this one; we have done over 2.5 million dollars in construction contracts; we have ministered in six countries; we have done one television and nine radio interviews; and we are constantly receiving new revelation in the love of the Lord and tremendous favor. We had a good life before this, but it was nothing compared to the blessings we have experienced lately.

> *Christ hath redeemed us from the curse of the law, being made a curse for us: for it is written, Cursed is every one that hangeth on a tree: that the blessing of Abraham might come on the Gentiles through Jesus Christ; that we might receive the promise of the Spirit through faith* (Galatians 3:13-14).

We are grafted into Abraham and thus into all the promises that pertain to him. That is part of our spiritual heritage, but we need to claim it to possess it.

Prayer:

*Lord, by faith we are grafted in to Abraham and into You, and we call down the blessings and promise of Abraham. "**For the promise, that he should be the heir of the world, was not to Abraham, or to his seed, through the law, but through the righteousness of faith**" (Rom. 4:13). Therefore we receive the world and all that is in it as our inheritance. Give us wisdom to be good stewards of all that belongs to us.*

What do you need to call down from your generational blessings? Begin to call in your ancestral heritage. Pursue God for what belongs to you, for *"the blessing of the Lord makes rich, and He adds no sorrow with it"* (Prov. 10:22 NKJV).

It is our sincere wish that this book will release and empower you to advance toward your destiny. God had a calling and a purpose for your ancestral family. That calling is without repentance, even if your ancestors never walked in the fullness of it, and can be passed down and be fulfilled in you and your children. God intended families to be the vehicle for the expression of His love and goodness. This is actually the glory that will cover the whole earth. It is our prayer that every hindrance be removed from your life so that you step into every blessing that God has for you.

Prayer:

Lord, we are asking You to separate from us every hindrance, every spiritual stronghold, everything that separates us from Your blessing. We give You permission to separate the chaff from our lives. Open the heavens that we may receive a blessing from You. Help us to walk into the callings that You preordained. Enable us to expand Your kingdom and bring glory to You the rest of our lives. Let Your Spirit so rule our hearts that we know intimately our Father's great love for us and have faith to receive the blessings. We declare that You are good, God, so good!

We pray for you, the reader, that you will go after all that belongs to you. We pray, in Jesus' name, that all the gifts, the callings, the lost inheritances, the influence, and creativity that belong to you, may pass down from the generations before. We thank God that through repentance and the asking of forgiveness, you have removed the blockages to your blessings. We ask for your blessings to overtake you and run you down. We pray that you will truly depart from your sins and enter into the blessing of the Lord.

I bow my knees to the Father of our Lord Jesus Christ, from whom the whole family in heaven and earth is named, that He would grant you, according to the riches of His glory, to be strengthened with might through His Spirit in the inner man, that Christ may dwell in your hearts through faith; that you, being rooted and grounded in love, may be able to comprehend with all the saints what is the width and length and depth and height—to know the love of Christ which passes knowledge; that you may be filled with all the fullness of God. Now to Him who is able to do exceedingly abundantly above all that we ask or think, according to the power that works in us, to Him be glory in the church by Christ Jesus to all generations, forever and ever. Amen (Ephesians 3:14-21 NKJV).

Call unto Me, and I will answer you, and show you great and mighty things, which thou knowest not (Jeremiah 33:3).

The Lord bless you, and keep you; the Lord make His face shine on you, and be gracious to you; the Lord lift up His countenance on you, and give you peace (Numbers 6:24-26 NASB).

ENDNOTES

Acknowledgments

1. http://www.quotationspage.com/quotes/Sir_Winston_Churchill/.

Introduction

1. Spiros Zodhaites, *The Complete Word Study Dictionary: Old Testament* (Chattanooga, TN: AMG Publishers, 1994), s.v., 1004.

2. Ibid., s.v., 1129.

Chapter 1

1. William Shakespeare, *Macbeth,* 4.1.

2. http://en.wikipedia.org/wiki/Second_law_of_thermodynamics.

3. Spiros Zodhaites, *The Complete Word Study Dictionary: Old Testament* (Chattanooga: AMG Publishers, 1994), s.v., 779.

4. *Webster's New Twentieth Century Dictionary*, s.v., "execrate."

5. Zodhaites, *Old Testament*, s.v., 3994.

6. Ibid., s.v., 7045.

7. Ibid., s.v., 7043.

8. Spiros Zodhaites, *The Complete Word Study Dictionary: New Testament* (Chattanooga: AMG Publishers, 1992), s.v., 2889.

9. Dennis Wiedrick, Conference, Edmonton, 1997.

10. Zodhaites, *Old Testament*, s.v., 5771.

11. Ibid., s.v., 5753.

Chapter 2

1. *Webster's New Twentieth Century Dictionary*, s.v., "occult."

2. Pastor David L. Brown, Ph.D., "The Dangers of Hypnosis"; http://logosresourcepages.org/Occult/hypnosis.htm.

3. http://en.allexperts.com/q/Physics-1358/Parakinesis.htm.

4. Ken & Jeanne Harrington, Toxic Thinking Seminar, treasurechestministries.ca; Joyce Meyer, *Battlefield of the Mind* (Nashville: FaithWord Publishers, 2002).

5. Spiros Zodhaites, *The Complete Word Study Dictionary: New Testament* (Chattanooga: AMG Publishers, 1992), s.v., 4625.

6. *Webster's New Twentieth Century Dictionary*, s.v., "offend."

7. Jim den Otter, Spruce Grove Community Church, July 2009.

Chapter 3

1. "The Curse of Vanishing Wealth"; http://moneycentral.msn.com/content/retirementandwills/planyourestate/p147046.asp.

2. Spiros Zodhaites, *The Complete Word Study Dictionary: New Testament* (Chattanooga: AMG Publishers, 1992), s.v., 952.

3. Spiros Zodhaites, *The Complete Word Study Dictionary: Old Testament* (Chattanooga: AMG Publishers, 1994), s.v., 3341, 3340.

4. Zodhaites, *New Testament*, s.v., 2206.

5. Perry Cochell and Rodney Zeeb, *Beating the Midas Curse* (Portland, OR: Heritage Institute Press, 2005).

6. "The Curse of Vanishing Wealth"; http://moneycentral.msn.com/content/retirementandwills/planyourestate/p147046.asp.

Chapter 4

1. Wendy Bumgardner, "Why Diets Don't Work"; http://walking.about.com/cs/diet/a/dietsdontwork.htm.

2. Morehouse Conference on African-American Fathers; www.Americanvalues.org/ html/r-turning_the_corner.html.

3. Center for Marriage and Families, David Blankenhorn & Alex Roberts, Research brief No. 9, Future of the Black Family Series, March 2008; http://center. americanvalues.org/?p=72.

4. Statistical Source: Current DHHS report on nationwide child abuse.

5. Statistical Source: *Technical Analysis Paper No. 42,* U.S. Dept. of Health & Human Services, Office of Income Security Policy.

6. Statistical Source: *1988 Census "Child Support and Alimony: 1989 Series P-60, No. 17, 6-7,"* and *"U.S. General Accounting Office Report,"* GAO/HRD-92-39FS January, 1992.

7. Judith Wallerstein and Joan B. Kelly, *Surviving the Breakup* (New York, NY: Basic Books, 1996).

8. Stanford Braver, "Frequency of Visitation," *American Journal of Orthopsychiatry.* http://www.scribd.com/doc/425877/The-Effects-of-Divorce-and-Sole-Custody-on-Children.

9. U.S. D.H.H.S., Bureau of the Census.

10. Center for Disease Control.

11. *Criminal Justice and Behavior,* Vol. 14: 403-26.

12. *National Principals' Association Report on the State of High Schools.*

13. U.S. Dept. of Justice, *Special Report Sept., 1988.*

14. *Fulton County Georgia jail populations & Texas Dept. of Corrections, 1992.*

15. Separated Parenting Access & Resource Center; http://deltabravo.net/custody/ stats.php.

Chapter 5

1. By the hand of Moses (Exod. 35:29; Lev. 8:36; 10:11; 26:46; Num. 4:37,45,49; 9:23; 10:13; 15:23; 16:40; 27:23; 36:13; Josh. 14:2; 20:2; 21:2,8; 22:9; Judges 3:4; 1 King 8:53,56; 2 Chron. 33:8; 35:6; Neh. 9:14; Ps. 77:20).

2. *Webster's New Twentieth Century Dictionary,* s.v., "adversary."

3. Ibid., s.v., "advocate."

4. Merrill F. Unger, *Unger's Bible Dictionary,* s.v., "talent=125 troy wgt"; www.ccsilver. com/reftable/conversion.html (silver @ $17.50/oz.).

5. Ibid., s.v., "Denarii @ 96/lb troy wgt."

Chapter 6

1. Center for Disease Control, Vol. 52, No. 19 and *Births: 2006*, as quoted in Linda Thom, "Illegitimacy Rates Surge–Driven By Third World Immigration"; http://vdare.com/thom/090226_immigration.htm.

2. John and Paula Sanford, *Healing the Wounded Spirit* (South Plainfield, NJ: Bridge Publishing, Inc., 1985), 128.

3. *Funk & Wagnalls Standard College Dictionary*, Canadian Edition (Toronto: Longmans Canada Limited, 1963), s.v., "shame."

4. United Feature Syndicate Inc.

Chapter 7

1. http://www.treasurechestministries.ca.

2. Vladimir Kvint, *Forbes Magazine* (Jan. 21, 1991); http://www.vkvint.com/documents/food_for_peace.pdf.

3. Ken and Jeanne Harrington, *Shift! Moving From the Natural to the Supernatural* (Shippensburg, PA: Destiny Image, 2009), 279.

4. http://www.investopedia.com/articles/00/100900.asp.

5. Baron John Emerich Edward Dalberg Acton (1834–1902) in a letter to Bishop Mandell Creighton, 1887.

6. *The Oxford International Dictionary* (Toronto: Leland Publishing Company, 1957), s.v., "lust" (verb #3).

7. Spiros Zodhaites, *The Complete Word Study Dictionary: Old Testament* (Chattanooga: AMG Publishers, 1994), s.v., 5647.

8. Ibid., s.v., 8104.

9. Robert Young, *Analytical Concordance to the Holy Bible* (London: Lutterworth Press, 1973), s.v., "nations," (Heb-goi).

10. *Webster's New Twentieth Century Dictionary,* s.v., "ethnic."

11. Emma Lazarus, "The New Colossus" (1883); http://www.statueliberty.net/statue-of-liberty-poem.html.

12. Abraham Lincoln, "The Gettysburg Address" (1863); http://blueandgraytrail.com/event/Gettysburg_Address_%5BFull_Text%5D.

13. *Webster's New Twentieth Century Dictionary,* s.v., "denominationalism."

14. Spiros Zodhaites, *The Complete Word Study Dictionary: New Testament* (Chattanooga: AMG Publishers, 1992), s.v., 5331, 5332, 5333.

15. http://www.pantheon.org/articles/d/delphi.html.

16. Zodhaites, *New Testament,* s.v., 4436.

17. http://www.npgaw.org/problemgamblinginformation/factsfigures.asp.

18. http://www.milwaukeemagazine.com/currentIssue/full_feature_story. asp?NewMessageID=13120.

19. http://www.merriam-webster.com/dictionary/fanatic.

20. http://money.cnn.com/2009/12/09/news/companies/tiger_woods_endorsements. fortune/index.htm.

21. http://www.bloomberg.com/apps/news?pid=newsarchive&sid=aFoJrWiRJoMg.

22. http://win.niddk.nih.gov/statistics/index.htm.

23. http://www.gotquestions.org/seven-deadly-sins.html; pride, envy, gluttony, lust, anger, greed, and sloth.

24. http://www.youtube.com/watch?v=sIFYPQjYhv8&feature=fvst.

25. http://www.youtube.com/user/Socialnomics09.

Chapter 8

1. *Webster's New Twentieth Century Dictionary,* s.v., "cult/culture."

2. Ibid., s.v., "magic."

3. http://www.watchtower.org/e/20090201/article_04.htm.

4. http://www.irr.org/MIT/is-mormonism-christian.html.

5. Mary Baker Eddy, *Science and Health With Key to the Scriptures* (Boston, MA: Christian Science Board of Directors, 1994), 465.

6. Ibid., 468.

7. Ibid., 374; http://www.allaboutcults.org/christian-scientist.htm.

8. *Webster's New Twentieth Century Dictionary,* s.v., "superstition."

9. http://www.behind-the-tm-facade.org/transcendental_meditation-religion.htm.

10. http://www.paulmason.info/gurudev/Beacon.htm, "Theory of Spiritual Development," Paragraph #21.

11. http://www.lightlink.com/trance/secrets/mantras.shtml.

12. http://www.davidicke.com/forum/showthread.php?p=338079.

13. http://www.trancenet.net/secrets/beacon/notes.shtml.

14. http://secondsun.webs.com/E-books/%5BAlbert%20Pike%5D%20Morals%20 and%20Dogma.pdf, Albert Pike, "Morals and Dogma" (Charleston: The Supreme Council of the Thirty Third Degree for the Southern Jurisdiction of the United States, 1871), 109.

15. Harold J. Berry, *What They Believe* (Lincoln, NE: BTTB, 1988), 71-96.

16. Albert G. Mackey, *Manual of the Lodge* (Richmond, VA: Macoy and Sickles, 1802), 96.

17. http://www.isaiah54.org/freemasonry.html.

Chapter 9

1. Spiros Zodhaites, *The Complete Word Study Dictionary: Old Testament* (Chattanooga: AMG Publishers, 1994), "rebelled", 4784.

2. *Webster's New Twentieth Century Dictionary,* s.v., "stubborn."

3. Zodhiates, *Old Testament,* s.v., "limited"/ *tâvâh,* 8428 (8427).

4. Isaac Asimov, http://www.brainyquote.com/quotes/quotes/i/isaacasimo140809. html.

Chapter 11

1. http://www.addictionsearch.com/treatment_articles/article/ritalin-abuse-addiction-and-treatment_43.html.

2. http://www.associatedcontent.com/article/5731/prescription_drug_abuse_in_the_elderly.html?cat=5.

3. http://pb.rcpsych.org/cgi/reprint/13/4/184.pdf.

4. *Webster's New Twentieth Century Dictionary,* s.v., "amoral."

Chapter 12

1. http://www.catholic.com/library/Myths_About_Indulgences.asp.

2. http://www.nytimes.com/2009/02/10/nyregion/10indulgence.html.

3. Sir Francis Bacon, *Religious Meditations, Of Heresies,* 1597.

Chapter 13

1. Vince Lombardi (1913–1970).

2. http://www.archives.gov/education/lessons/sioux-treaty/.

3. http://afp.google.com/article/ALeqM5iVC1KMTOgwiSoMQyT2LwZc9HyAgA.

4. http://www.thecanadianencyclopedia.com/index.cfm?PgNm=TCE&Params=A1A RTA0003983.

5. http://www.arena.org.nz/The%20Treaty%20of%20Waitangi.htm.

6. http://en.wikipedia.org/wiki/M%C4%81ori.

7. http://www.acf.hhs.gov/programs/cb/pubs/cm07/figtab3.htm.

8. McCreary Centre Society, Healthy Connections: Listening to BC Youth, 1999, p. 17.

9. Child Sexual Abuse Statistics, compiled by the National Advisory Council of Women, quoted by University of Victoria's Sexual Assault Centre; http://www.safekidsbc.ca/statistics.htm.

10. http://www.findcounseling.com/journal/child-abuse/child-abuse-statistics.html.

11. E. Walker, J. Unutzer, C. Rutter, A. Gelfand, K. Saunders, M. VonKorff, M. Koss, and W. Katon, *Costs of Health Care Use by Women HMO Members With a History of Childhood Abuse and Neglect,* Archives of General Psychiatry 56 (1999), 609-613.

12. http://pediatrics.about.com/od/childabuse/a/05_abuse_stats.htm.

13. http://singleparents.about.com/od/parenting/a/abandonment.htm.

14. http://www.threeworldwars.com/overview.htm.

15. http://www.spendonlife.com/guide/identity-theft-statistics.

16. http://www.sequence-inc.com/index.php?option=com_content&view=article&id=287:bernard-madoff-ponzi-schemes-and-pyramid-schemes&catid=15:recent-articles-a-press&Itemid=64.

17. http://www.americasquarterly.org/node/277.

18. "Gold Dust Memo" and "More on Albania Pyramid Scheme Ponzi"; http://www.crimes-of-persuasion.com/Crimes/InPerson/MajorPerson/albania_ponzi.htm.

19. Oliver Teves, "Cleaning Out a Country–Philippines Pyramid Scheme" (April 25, 2003); http://www.crimes-of-persuasion.com/Crimes/InPerson/MajorPerson/albania_ponzi.htm.

20. Lao-tzu (604 B.C.–531 B.C.), *The Way of Lao-tzu.*

21. William Congreve (1670–1729), "Grief walks on the heels of pleasure: married in haste, we repent at leisure," *The Old Bachelor,* 1693.

Chapter 14

1. http://news.sky.com/skynews/Home/UK-News/Sexual-Partner-Calculator-British-Adults-Average-28m-Indirect-Partners/Article/200909415386485.

2. http://www.merriam-webster.com/dictionary/fornication.

3. http://internet-filter-review.toptenreviews.com/internet-pornography-statistics.html.

4. Rape Crisis, Auckland 2003 statistics; Hayes, Robert. (1990, Summer). "Child Sexual Abuse." *Crime Prevention Journal;* http://www.rapecrisis.org.nz/pdf/Incest%20(Read-Only).pdf.

5. Aphrodite Matsakis, *When the Bough Breaks* (Oakland, CA: New Harbinger Publications, 1991); http://www.ncvc.org/ncvc/main.aspx?dbName=DocumentViewer&DocumentID=32360.

6. M. Hirschfeld, *Transvestites: The Erotic Drive to Cross Dress,* trans. M. A. Lombardi-Nash (Buffalo, NY: Prometheus Books, 2003).

7. http://www.webmd.com/sex-relationships/features/explaining-pedophilia?page=4.

8. http://wiki.ccv.edu/index.php/Kimberly_Bloomer,_What_Causes_Pedophilia%3F.

9. http://www.yellodyno.com/html/child_molester_stats.html.

10. http://www.cnn.com/2009/WORLD/asiapcf/02/16/un.trafficking/index.html.

11. http://www.christendom-awake.org/pages/mshivana/tobpaper.htm.

12. http://people.howstuffworks.com/love7.htm.

Chapter 15

1. http://www.thefreedictionary.com/malign.

2. Edmund Burke (1729–1792).

3. Haman was a descendent of Agag (Esther 3:1), the Amelekite king that Samuel slew (1 Sam. 15:32). Thus he was a sworn enemy of the Jews and his existence was the result of King Saul's disobedience. God, foreseeing this event, had commanded that Amalek be fought against until they were destroyed (see Exod. 17:14-16).

Chapter 16

1. Spiros Zodhaites, *The Complete Word Study Dictionary: New Testament* (Chattanooga: AMG Publishers, 1992), s.v., 3126.

2. http://www.fbi.gov/hq/cid/ngic/violent_gangs.htm.

3. http://www.mysteriesofcanada.com/Canada/history_of_the_chinese_in_canada. htm.

4. http://www.epm.org/artman2/publish/persecuted_church/The_Persecution_of_ Christians_Today.shtml.

5. John Emerich Edward Dalberg-Acton (1843–1902).

6. http://www.spendonlife.com/guide/2009-identity-theft-statistics.

7. http://www.privacyrights.org/ar/idtheftsurveys.htm.

8. Ibid.

Chapter 18

1. King James center column reference (Exod. 17:7).

2. Alfred Jones, *Jones' Dictionary of Old Testament Proper Names* (Grand Rapids, MI: Kregel Publications, 1997), s.v., "Amalek."

3. See Romans 13:13; 1 Corinthians 3:3; 2 Corinthians 12:20; Philippians 1:15; 1 Timothy 6:4; James 3:14; and James 3:16.

Chapter 20

1. Spiros Zodhaites, *The Complete Word Study Dictionary: Old Testament* (Chattanooga: AMG Publishers, 1994), s.v., 1293, 1288.

2. http://www.census.gov/prod/2009pubs/acsbr08-2.pdf.

3. Spiros Zodhaites, *The Complete Word Study Dictionary: New Testament* (Chattanooga: AMG Publishers, 1992), s.v., "substance," 5287.

4. Ibid., "person," 5287.

5. 300 denarii = 300 days wages, approx. $50,000; http://www.census.gov/ prod/2009pubs/acsbr08-2.pdf.

6. Two mites equal approx. $3.75; *Thompson Chain Reference Bible* (Indianapolis, IN: Kirkbride Bible Company, 1967).

7.   http://www.allaboutscience.org/second-law-of-thermodynamics.htm.

8.   http://www.about-bristol.co.uk/ash-01.asp.

9.   Zodhaites, *Old Testament,* s.v., 3027.

10. *Apocalypto,* Icon Productions, Mel Gibson, Director, 2006.

Chapter 21

1.   http://www3.telus.net/st_simons/nsnews019.html.

2.   Spiros Zodhaites, *The Complete Word Study Dictionary: Old Testament* (Chattanooga: AMG Publishers, 1994), 6918, 6942.

3.   Spiros Zodhaites, *The Complete Word Study Dictionary: New Testament* (Chattanooga: AMG Publishers, 1992), s.v., 40, 53.

4.   Zodhaites, *Old Testament,* s.v., 4175.

5.   Ibid., 3384.

6.   Ibid., 6666.

7.   Dottie Rambo and Dave Hunsinger, "Multiply" from *Down By the Creek Bank* (Heartwarming Music and John T. Benson Publishing Company: 1978).

Conclusion

1.   Robert Young, *Analytical Concordance to the Holy Bible* (London: Lutterworth Press, 1973), s.v., "superfluous."

2.   *Webster's New Twentieth Century Dictionary,* s.v., "redundant."

3.   Adolphus Frederick Eoll, *Father's Biography* (Family Documents, 1940).

ABOUT KEN AND JEANNE HARRINGTON

Treasure Chest Ministries

www.treasurechestministries.ca

Ministry contact:

Brenda G. Smith—Treasure Chest Ministries
Box 3458
180 Century Road
Spruce Grove, AB T7X 3A7
780-962-5699
info@treasurechestministries.ca

Workshops / Seminars:

Breaking Generational Curses and Enacting Your Blessings

Healing Toxic Thought Patterns

Stirring up the Prophetic

Character…the Door to Your Destiny

Use contact information above to attend all seminars.

Resources:

www.treasurechestministries.ca

In the right hands, This Book will Change Lives!

Most of the people who need this message will not be looking for this book. To change their lives, you need to put a copy of this book in their hands.

> *But others (seeds) fell into good ground, and brought forth fruit, some a hundred-fold, some sixty-fold, some thirty-fold* (Matthew 13:8).

Our ministry is constantly seeking methods to find the good ground, the people who need this anointed message to change their lives. Will you help us reach these people?

> *Remember this—a farmer who plants only a few seeds will get a small crop. But the one who plants generously will get a generous crop* (2 Corinthians 9:6).

EXTEND THIS MINISTRY BY SOWING
3 BOOKS, 5 BOOKS, 10 BOOKS, OR MORE TODAY,
AND BECOME A LIFE CHANGER!

Thank you,

Don Nori Sr., Publisher
Destiny Image
Since 1982